Exploring and Applying the Parables of Jesus found in the Gospel of Luke

John Belham

PARVA PRESS

Copyright © 2022 by John Belham

The right of the author has been asserted.
All rights reserved. No part of this publication may be reproduced, distributed or transmitted in any form or by any means, without prior written permission.

Parva Press
Web: https://www.parables.org.uk
E-mail: parvapress@parables.org.uk

Publisher's Notes
A selection of these parables and their associated podcasts have been previously published in individual instalments by Parva Press

Principal Scripture quotations are from the ESV* Bible (The Holy Bible, English Standard Version*) copyright © 2001 by Crossway, a publishing ministry of Good News Publishers. Used by permission. All rights reserved.

Supporting references marked RSV and some allusions are drawn from the Revised Standard Version of the Bible, Copyright 1952 (2nd edition 1971) by the Division of Christian Education of the National Council of the Churches of Christ in the United States of America. Used by Permission. All rights reserved.

Book Layout © 2017 BookDesignTemplates.com

British Library Cataloguing in Publication Data.
A catalogue record for this publication is available from the British Library.

ISBN 978-0-9537489-2-1

To the glory of God
and the stirring, strengthening
and encouraging of his people

"He who has ears to hear, let him hear."

CONTENTS

Introduction 1
   Alphabetical list of the parables explored 3
The Sower 5
   The Parable of the Sower: a key to the parables 6
The Scribes and Pharisees – a background note 25
The Lamp put on a Stand 29
   The parable applied to himself and his teaching 30
   The parable addressed to those who did not wish to see 39
   The parable addressed to disciples 45
The Good Samaritan 51
The Friend at Midnight and the Good Gifts of a Father 61
The Rich Farmer or the Rich Fool 75
The Faithful Servants 85
The Barren Fig Tree 101
The Mustard Seed or the Mustard Tree 115
The Leaven 141
   Understanding this parable as a parable of growth 142
   Understanding this parable as a parable of the spreading of evil . 147
The Narrow Door that will be Closed 161
The Wedding Feast and the Great Banquet 175
   The wedding feast 178
   The Great Banquet 182
The Tower, the King going to War and the Salt 193
   The Man Building a Tower 196

The King Facing Defeat	201
The Tasteless Salt	208
The Lost Sheep, Lost Coin, Prodigal Son and his Elder Brother	215
The reason why this series of parables was told and the first two parables explored	216
The Prodigal Son	228
The Return of the Elder Brother	241
The Dishonest Manager	251
The Rich Man and Lazarus	263
The Widow and the Judge	279
The Pharisee and the Tax Collector	289
The Ten Pounds or Ten Minas	297
The Vineyard Tenants	313
The Budding Fig Tree	327
Three Striking Sayings or Short Parables Spoken by Jesus at the Very Beginning of his Ministry	345
The New Patch and the New Wine	345
The Blind Leading the Blind	361
The Wise and the Foolish Builders	379
Postscript	395
Principal Sources	397
The Cover Images, the Author, and our other Publications	401
Exploring and Applying the Lord's Prayer	403

Introduction

Our aim is to explore a number of the well-known parables found in the gospel of Luke, exploring each parable in its original setting, and then seeking to apply its teaching to our current situation in the world of today.

Beginning with the Sower, the parables are presented in the order in which Luke recounts them. The book is not intended to be an academic text, but a book for group or personal consideration. At the time of publication, spoken podcasts of many of the parables can be found at https://www.parables.org.uk

The Lord scattered parables and memorable pictures large and small throughout his teaching. Sometimes his vivid word pictures were in clusters of two or three, yet together forming a single portion of his teaching and so it is often helpful to explore them together.

This selection of the major parables recorded by Luke is offered with the prayer that it might be used of God for the challenging, stirring and building up of his people.

Questions for personal reflection or discussion

The questions at the end of each parable are offered: Firstly, to help us to see and take hold of the promises our Lord gave. Secondly, to help us to recognise his warnings – and to heed them.

Acknowledgement

The author gratefully acknowledges his debt to the many godly commentators who, over the centuries, have mined the treasures of these parables. He acknowledges his eternal debt of gratitude to the One who first told them.

Approach

Writing in the 1800s, Richard Trench, Dean of Westminster and then Archbishop of Dublin, commented that each parable is like '. . . a casket, itself of exquisite workmanship, but in which jewels yet richer than itself are laid up . . .'

I tremble to handle the words of my Lord, but prayerfully aim to look within:

- To find the simplest, clearest and most straightforward understanding of each parable.
- To take note of the occasion that gave rise to the Lord telling the parable, and the particular people to whom it was addressed.
- To note the way our Lord himself interpreted and applied it, and the way it was understood by the apostles, who profited from the teaching and put it into practice in their lives.
- To avoid interpretations that, although the parable might be understood in that way at a much later date, including our own, were clearly not intended to be understood that way by his hearers at the time the parable was told.
- To avoid reading into the parables the kind of 'creative' interpretations our over-active imaginations can so easily supply!

Alphabetical list of the parables explored

(Kept in the groups in which they were taught)

The Barren Fig Tree – 101
The Blind leading the Blind – 361
The Budding Fig Tree and all the trees coming into leaf – 327
The Dishonest Manager – 251
The Faithful Servants – 85
The Friend at Midnight and the Good Gifts of a Father – 61
The Good Samaritan – 51
The Lamp put on a Stand – 29
The Leaven – 141
The Lost Sheep, Lost Coin, Prodigal Son and his Elder Brother – 215
The Mustard Seed, or, the Mustard Tree – 115
The Narrow Door that will be closed – 161
The New Patch and the New Wine – 345
The Pharisee and the Tax Collector – 289
The Rich Farmer, or, the Rich Fool – 75
The Rich Man and Lazarus – 263
The Sower – 5
The Ten Pounds, or Ten Minas – 297
The Tower, the King going to War, the Salt – 193
The Vineyard Tenants – 313
The Wedding Feast and the Great Banquet – 175
The Widow and the Judge – 279
The Wise and the Foolish Builders – 379

The Sower

And when a great crowd was gathering and people from town after town came to him, he said in a parable, "A sower went out to sow his seed. And as he sowed, some fell along the path and was trampled underfoot, and the birds of the air devoured it. And some fell on the rock, and as it grew up, it withered away, because it had no moisture. And some fell among thorns, and the thorns grew up with it and choked it. And some fell into good soil and grew and yielded a hundredfold." As he said these things, he called out, "He who has ears to hear, let him hear."

And when his disciples asked him what this parable meant, he said, "To you it has been given to know the secrets of the kingdom of God, but for others they are in parables, so that 'seeing they may not see, and hearing they may not understand.'"

"Now the parable is this: The seed is the word of God. The ones along the path are those who have heard; then the devil comes and takes away the word from their hearts, so that they may not believe and be saved. And the ones on the rock are those who, when they hear the word, receive it with joy. But these have no root; they believe for a while, and in time of testing fall away. And as for what fell among the thorns, they are those who hear, but as they go on their way they are choked by the cares and riches and pleasures of life, and their fruit does not mature. As for that in the good soil, they are those who, hearing the word, hold it fast in an honest and good heart, and bear fruit with patience."

> The gospel of Luke chapter 8 verses 4 to 15,
> English Standard Version

The Parable of the Sower: a key to the parables

The parable of the man sowing his seed is one of the best known of all the parables. With minor variations, it is found in each of the first three gospels, and marks the beginning of our Lord's public preaching of the word of God by way of parables.

May I invite you to look: Firstly, at the setting. Secondly, at the quotation between the parable and the Lord's explanation of it, for, taken together with this particular parable, that quotation offers a key to understanding the reception given to all the parables and explains why the Lord chose to teach in this way. Thirdly, at the parable itself, 'soil by soil'.

(To make group study easier, there is a break after looking at the fate of the seed falling on the pathway.)

The setting

Great crowds flocked to the Lord Jesus. People were there for various and mixed reasons, many out of curiosity, some to see amazing miracles of healing, and others to hear the Lord's teaching. Those who were sick would be desperately hoping for healing as would those who brought them. So many of these wanted to press forward to catch his personal attention that it became almost impossible for him to preach and teach. In Matthew's and Mark's account of this parable, we read of our Lord taking a boat and moving out a little from the shore in order to distance himself from the crowds. He was then much freer to teach – the shore-line makes a perfect auditorium; on a still day speech can carry a great distance.

Why did the Lord use parables?

When his disciples asked Jesus about the meaning of the parable, he said to them, 'To you it has been given to know the secrets of the kingdom of God, but for others they are in parables, so that "seeing they may not see, and hearing they may not understand."' This passage from Isaiah is quoted or alluded to several times in the New Testament, in the context of the truth being hidden from those listening with determined hardness of heart and unbelief. The parables let them have their own way. It is a fact that as our Lord spoke there were people in the crowd who did not wish to understand, let alone turn or believe.

The Lord taught in parables so that these striking word pictures might catch the people's attention and awaken their interest. However, he also did so because, by using parables, the roles are reversed. We like to sit in judgement on what we hear, and assess it by our own opinion. But parables do the reverse, we are judged by our reception of them.

The parables distinguish between different groups of hearers. A great many of Jesus' hearers loved to hear his stories, yet 'had no ears' to really hear what he was saying; his teaching about the kingdom of heaven just meant nothing to them. Others really did begin to hear and understand but reacted strongly against it; the implications with regard to their lifestyle and social status were too disturbing. They would not hear because they did not wish to do so. Still others, coming with an open mind and stirred to enquire further, were eager to understand and respond to his teaching.

The disciples wanted to dig deeper, they wanted to understand. Then, as now, for those with this God-given spiritual hunger, the parables offer great insight. They display the King and his kingdom; they show how to enter the kingdom of heaven and how to live as a member of it. They also show the evil one's activity and how, even with the best of intentions, we can be deflected, grow cold or stubbornly resist the Lord God and his purposes.

The parable applied
The parable has been called 'the parable of the soils' because what differs is not the seed but the reception it receives. Typically, as the

ancient sower sowed his seed he would scatter it over the whole area by flinging handfuls of seed taken from his basket or sling. He would then plough shallowly to embed the seed in the soil. Modern farming allows for very precise drilling but here is indiscriminate sowing and so, inevitably, the eventual fruitfulness of the seed is according to the nature of the ground on which it falls.

As it was with Jesus' original hearers, wherever the word of God is taught this parable will be working itself out in the lives of those who receive it. The challenge of the parable to the Lord's hearers then, and to ourselves today, is to ask, 'What kind of hearer; what kind of soil am I – at present?' 'At present', simply because there is nothing fixed. Many of us will find that we are not one kind of soil for the whole of our lives. We may pass through times in our lives when the reception we give to the word of God will be all too vividly portrayed as one or another of the poorer soils of the parable, and there may also be times in our lives which, under the hand of God, are wonderfully fruitful.

To the disciples and those who gathered with them to ask its meaning, he spelled out the parable in detail. The sower, said the Lord Jesus, sows the word. This is what the Lord himself was doing; he was proclaiming the kingdom of God. That same word would subsequently be sown by his chosen apostles and those who came to believe through their witness. So Luke could write of the apostle Paul, that he spent his time in Rome '. . . preaching the kingdom of God and teaching the things concerning the Lord Jesus Christ . . .' In our own day, it is sown wherever the kingdom of God, in accord with the teaching of our Lord and his apostles, is faithfully proclaimed from a public platform, shared with a friend or whispered at a child's bedside.

Seed on the path: those who hear and yet the word is taken away

Seed falling on or beside the pathway is trodden underfoot and eaten by the birds. Here the Lord portrayed seed falling where it has little or no opportunity of germinating, taking root, or eventually proving fruitful.

Among the people crowding round the Lord, were there people like that? The religious leaders, the scribes and Pharisees, were always present but 'in a professional capacity'. They were there to see what was going on. They were there to test and sit in judgement over what he said. Later in his ministry, they would be there to see if they could trap him by his words because they came to hate all that he said, all that he stood for and all that he was. They had absolutely no intention of letting his words affect them; no intention of letting the seed grow in their hearts and lives. They certainly heard with their ears. They certainly saw the signs he did with their own eyes but they did not wish to 'hear and understand' or to 'turn and be healed' let alone to 'believe and be saved' – or to perceive who he really was; the Son of God amongst them, the promised Messiah. They determinedly did not wish to recognise that. Their hearts and minds were absolutely rock-like; quite as hard as any pathway. Sadly, they reflect the terrifying fact that it is possible to be eminent in religious affairs and yet with a mind closed to gospel truth; held in great esteem in the hearts of men and yet very far from the heart of God.

Helmut Thielicke speaks of 'asphalted hearts'; people who are hard, busy, efficient, often very influential but ultimately, spiritually blind. Falling on the ears of such people the word of God is simply not received; they seem totally impervious. Each of the first three gospels records the birds taking away the seed, but Luke alone draws attention to the trampling of the seed under foot. The seed has as much chance of growing into a fruitful plant as a wheat or sunflower seed would have on a busy modern road. To those who pass by, the seed is of no value and so is trodden underfoot or crushed by a passing vehicle. Lying exposed on the road the seed is very vulnerable to sharp eyes and ready beaks; as it first falls, or even after it has been crushed, the birds are quick to enjoy the morsel.

Is it hard to think of people among our own friends and acquaintances of whom that is true? Maybe, very painfully, we see it in those very near to us, even among family members. Anything godly is 'as water off a duck's back'; they seem to be all but 'Teflon-coated' like a non-stick frying pan. With them, godly things are brushed aside, trampled and crushed without any awareness at all. Satan delights in such a reception of the word of God and, like birds with fallen seed, makes sure that even the crushed and trodden fragments of a disturbing or awakening, godly 'seed thought' are speedily removed!

But what of ourselves?

Clearly, from the parable, we have an adversary who is determined that we should not 'believe and be saved', receive and fruitfully hold fast the word of God. Here is an adversary who delights when we, those around us, or our circumstances cause 'the seed' to be crushed in the busy rush of life and so rendered fruitless. We have an adversary who watches for every opportunity to snatch away the word of God and so prevent our thinking about it or putting it into practice in our lives.

This path-like hardness of heart toward the things of God gives the evil one his opportunity to render the seed of God's word fruitless. It may be a life-long attitude or it may be for a time, perhaps months or years. Times of hardness come when we 'do not wish to know'; when we are determined not to turn from a hardened-hearted, God-ignoring, course of action, 'doing it my way', living in the manner we choose. Or it may be a particular phase of life when, by our choice or by our circumstances, we are surrounded by those who are deliberately ungodly and who scoff at the things of God. Keeping such company is the spiritual danger described in the opening verse of Psalm One. The computer, television or mobile phone can bring such ungodly thinking and scoffing very directly to our ears and eyes. 'Television taught me to laugh at Christianity and scoff at Christian leaders,' was the testimony of one student after becoming a Christian. Or there may be particular days in which, for one reason or another – perhaps because of some great disappointment, or preoccupation, or ill health – we simply are not receptive. We have closed ears and closed hearts to the things of God. They do not thrill us or stir us; we are cold and indifferent to them.

It is not for nothing that godly folk of a former generation taught us to pray, '. . . from hardness of heart and contempt of thy Word, Good Lord, deliver us.' It is only by the goodness of God that we can be delivered – but what an encouragement to pray, for the Lord God is able to deliver both us and those we care about from such hardness of heart.

If hardness of heart is the evil one's delight, what of the items of news that often closely follow the hearing of a serious call or challenge from the word of God? The Lord in this parable plainly teaches us that Satan watches to snatch away the word. Is opportunity given him to do his devilish work when the hearing of God's word, for example in a meeting or church service, is immediately followed by announcements, notices and presentations? Refreshments, too, can be very valuable if we buy up the time to speak of the challenge of the word of God and to encourage each other in the faith. But over refreshments it is all too easy to let slip from our minds all godly thoughts, and chat about the weather, the price of fuel or our ailments. It has been well said that the devil loves coffee!

Alexander Whyte tells of a visitor to a crofter's cottage who, after family evening prayers, would have continued the earthly conversation that was taking place before prayers. He was gently but rightly told that after family prayers they kept silence. We do well to afford Satan and those who would trample on or snatch away spiritual things as few opportunities as possible!

'Lord, help us to see and hear what you are saying, and to have spiritual understanding and insight as we explore and respond to these your parables.'

Questions for personal reflection or discussion

1. What drew such crowds to the Lord Jesus?
2. We like to be judge of all we hear, is there an uncomfortable side to the parables?

The pathway
3. Do we have friends and family who just seem impervious to the things of God? How can we help them?
4. Times of hardness, coldness, indifference to the things of God, – have you been there yourself? Who and what can help us when facing such times?
5. Do we by choice or circumstance keep company with 'path-like' people? What helpful advice does Psalm 1 verse 1 offer?
6. In what ways could our Christian meetings better make room for the word of God to do its work rather than the evil one to do his?

References

Other accounts of the parable – Matthew 13:1-23, Mark 4:1-20
The word of the Lord to Isaiah – Isaiah 6:9-10, John 12:40, Acts 28:26-27
Those who gathered with them – Mark 4:10
Paul, preaching the kingdom of God – Acts 28:31
'From hardness of heart' – from the Litany, Book of Common Prayer

The Parable of the Sower – part 2

(The questions for these soils can be found on page 21.)

Rocky, shallow soil: those who hear and yet in testing times fall away

In the Holy Land the soil depth is often very shallow and such soil dries out all too easily. Matthew and Mark point us to the lack of soil depth, Luke to the lack of moisture as it dries out. Despite a promising start in the early rains, seed corn falling on such soil will produce plants that are unable to withstand the drying heat of summer. It is an uncomfortable question, but can you think of those who were deeply moved by the word of God, and who, to all appearances, joyfully embraced the Christian faith, maybe with tears or with elation, and yet are now very far from the things of God? They 'believe for a while' but circumstances have not been easy; the going has been too tough, faith has withered and they have given up.

There in the crowd listening to the Lord it would have been exactly the same. In John chapter six we read of whole sections of the crowd, who had been following Jesus, now finding it too hard. They could not bear the things he was saying so drew back and no longer followed him. We read of Peter who, at Jesus' invitation, enthusiastically began to walk on the water . . . and then doubted. Taking his eyes off the Master, the waves were too boisterous and the challenge too great. Or Peter, again, having professed utter loyalty, after the Lord's arrest faced 'a time of testing' and found himself denying his Lord with oaths. For our great encouragement, the example of Peter demonstrates that we can for a time be one of these unproductive soils, and yet neither fixed as such nor discarded by the Lord. We can be different soils at different times. The restored and forgiven Peter went on to be very fruitful indeed but at that particular point he could well have been 'shallow ground'.

I certainly confess to having been very shallow soil. Embracing the gospel when 12 or 13 years old, our family moved the following year – new home, new town, new school, and new church – none of which offered any real spiritual encouragement. For years I spiritually withered until, on the point of spiritual extinction, by the goodness of God, someone 'watered' me! Only by the grace and mercy of God can any of us stand and it is good to acknowledge that.

Sadly, we will all know folk who would say of Christianity, 'I know, I've been there and done that years ago.' Yet in view of times of testing, the knocks and disappointments of life or the sneers of ungodly folk around them, they would now consider themselves to have long outgrown the simple, child-like trust that true faith demands.

Opposition or personal tragedy can bring this about but so, too, can spiritual isolation within our own family or community or years of isolation from true Christian fellowship and teaching. It may be that we have become involved in socially active yet spiritually arid churches; churches that offer teaching that has deflected us from that of the Lord and his apostles, and where true fellowship in the gospel is scarce or non-existent and so faith has, 'withered away because it had no moisture.' Especially later in life, with decreasing mobility and the failure of sight and hearing, spiritual isolation can be quite desperate – as, of course, it can be for our fellow believers imprisoned for their faith. Only deeply rooted in his word and by the good hand of God can we come through times of testing such as these.

It is always appropriate to rejoice when the word of God is eagerly received and yet it is sobering to reflect, ten years on, on any group of keen and enthusiastic people, to all appearances Christian, and see the proportion of them who have, for one reason or another, given up and fallen away. There is scope here for much fruitless debate as to whether a true disciple can fall away. Only God knows the secrets of our hearts, and the purpose of the parable is not to enable us to judge, or categorise, let alone dismiss the early faith of others but, rather, to give us insight into our own heart's standing before God. The Lord's parable shows us the challenges we face and stirs us to examine our own hearts, turn for forgiveness, amend our own way of living and so guard our own reception of God's word and our own ongoing fruitfulness before him.

So, what of ourselves? It is good to remind ourselves that it is 'through much tribulation' that we enter the kingdom of God; that there will be 'times of testing'. For all kinds of reasons, testing and spiritually dry times will befall us, church leaders and people alike. There will be those who laugh and sneer, block our way and make life difficult for us. There may be people who would actively persecute, crush, imprison and kill us and those we love. Even as I write, a great many of our fellow Christians around the world are suffering persecution as dreadful as that. In the light of this parable and the many other warnings in scripture, it is clear that we need to be prepared for such 'times of testing.' If we are taken by surprise, such things can easily deprive us of our joy in the Lord and our fruitfulness before him.

How can we be prepared? From the parable, the clear challenge is to make sure that our own faith is not shallow; only carried along by the presence and the encouragement of friends more godly than ourselves, a 'fair-weather faith' that will not hold fast through testing, sad, or difficult days.

Using the picture the parable sets before us, to be stable, strong and fruitful we need to let the word of God in all its forms permeate and take root deeply in our lives. It is a life-long process and for it to happen, we do well to follow the early believers' pattern of devoting ourselves to the apostles' teaching, to prayer and fellowship; for us, that must mean making it a priority to spend time prayerfully reading and meditating on the word of God. Only then will we be able to hide in our hearts its promises and know and take seriously the commands of the word of God. We will also be able to learn from the examples of

Scripture, both from those who stood firm and from those who fell away; for the warnings are written there for our protection. We do well to guard a time of unhurried prayer in order to cultivate that close, personal walk or 'abiding in him' spoken of by our Lord in the fifteenth chapter of John's gospel. Finally, but very importantly, we need to treasure true Christian fellowship and partnership in the gospel so that we may support, encourage and pray for one another.

For such things as these it is difficult to find time in our busy lives yet it is worth making time – perhaps very early in the morning, or on our feet as we walk, or, arriving early for work, before we begin. Every opportunity we make for the word of God to permeate our lives, alone or in company with our fellow believers, will contribute to our being increasingly strongly rooted and so able to withstand testing times and be fruitful.

Thorny soil: those who hear and yet as they go on their way are spiritually choked

Thorns, thistles, weeds, not the best or most promising place for seeds to fall! Yet with the ancient practice of scattering seed, some of the seed would undoubtedly have landed in just such a situation. The potential for weeds to choke the good seed is always present even on the best land, especially at the field edges. The thorns that are particularly likely to overwhelm our fruitful walk with the Lord are named in the parable: cares, riches and pleasures. Here are competing interests and loyalties that legitimately demand our attention and yet, left unchecked, threaten to choke godly fruitfulness. It could be one great, all-consuming and spiritually-choking 'thorn bush' or a great number of small cares, concerns and other interests.

Among the crowd listening to the Lord Jesus, it seems to have been the disciple Judas's love for money that opened the way for the devil to tempt him and cause him to betray his Lord. His great desire for money blinded him to all else, gave the devil a foothold and rendered that man's life fruitless.

How many of us can think of friends who as teenagers or young adults 'received the word' and promised great fruitfulness and yet in middle life are totally absorbed in this world as they climb the career ladder, bring up a family and work every possible hour to finance their chosen life style. They are very busy indeed but there is simply no opportunity, time or emotional energy left for pursuing godly priorities. The challenge of godly fruitfulness is smothered. They, 'go on their way' preoccupied with the affairs and pleasures of this world and sadly, 'their fruit does not mature'.

Fine, we have seen it in others . . . but have there not been times when we have been there ourselves? Here in this picture of the thorny patch is a constantly necessary warning.

Could it happen to us? The trouble is that the weeds grow so slowly and steadily that they are quite unnoticed – until little by little we are swamped by them. It can happen to us. It can be happening to us! Like Judas, could the desire for more money be our undoing – or a thirst for power and influence – or a hunger for self-indulgent pleasure? We do well to recognise our own frailty and the nature of the world in which we live. It offers so many enticing 'thorns' which, if given the chance, will take root and grow very vigorously. John Calvin calls us to recognise how inclined our hearts are to grow weeds, and how careless we are about weeding!

We are enthusiastic about medical check-ups; perhaps we should be more enthusiastic about spiritual check-ups! These might take the form of honest and private answers to a spiritual questionnaire or, if invited to do so, an honest and godly friend might help us to spot a cluster of fruitfulness-reducing weeds we had not noticed or had simply assumed were just 'part of our current phase of life'. Keeping alert to the appearance of 'seedling thorns' by regularly meditating on

God's word, must offer us the best and most frequent use of our heavenly Father's appointed weeding instrument or 'hoe'!

How can we make the legitimate concerns of this world take only their rightful proportion of our time, effort and emotional energy? Only, surely, in our wealth creation, responsibilities and pleasures, by determinedly seeking first our heavenly Father's honour, his kingdom and his will; by 'seeking first the kingdom of heaven.'

Good soil: those who hear, hold fast and over time prove fruitful

Finally, the seed that fell on good ground, 'Those who, hearing the word, hold it fast in an honest and good heart, and bear fruit with patience.' Here is the picture of ground that is fertile, well watered and weeded. Spiritually it depicts people who bring a good and honest heart to the hearing of the word; people who are unprejudiced and willing to learn; people who have no other priority but to hear and embrace the word of God. They hear it, reflect on it, seek further insight into it and put it into practice in day by day living. Having so taken hold of it – even though doing so is at the expense of the things of this world – they pray for strength to hold it fast through the challenges of life, the scoffing and the times of doubt. These are the people whose lives are gradually changed as they 'grow in grace and in the knowledge of our Lord and Saviour Jesus Christ.' They trust him, obey him, walk closely with him and are empowered by the Holy Spirit to live and speak for him.

In the crowd of people listening to the Lord, who would be like that? After Pentecost, when Peter and John were arrested, the authorities were amazed by their holy boldness and wisdom – and noted that, although in their eyes they were 'ignorant and unlearned men', Peter and John 'had been with Jesus.' On the Day of Pentecost itself, Peter had spoken with God-given clarity and power, and three thousand people turned, believed and were baptised. On that day alone the harvest yield was very great. Later, as Peter was led by God to proclaim the gospel in Cornelius's house, the harvest of God amongst the non-Jewish people was begun. Peter's ministry in those early days was dramatically fruitful.

In more recent history, John and Charles Wesley, George Whitefield, and Charles Spurgeon were each wonderfully fruitful in their generation as was Billy Graham in the last century. Many others have been exceedingly fruitful, as Matthew and Mark record, '. . .some thirty, some sixty, some a hundredfold.'

For ourselves, the challenge of the good soil is to be receptive and fruitful ground. From the parable, that means being eager to hear and understand the word of God. It will mean being willing to 'turn and be healed'; willing and eager to 'believe and be saved'. It will mean receiving the Lord Jesus for the one he truly is; submitting to him as the Son of God and accepting his great work on the cross as essential for our acceptance before Almighty God. It will mean putting the Lord's commandments and teaching into practice in our own lives. Then, as one of a company of Christians, each playing our part, it will mean being his willing servants; salt and light in our society and in our world. To be so, we are called to pray that he would fill us, daily, with his Holy Spirit so that we are able to be his ambassadors as we are out and about among friends, neighbours, colleagues and family. That may, or may not, lead to a recognised pastoral, preaching or teaching ministry.

I love that final expression found only in Luke, 'bear fruit with patience.' Here is nothing instant, it is like the seed growing, it takes time, great patience and persistence and even then the true harvest is not apparent until all is gathered in. Only then can it be accurately assessed, and then only by the Lord of the Harvest himself.

Overall conclusion to the parable

The sharp challenge of the parable is to take care how we hear. We might usefully ask, 'What kind of soil am I today? What kind of soil am I likely to be in five years time?

Do I have, and will I have, an open heart to turn and be forgiven?

Do I now, and will I then, rejoice in the salvation of God?

Will the gospel seed have been snatched away; will the devil have stopped me believing and being saved?

Will I have fallen away in difficult days because I have not let his word root deeply in my life?

Will I have gone on my way, the things of this world smothering and choking my love of the things of God?

Will I be found, at the last, to have played my part for the kingdom of heaven; been fruitful before the Lord God?'

All God's work in our lives, awakening us, keeping us and enabling us to be fruitful, is of his goodness; by his Holy Spirit and his living word active in our lives. And yet very clearly, from this parable, we have our part to play:

– By hungering for these things, making time for them, welcoming them and being actively receptive of them.

– By letting God's word take root deeply in our thinking, and be expressed in our day by day living and in our treatment of those about us.

– By keeping our lives well weeded before the Lord and constantly guarding godly priorities.

– In short, by seeking first the kingdom of God.

'Lord Jesus cause us, like the disciples, to hunger to understand and respond to the word you have sown. Cause us to see for ourselves where we stand before you. Fill us with the Holy Spirit of God and stir us to joyfully hold fast your word and steadfastly hunger, pray and labour for fruitfulness before you.'

Questions for reflection or discussion

The parable taken as a whole
1. In what ways does the parable help us to see how the gospel is received, so that we can encourage ourselves and those around us to hold fast and be fruitful?
2. What can we do, personally, to guard ourselves from being poor soil and encourage growth and fruitfulness?

Rocky soil
1. Are we discerning in our reaction to what we hear and see in the world around us – at work, on television, among our friends and on social media?
2. Whenever we hear a Christian lecture, sermon or talk, how can we tell if the apostolic teaching is being faithfully proclaimed? In what ways can the Bereans – who searched the Scriptures to see if Paul's preaching was faithful (Acts 17:11) – help us to be discerning?
3. Would we admit to times of spiritual dryness, when faith all but withered away?
4. What encouragement is there to be found in the apostle Peter as his life reflects these soils?
5. What habits and attitudes can we be developing to help us to be strongly rooted?

Thorny soil
1. Which particular weeds do you see choking the fruitfulness of Christians in our culture?
2. Is it nearly impossible to be fruitful for the Lord when bringing up young children . . . or are they a field for our fruitfulness? And are the contacts and opportunities they bring us an opportunity for further fruitfulness?

3. How common is it to go through times and seasons when the pressures of life, at work or at home, make us 'pretty weedy'?

4. Could we usefully spend time considering the spiritually choking 'thorn bushes' that are growing around our life, and taking such action as we can?

5. What kinds of testing times might come to us and how can we help one another through them?

Good soil

1. To what extent do we hunger and pray that God would raise up exceedingly fruitful people for the honour of his name and the building of his kingdom in our own day?

2. How can we 'grow in grace and in the knowledge of our Lord and Saviour Jesus Christ'?

3. Are we faithfully playing the part that the Lord has called us to play at this time?

4. How can we encourage one another to be increasingly fruitful?

Footnote

There is a modern understanding which holds that our Lord is teaching that, despite all the ploys of the evil one, either directly, (under the picture of the birds snatching away the word), or indirectly through the fallen nature of this world, (under the picture of scorched earth and thorns choking the word), the proclamation of the word of God will produce a varied but abundant harvest.

Such an interpretation emphasises the Lord God's sovereignty, and would strongly encourage the faithful 'sowing of the word' in every generation. The explanation given to the disciples, who wanted to hear and understand the parable – and so asked what it meant – would help to prepare them for their own 'sowing of the word' in later years. The challenge to patient 'sowing' of the word in the face of a mixed reception has been relevant all down the centuries. Often the harvest, springing from the seed a person has faithfully sown, ripens long after they have gone to be with their Lord.

However, on its own, this interpretation does seem to relieve the hearers of their responsibility to carefully hear, understand and act upon the word sown.

I have held to the classic understanding that the Lord's primary intention was to awaken his hearers to their responsibility of hearing and responding to his teaching, as immediately after the parable, we read 'As he said these things, he called out, "He who has ears to hear, let him hear."' Luke also records Jesus saying, 'Take care then how you hear . . .' just two verses later.

References

Peter walking on water – Matthew 14:28-31
Peter denying his Lord – Mark 14:66-72
People giving up following Jesus – John 6:66-69
Devoted to the apostles' teaching – Acts 2:42
Judas' interest in money – John 12:3-8
Grow in grace and knowledge – 2 Peter 3:18
Peter and John arrested – Acts 4:1-4 and 13
Peter on the Day of Pentecost – Acts 2:14-42
Peter in Cornelius' House – Acts 10:1-48
Take care how you hear – Luke 8:18
Steadfast, immovable – 1Corinthians 15:58

The Scribes and Pharisees – a background note

As so many of our Lord's parables were spoken in response to the behaviour, questionings or murmurings of the scribes and Pharisees, it may be helpful to offer this brief sketch of their background and thinking.

The scribes and Pharisees could trace their origins back some 500 years, to the time of the return of a remnant of Jewish people to Jerusalem after their exile in Babylon. In particular to Ezra, who '. . . had set his heart to study the law of the LORD, and to do it, and to teach his statutes and ordinances in Israel.' They were experts in the law and are often referred to in the New Testament simply as lawyers. Seen as 'holy men', they were zealous to keep the law in every detail, and to teach it to others.

The scribes and Pharisees became particularly important in the time of Antiochus Epiphanes, king of Syria, who compelled all his subjects to conform to one culture and one faith – that of Greece. He attacked and overcame Jerusalem, and re-dedicated the temple to Zeus in 167 B.C. It was in these very difficult times that the Pharisees rightly and nobly became the guardians of Israel's true faith.

When Jesus walked among God's people, the scribes and Pharisees still regarded themselves as those guardians. They were correct and godly in so many ways, but they had become a politically astute class of able men of respected social position. Perhaps because of their position in society, they had lost, or in that generation perhaps never had, that simple, humble and close walk with the Lord God that characterised, for example, Simeon, and also Anna. Together with others, both Simeon, and Anna were watching and waiting for the 'consolation of

Israel', for God himself to visit and redeem his people. Led by the Holy Spirit, when Mary and Joseph brought the young child Jesus into the temple, they each independently instantly recognised the Lord's Anointed One. In general, the scribes and Pharisees did not have that kind of spiritual insight.

Aware of their need to protect their own position, the Pharisees had no eyes to recognise Israel's long-promised Messiah – especially as God's Anointed One was clothed with humility, and was neither drawn from the ruling class, nor one of their own class, nor a charismatic warrior hero who might liberate Israel from the occupying forces of Rome. The people of Israel longed for their promised deliverer, but had come to associate that with freedom from subjection to Rome. Over the years, a number of military leaders had arisen who claimed to be Israel's long promised Messiah.

For this reason, Jesus did not publicly claim the title, Messiah. Under the Holy Spirit's leading, he let people discover it for themselves. Privately to his disciples he acknowledged it to be the truth, but to them, and to others who recognised who he really was, he asked or commanded them to keep silence.

All through his ministry, the Pharisees and scribes watched and listened, but Jesus did not fit with their expectations of the Messiah. Their hearts were hardened as they examined him on the basis of their own practices, especially the keeping of details of the law – as it had become interpreted by themselves. So their primary tests in assessing Jesus were questions, such as, 'With whom does he mix, with 'holy' people like ourselves, or with those we regard as 'sinners'?' and 'Does he keep our detailed rules concerning the Sabbath?' He was, in their eyes, an 'irregular Rabbi'. He was not one of the ruling religious class, did not observe their traditions and clearly had no intention of throwing off Rome by military might. How could such a man possibly be Israel's true Messiah? Not until finally, put under oath by Caiaphas, did Jesus publicly acknowledge it to be the truth – and was condemned to death for doing so.

However, in the light of the fulfilment of so many of the prophecies of Scripture concerning the promised Messiah, for the people of that time who had eyes to see and ears to hear, his life, his words and his miraculous signs, his death and resurrection, made it increasingly plain who he really was – and is.

References

Ezra – Ezra 7:10
Simeon – Luke 2:25-35
Anna – Luke 2:36-38
Details of the Law, interpreted by themselves – Matthew 15:7-9
With whom does he mix? – Luke 15:1-2
Caiaphas – Matthew 26:57 and 62-64

The Lamp put on a Stand

"Now the parable (of the sower) is this: The seed is the word of God. The ones along the path are those who have heard; then the devil comes and takes away the word from their hearts, so that they may not believe and be saved. And the ones on the rock are those who, when they hear the word, receive it with joy. But these have no root; they believe for a while, and in time of testing fall away. And as for what fell among the thorns, they are those who hear, but as they go on their way they are choked by the cares and riches and pleasures of life, and their fruit does not mature. As for that on the good soil, they are those who, hearing the word, hold it fast in an honest and good heart, and bear fruit with patience.

"No one after lighting a lamp covers it with a jar or puts it under a bed, but puts it on a stand, so that those who enter may see the light. For nothing is hidden that will not be made manifest, nor is anything secret that will not be known and come to light. Take care then how you hear, for to the one who has, more will be given, and from the one who has not, even what he thinks he has will be taken away."

Then his mother and his brothers came to him, but they could not reach him because of the crowd. And he was told, "Your mother and your brothers are standing outside, desiring to see you." But he answered them, "My mother and my brothers are those who hear the word of God and do it."

Luke 8:11-21, English Standard Version

The Lamp put on a Stand

Matthew, Mark and Luke all record the Lord using this picture of a lamp. Leon Morris comments that the purpose of lighting a lamp is to give light, and so a lamp is not hidden but placed prominently and publicly so that as many people as possible may benefit. To be able to see, common sense demands that a light be placed high on a stand or hung from above, rather than covered over or hidden.

Luke records our Lord using the illustration of the light on a stand on more than one occasion, and it becomes clear that Jesus used it in three quite different ways. Firstly, he applied it to himself, his words and those hearing him. Secondly, he applied it to people who refused to benefit from the light. And thirdly, he applied it to describe the disciples who were to become his chosen messengers; lights in this dark world.

The parable applied to himself and his teaching

How did the parable of a lamp placed on a stand apply to the Lord Jesus himself?
The temple religious leaders were first alerted to the Messiah's imminent birth by Zechariah. Zechariah, ministering in the temple, was left speechless after an angel appeared to him. From that moment, until Zechariah named his son, by writing, 'His name is John,' he had been completely dumb. Suddenly and dramatically he was able to speak, and opening his mouth he prophesied that the Lord God would visit and redeem his people Israel and that his son, known to us as John the Baptist, would be the Lord's herald, going before him to prepare his way.

Not long after this, King Herod, the religious leaders and the people of Jerusalem were set astir by the wise men or magi, who had come from the east, publicly asking, "Where is he who has been born king of the Jews?" King Herod, immediately aware of a potential threat to his position, demanded to know from the religious leaders where *the Messiah* was to be born. As often happens under the hand of God, here was the secular and thoroughly ungodly ruler, Herod, alerting the religious leaders to the significance of the magi's question.

A little later, again in the temple in Jerusalem, the aged Simeon prophesied that the young infant, Jesus, would become '. . . a light to lighten the nations, and the glory of God's people Israel.'

Attention to Jesus' birth, and that he was the Lord God's anointed, the Messiah, had been clearly drawn to both state and religious leaders.

Jesus' teaching was also very public, as were his person, his compassion, and his wonderful signs. The Lord Jesus, through his life and teaching, gave his hearers the greatest possible opportunity to hear the word of God. He really was like 'a lamp on a stand', drawing great crowds of people from every walk of life to hear him.

Very publicly, the Lord declared his Father's words. Very publicly, at the Passover feast, he was crucified. And his cross, his resurrection and his teaching have been publicly proclaimed throughout the world by the apostles and by those who have faithfully followed in their steps.

He who told this parable is, as he said, greater than Solomon and more than a prophet – he is 'the light of the world' and Israel's glory.

How did the Lord apply the parable to himself and his teaching of the word of God?

The parable of the sower sowing his seed is very well known and greatly loved, but it is important to note that both Mark and Luke record Jesus telling the parable of the lighted lamp immediately after the parable of the sower. The parable of the lamp reinforces the teaching Jesus had been pressing home on the disciples and those in the crowd listening to him. The sower and the lighted lamp are two parables with a single challenge. And so, it is instructive to briefly reflect on the parable of the sower, in order to compare it with the parable of the lamp.

In the parable of the sower, what is the seed picturing? To the disciples, Jesus explained, "Now the parable is this: The seed is the word of God."

Who is pictured sowing this seed, the word of God? Scholars generally agree that it must be the Lord Jesus himself, and later on, his appointed apostles, and down the centuries those who would faithfully teach what they taught.

From the explanation the Lord gave to the disciples, with the repeated '. . . they are those who, hearing the word . . .' it is clear that the different situations into which the seed fell represent the hearers; the differing groups of hearers, each giving the word of God a very different reception. Is it difficult to think of people we know who, just at the present time, appear to fall into each of these groups? The person who, should you mention godly things, will immediately close or change the conversation. The person who for a spell was so enthusiastic about the things of God, but now . . . The person who showed such early promise and yet, in the years that have followed, has became totally absorbed in pursuing many other interests. And finally, those whose patience and steadfastness before the Lord set us a challenge and great example to follow.

Following the same pattern, but applying it to the parable of the lighted lamp . . .

A lamp is put on a stand so that all may benefit from its rays, and so, like the sower sowing seed that fell everywhere, the light sheds its rays everywhere.

What is the light the lamp is giving? Jesus immediately refers to hearing, and so, like the seed, the light being scattered is clearly the word of God.

Who is the lamp? From the setting, it must first be our Lord himself.

Who would dream of hiding a lamp so that its light could not shine out and be of benefit to all around? Satan is always ready and eager to snatch away or obscure the word of God. And there are hearers who, for one reason or another, do not wish to see or know themselves, nor wish others to benefit from it. People like these may well be determined to 'cover' or 'hide' the word of God; suppressing both the truth and those who declare it.

As in the parable of the sower, it is the responsibility of all who are offered the light to benefit from it. Or, as the Lord Jesus directly said as he told the parable of the lamp, "Take care then how you hear."

The great thrust of the teaching of the parables of both the sower and the lamp
Three verses clearly state the point Jesus was making. As he finished telling the parable of the sower to the great crowd, we read, 'As he said these things, he called out, "He who has ears to hear, let him hear."' As he told the parable of the lighted lamp, he said, "Take care then how you hear . . ." And at the conclusion of the section, Luke records him saying, "My mother and my brothers are those who hear the word of God and do it." Jesus was emphasising the great responsibility of his disciples, and the crowd who were listening to him, to listen carefully.

How were they to listen? They were not to be satisfied with 'hearing an excellent speaker with such arresting stories' – nor to have their minds preoccupied with the astonishing acts of healing and compassion they saw, but to listen and heed the words of the Lord Jesus, as truly being 'the word of God'. They were to take note and to put into practice what they were hearing; to let his teaching touch every part of their thinking and living so that they were not 'hearers only', but 'doers of the word.'

All were free to benefit from it – yet so few did. Hence, the repeated challenge 'to take heed.'

Is the parable a word for us, in our day?
At night, a modern house deprived of its electricity supply will be plunged into darkness. Not until it is restored can each room be filled

with light. Until then we stumble around in the semi-dark or with a feeble torch or candle. We may be in darkness for reasons beyond our control, or maybe because we 'never got around to' putting money in the meter or arranging to pay the bill. Like Jesus' original hearers, a very great number of people today never 'get around to' seriously thinking who Jesus truly is or heeding the word of God he proclaimed, and so continue to stumble about very uncertainly in an increasingly dark world with only the fading torchlight of a previous generation's godly ways, or the dim, and often misleading, glow of the thinking and opinions of society around us.

In a house that is fully lit, nothing remains hidden by the darkness. All becomes open and plain to see. In a similar way the word of God shines light into our lives, in order that we may be warned and stirred to put each part right before God our heavenly Father, and then, as the apostle John writes, to continue walking in the light as disciples.

'Take care then how you hear . . .'
By teaching his disciples, whom he later called his 'sent ones', his apostles, and equipping them with the Holy Spirit at Pentecost, the Lord Jesus made provision for light to shine throughout the whole world and in every generation. In our day, whenever we hear or read the word of God, faithfully written or spoken, it is our responsibility, just as much as it was for his first hearers, to take note and put it into practice in our lives.

It may be a word to encourage us in the Christian faith, for example, to help us to hold fast in difficult times. It may be a seed thought that stirs us to question some way of thinking, attitude or behaviour of our own in the light of Scripture. If we find that it may not be pleasing before our heavenly Father, true disciples are called to ask for his forgiveness and the enabling of the Holy Spirit to begin to take steps to turn from it.

In order to grow in faith and in faithful living before God, we need to heed and to act on his word each time we hear it. Norval

Geldenhuys draws our attention to our Lord's words and explains that, to those who listen to the word of God with a believing, surrendered and obedient heart more will be given. But the indifferent will lose even the little they thought they possessed.

The great benefit of taking care how we hear
Such heeding of the word of God has certainly proved to be the key in the lives of Christian disciples down the centuries. We read of the Thessalonians welcoming the gospel of God as proclaimed by Paul and Silas and turning from idol worship, to worship the living God. Centuries later Martin Luther, translating Scripture and paying prayerful attention to the words within, re-discovered the true apostolic gospel of grace. And today, if we thoughtfully read the word of God, the eyes of our understanding will be increasingly opened and our thinking lit up. The word of God will bring light to every part of our lives, and godly thinking, speaking and actions will begin to grow.

The Lord Jesus really is the light of this dark world. Those willing to see and hear, discover who he truly is and what he has done for us. If we go on to live according to his word and teaching, his light will gradually illuminate the whole of our lives; our thoughts and understanding, our motives and actions, and our overall aim in life. It will also illuminate our perception of this world and of all that is going on around us; we will be given an increasingly godly understanding of the times in which we are living.

Even so, Matthew Henry presents those who would willingly hear with the very perceptive challenge to watch our hearts as we hear or read God's word:

– To watch out for things in our current thinking or circumstances that would stop us from benefitting from the word.

– To watch over our hearts for any hidden prejudices, or dearly held errors or life-style choices, that would hinder our willingness to accept reproof or correction.

– To watch out for a lack of attention or carelessness that would entertain us, or fulfils a set task, but cause us to learn very little.

– To watch out for such a superficial hearing or reading that we lose or soon forget even the little we thought we had gained from it.

Beware, 'For nothing is hidden that will not be made manifest, nor is anything secret that will not be known and come to light. Take care then how you hear. . .'

If Jesus' hearers then, or we in our day, knowingly or carelessly suppress or neglect the light he has made freely available to us, that suppression or neglect, the true source of our failure, will finally stand in judgement of us.

This is, perhaps, not a comfortable thought! Nor is it a comfortable line in the parable! (Is it a surprise that so many preachers and commentators pass lightly over it?)

We may choose to pay little or no attention to what the Lord God has caused to be written. Or we may be persuaded by others that it is no longer relevant, or that there are more 'advanced' understandings in our day. Nothing will be hidden on judgement day, all will be revealed; the secrets of all hearts will be known. The word of God, as proclaimed by the Lord Jesus and communicated to us by his chosen apostles, and the way we have responded to it, will ultimately be our judge. It will be the test that will reveal even the hidden motives of our hearts.

This uncomfortable understanding is nevertheless reinforced by the incident Luke records next, the attempt by his family to tear him from his teaching and proclaiming of God's word. Jesus responds that his true family, the family of God, are 'those who hear the word of God and do it.'

The obedience of faith

The light of the glorious gospel, comments J.C. Ryle, is not just to be admired or discussed but to be lived. It is something very valuable entrusted to us. It is certainly not comfortable to compare the warning Jesus gave here concerning the light, with the dreadful words addressed to the unfaithful servant in the parable of the talents, 'So take the talent from him, and give it to him who has ten talents. For to everyone who has will more be given, and he will have abundance; but from him who has not, even what he has will be taken away.' Before the Lord God, we have the responsibility for putting the word of God into practice in our lives. If we fail to make good use of the opportunity entrusted to us, we will lose it.

As John Newton points out, the word of God, because it is *the word of God*, is not *proposed* to us, for us to give our opinion, but *proclaimed* to us, for our submission and obedience to it. The truth is exactly as Jesus declared it to be, 'My mother and my brothers are those who hear the word of God and do it.'

Heavenly Father we thank you that you sent your Son to be the light of the world, and through him you have made your ways, your promises and your demands of us, plainly known. Stir us to hear and act on your word; to be among 'those who hear the word of God and do it.'

Questions for reflection or discussion

1. In what ways did God cause the Lord Jesus and his words to be placed very publicly 'like a lamp on a stand'?
2. In what ways does the parable of the sower sowing his seed have a common theme with the lamp spreading its light?
3. 'My mother and my brothers are those who hear the word of God and do it.' How can we, in our day, 'hear the word of God'? And what would it mean in practice to 'do it'?
4. To what extent do we unhurriedly read the word of God, and how can that help us to grow spiritually?

5. To what extent are we 'hearers of the word' rather than 'doers of the word'?

6. Even when we put ourselves in a place where we could learn from the word of God, to what dangers does Matthew Henry alert us?

7. How easy is it for us to lose even the little we have learned?

8. In what ways can current social thinking and opinion be misleading, deflecting us from godly ways?

9. In what ways are we living on the 'spiritual capital', the godliness, of a former generation?

10 From the T.V. and Radio, on our computers and 'phones, in conversations and in church, we are constantly hearing the words and opinions of others. With such a demanding background, what steps can we take to make sure that we actually hear the words of the Lord Jesus and do them?

References

Zechariah – Luke 1:8-23

John, the Lord's herald – Luke 1:57-80

The one born king of the Jews – Matthew 2:1-4

A light to lighten the nations – Luke 2:32

Not hearers only, but doers of the word – James 1:22

Walking in the light – 1 John 1:5-7

Thessalonians – 1 Thessalonians: 1:9-10, and 2:13

Talents – Matthew 25:29

The Parable of the Lamp put on a Stand – the second way in which Jesus applied this parable

When the crowds were increasing, he began to say, "This generation is an evil generation. It seeks a sign, but no sign will be given to it except the sign of Jonah. For as Jonah became a sign to the people of Nineveh, so will the Son of Man be to this generation. The queen of the South will rise up at the judgement with the men of this generation and condemn them, for she came from the ends of the earth to hear the wisdom of Solomon, and behold something greater than Solomon is here. The men of Nineveh will rise up at the judgement with this generation and condemn it, for they repented at the preaching of Jonah, and behold, something greater than Jonah is here.

"No one after lighting a lamp puts it in a cellar or under a basket, but on a stand, so that those who enter may see the light. Your eye is the lamp of your body. When your eye is healthy, your whole body is full of light, but when it is bad, your body is full of darkness. Therefore be careful lest the light in you be darkness. If then your whole body is full of light, having no part dark, it will be wholly bright, as when a lamp with its rays gives you light."

Luke 11 29-36, English Standard Version

('Under a basket' is sometimes translated under a barrel or under a bushel.)

The parable addressed to those who did not wish to see

Here is the second way in which the Lord used this parable. The setting is of great crowds hungry to witness dramatic signs and miracles, yet failing to recognise or to hear the One who was plainly before them. Jesus described them as an 'evil generation' who would stand condemned on the last day. They would be condemned by such people as the Queen of Sheba who travelled a great distance to hear Solomon's wisdom, and by the men of Nineveh who had heeded the word of God proclaimed by Jonah, and turned, and repented before God. They had actively responded, whereas so many of Jesus' hearers, and in particular the Pharisees and their scribes, refused to do so.

Those willing to see did not need a sign. The light was shining all around them. By Jesus' deeds and words it was becoming apparent to those willing to see that here was one who was indeed greater than a prophet and greater than even Solomon. Here before them, proclaiming the word of God with the power of God, was the anointed Son of God, the long promised Messiah.

Admiral Lord Nelson, famously and deliberately, put his telescope to his blind eye in order not to see ships. In exactly the same way the scribes and Pharisees – despite the clear prophecies of Scripture, the testimony of Simeon, Anna and John the Baptist, and the evidence before their eyes – had no eyes to see or recognise who Jesus really was, or to allow the light of his words to shine into their wilfully darkened minds. Even as he hung on the cross, this 'evil generation', as Jesus described them, was still taunting him with the same demand for a dramatic sign, 'If you are the son of God, come down from the cross.'

Behold something greater than Solomon is here
If the Queen of Sheba travelled so far to hear the wisdom of Solomon, and the men of the ungodly city of Nineveh turned in repentance on hearing Jonah, how much more should those hearing the very words of God from the lips of the Son of God, turn, repent and believe. In the day of God's judgement, that queen and the men of Nineveh will testify against such wilful rejection of God's word.

John Newton puts the challenge we all face, very clearly. 'The Scripture,' the word of God, 'is the rule by which we must all be judged at last; it is therefore our wisdom to judge ourselves by it now.' The ungodly men of Nineveh, hearing the words of God's prophet Jonah, had greater wisdom than the religious leaders, the 'experts in the word of God', hearing the words of their own long-promised Messiah, the Son of God!

Your eye is the lamp of your body
The eye is the lamp of our body in the sense that seeing enables our minds to be aware of our surroundings and so makes it possible for us to move appropriately. As they inform our minds, the eyes guide our hands and our feet, warn us to bend under a low branch, raise our foot over a step or perform intricate tasks. Although many people are forced to depend on sounds and feeling to guide them, without sight we really are in darkness.

In Jesus' day – as in so many poor communities today – there were a great many people who were blind, whose sight was damaged from birth, or by disease, or by injury. Note how many times blind people feature in the Gospel accounts, and note how each of them was desperate to be able to see. In order to survive, those who were unable to see were reduced to begging. And so Jesus' picture of a life without light would have been especially relevant and easily understood.

Therefore be careful lest the light in you be darkness – a hindrance to spiritual discernment
A person may be determined to follow some ungodly agenda or lifestyle. Is it then surprising that they are keeping themselves in the darkness of unbelief; closing their mind to the word of God? This is the reason our Lord warns the religious leaders to look to their own hearts which had become darkened by wilful unbelief, 'Therefore be careful lest the light in you be darkness.' John Calvin warns us to make sure that our minds, which ought to shine like a godly lamp to guide all our thoughts and actions, are not keeping us in ungodly darkness and so misleading the whole of our life. Here, too, is the danger of ignoring the promptings of our conscience; hardening our hearts because we are determined to follow our own ways.

It is possible to have a mind darkened by the many influences of the world around us, by the evil one, or by our own determined will. In that state, we cannot, or will not, see the truth of God, which seems foolishness to us, a stumbling block to our progress, and a hindrance that gets in the way of our dearly held plans and purposes – and so it must be suppressed and if possible destroyed. This was how the scribes and Pharisees came to view the Lord Jesus and his teaching. It was for this same reason that Paul, the great missionary apostle, was hated and hounded.

It is also how today, many politicians and leaders of lobbying and of special interest groups – who are demanding their perceived 'rights' the world over – view Christianity and the Christian heritage. The light of the word of God is publicly shining, but many do not wish to see. We dislike what God has caused to be written, and want it smothered in some way; put out of the public domain and confined to private worship. Yet it is the light of the word of God that has, to our great benefit, so wonderfully moulded the English speaking world, and the whole of Western civilization.

In every generation the proof of true faith is a humble obedience to the Lord God and an acceptance of his word.
The scribes and Pharisees were quite content for Jesus to be a popular teacher, quite content that he should display mighty acts of compassion – but absolutely not that he should be recognised as the anointed Son of the Most High, the Messiah.

Many Christian leaders in the church today cannot and will not accept the teaching that, in a personal sense, Christ Jesus died as a ransom; died in the place of each one of us to pay the price of our forgiveness. Yet, for those with eyes to see, by promise, pattern and prophesy, by the witness of John the Baptist and of the apostles, this is the consistent testimony of the word of God from Genesis to Revelation.

In this age, many of us are happy for God to be in his heaven and ready to bless us – just as long as the teachings of our Lord and his chosen apostles do not challenge our thinking or limit our choices. But sometimes obedience to our Lord and his word will restrict our pursuit of pleasure or of wealth. It may cause us to follow a very different direction from the one we would have chosen. And it may cause us to walk a very different path from those following the widely-held thinking of our time.

Why are we presented with these tests of obedience? Each one of them lays low our human pride and challenges us to humbly accept the word of God and his chosen way – or to reject it. Will we walk in the light of his word, or will we choose to ignore it, turn our back on it, or even suppress it, in order to follow our own dark path?

Words of great encouragement, a life full of light.
'If then your whole body is full of light, having no part dark, it will be wholly bright, as when a lamp with its rays gives you light.'

What an encouragement and contrast Jesus gives to those who will welcome the light of the truth of God and turn and live by the light – the whole of our lives gradually becoming filled with the enlightenment of the word of God, 'full of light, with no part dark . . .'

The Lord Jesus, the Son of God, will be acknowledged for who he is and what he came to do, and indeed for what he is poised to do as he returns in great glory as Lord and Judge. We will count it all joy to live for him, as John Newton, again, makes plain, if our minds are enlightened by the Spirit of God, 'the truth of the word of God is recognised, welcomed and increasingly informs our every thought, word and deed.'

Heavenly Father, soften hardened hearts that do not wish to see or hear. By your Holy Spirit, cause darkened minds to be opened. We ask these things for the glory of your name.

Questions for reflection or discussion

1. What prevented the scribes and Pharisees accepting Jesus for who he was? What prejudices, early teachings or expectations can blind us from discovering who he truly is?
2. Why was Jesus, and why was his teaching, so hated and rejected? Why is true biblical Christianity treated by so many in our day, as if it should be silenced, suppressed and ultimately eliminated?
3. Do we judge the word of God by our own opinions? Do we let the word of God judge our opinions? Who and what does Jesus say will finally be our judge?
4. If '. . . the word of God is recognised, welcomed, and increasingly informs our every thought, word and deed,' would we gradually find that there are long-held ideas that we discover are not right, and ways of living and behaving that we need to change?

References

'If you are the Son of God, come down from the cross' – Matthew 27:40

Go and preach the gospel – Mark 16:15

Some examples from the Scriptures of the teaching that the Son of Man died in our place to pay the price of our forgiveness:

By promise – Genesis 3:15

By pattern, under the picture of a lamb sacrificed in our stead – Exodus 12:1-14 (See also 1Corinthians 5:7)

By prophesy – Isaiah 53:1-9. John the Baptist – John 1:29-34.

The teaching of Jesus – Mark 10:45

The teaching of the apostles, Peter – 1Peter 1:18-20, Paul – Romans 5:6-11, John – Revelation 5:6-10

The Parable of the Lamp put on a Stand – the third way in which Jesus applied this parable

"Blessed are you when others revile you and persecute you and utter all kinds of evil against you falsely on my account. Rejoice and be glad, for your reward is great in heaven, for so they persecuted the prophets who were before you.

"You are the salt of the earth, but if salt has lost its taste, how shall its saltiness be restored? It is no longer good for anything except to be thrown out and trampled under people's feet.

"You are the light of the world. A city set on a hill cannot be hidden. Nor do people light a lamp and put it under a basket, but on a stand, and it gives light to all in the house. In the same way let your light shine before others, so that they may see your good works and give glory to your Father who is in heaven."

Matthew 5 11-16, English Standard Version

The parable addressed to disciples

The third situation in which Jesus uses this parable is recorded in Matthew chapter five, at the beginning of the Sermon on the Mount. Jesus is describing disciples as he has portrayed them in the famous beatitudes as being poor in spirit, mourning for their failures, meek, hungering and thirsting after God's right way, merciful, pure and peacemakers. And yet, although they would clearly be the best of citizens, seeking only the wellbeing of those around them and of the whole of society, he warned them that for his sake they would be hated and slandered, reviled and persecuted.

Then he told his disciples, nevertheless, 'You are the salt of the earth . . .' 'You are the light of the world.' He then gave the picture of a city on a hill which cannot be hidden, told this parable of the lamp, and concluded, 'In the same way let your light shine before others, so that they may see your good works and give glory to your Father who is in heaven.'

It is clear that the Lord Jesus intended his disciples to become unashamedly salt and light in a dark and decaying world. From the Day of Pentecost onwards, emboldened and empowered by the Holy Spirit, his chosen apostles, joined by the apostle Paul, fulfilled that commission at great cost to themselves, filling the cities with their teaching and turning the ancient world 'upside-down'.

Light in more recent times
In 1535 John Calvin fled his native France to escape religious persecution and sheltered in Basle before beginning his great work in Geneva a year later. He wrote of this parable, 'We are all children of the light, once we have received illumination by faith, and we are told to carry flaming torches in our hands, or we shall be lost in the darkness, and further to show others the path of life.' This is how Calvin saw the Gospel's work in the dark world of his day. It enlightens the minds of those who receive it and stirs them to long to share that enlightenment with those around them. What a world-wide light was held high by his faithful preaching and teaching! The city of Geneva became a beacon of godly government throughout Europe, the word of God permeating every department of its communal life. Although Geneva is built in a valley around a great lake, under the faithful preaching of the word of God, it really became as 'a city set on a hill.'

In England those who caught the reformation vision were, by their lives and their preaching, a shining light in the darkness of a benighted church and land. Brought to faith by the confession of Thomas Bilney, Hugh Latimer became the great preacher of the Reformation and held high the apostolic gospel as the Lord God gave him opportunity. He did so to the end of his life, even in the face of persecution and his untimely death under Queen Mary. His words spoken to Nicholas Ridley as they were bound together by an iron fetter to be burned at the stake in Oxford in 1555 are a world-famous witness to the light to the gospel of grace. "Be of good comfort, Master Ridley, and play the man: we shall this day light such a candle, by God's grace, in England, as I trust shall never be put out."

'This little light of mine . . .' the application of this parable to the local church and to each one of us

There is a delightful walk in lanes between woods and fields, known as 'the candlestick'. It is so called because the lanes form a circular walk to and from the church. The church has long been known as 'the candlestick' because its task is to hold, and to hold out, and to hold high the gospel of God. Matthew Henry rightly notes that the ministers and people of God must be as shining lights. Not only by our lips giving praise to God, but also in our lives by serving one another and those around us. 'So that they may see your good works and give glory to your Father who is in heaven.' They will only do so when our lips and our lives are all of a piece. By our deeds and by our words we are called to give glory to God – in order that those around us might turn and give glory to him, too.

As the scribes and Pharisees carefully and critically 'watched' our Lord, so the world watches those who bear his name. Our words and our ways of living shine as a light on a stand, or a city on a hill. The things that commend the gospel – and the things that do not – are plain for all around us to see. Naturally enough, they hardly notice the good, but do notice the things that do not commend the gospel. On a bigger scale, scandals involving God's people with money, sex or deceit are always guaranteed a place in the news!

From this parable, each one of us is personally challenged not to 'hide our light under a bushel.' We are all different and of different temperaments and abilities, but we all have a part to play in the forwarding of the kingdom of heaven, as the Lord God gives us opportunity.

How encouraging are the Lord's words about the lady breaking open her most precious flask of ointment, 'She has done what she could . . .' At great personal cost, she did what she could, while she could, and she did it for the Lord. That is our challenge. We may be called to be like Peter, preaching to thousands, or like Paul, travelling the empire to debate, persuade and plant churches in every city. Or we may, like Philip, be called to explain who Jesus really is and what he has done for us on the cross, to one individual; to someone in a chariot, on a train or in an aeroplane. Or we may be given opportunity to be like Tabitha who offered godly practical help to those around her. The challenge is always the same: to do what we can, while we can, and to do it for the Lord.

Some years ago, I thanked a neighbour who, over a number of years, had helped, encouraged and supported six or eight lonely and elderly people as their lives drew to a close. Her response, "I'm just letting my little light shine."

In overall conclusion
The shining light of the Lord Jesus and his word – our Lord's three applications of the parable of the lamp:

– The challenge to take note of who Jesus truly is, and to take care how we hear the word of God from his lips, and to be diligent to do it.
– The danger and error of suppressing the truth, or of personally turning a wilfully blind eye or a wilfully deaf ear.
– The great commission given to those who are his – to be lights for the Lord, holding high the word of God, both as a company of people and individually, 'You in your small corner and I in mine.'

Lord God, we thank you that you have caused your word to be held high, first by your Son and then by faithful men and women down the centuries, even to ourselves in our land and generation. Give us ears to hear and hearts to welcome and obey your sovereign word, and by your grace enable us to be bearers of your light and truth in our own day.

Questions for reflection or discussion

1. If true Christians are honest, caring, kind and hard-working – how is it that even the best of them will, from time to time, meet with the kind of rejection that Jesus described?
2. In what ways have the apostles, and other New Testament writers like Luke, by their preaching and writings continued to be a light in this world? Even having this parable before us bears witness to it!
3. The local church, both leaders and people, is called to be a 'candlestick'. How well does our church measure up to this description? As a body of believers and as individuals, in what ways could we be more faithful as lights in this increasingly dark world?

References

Filling cities with their teaching – Acts 5:28
Turning the world upside down – Acts 17:6
Critically watched our Lord – Luke 6:7
'She has done what she could' – Mark 14:3-9
Peter – Acts 2:14-42
Paul – for example, Acts 14:21-28
Philip – Acts 8:26-39
Tabitha, also known by her Greek name, Dorcas – Acts 9:36

The Good Samaritan

And behold, a lawyer stood up to put him to the test, saying, "Teacher, what shall I do to inherit eternal life?" He said to him, "What is written in the Law? How do you read it?" And he answered, "You shall love the Lord your God with all your heart and with all your soul and with all your strength and with all your mind, and your neighbour as yourself." And he said to him, "You have answered correctly; do this, and you will live."

But he, desiring to justify himself, said to Jesus, "And who is my neighbour?" Jesus replied, "A man was going down from Jerusalem to Jericho, and he fell among robbers, who stripped him and beat him and departed, leaving him half dead. Now by chance a priest was going down that road, and when he saw him he passed by on the other side. So likewise a Levite, when he came to the place and saw him, passed by on the other side. But a Samaritan, as he journeyed, came to where he was, and when he saw him, he had compassion.

He went to him and bound up his wounds, pouring on oil and wine. Then he set him on his own animal and brought him to an inn and took care of him. And the next day he took out two denarii and gave them to the innkeeper, saying, 'Take care of him, and whatever more you spend, I will repay you when I come back.' Which of these three, do you think, proved to be a neighbour to the man who fell among the robbers?" He said, "The one who showed him mercy." And Jesus said to him, "You go, and do likewise."

Luke 10:25 to 37, English Standard Version

The Good Samaritan

The key to this parable, which is only recorded by Luke, is to note that it is wrapped in a conversation and that a question during that conversation caused the Lord Jesus to tell it. In the light of this, may I invite you to look at the first part of the conversation, the parable, the concluding conversation, and pictures from the parable?

The conversation
The parable begins with the lawyer courteously and apparently innocently asking, 'What must I do to inherit eternal life?' The question was actually a cunning test put by an expert representing the religious leaders, to see if the Lord Jesus was challenging their teaching. If he was bringing any different teaching, the lawyer's question would lay it bare and they could charge him with heresy. If he was teaching what was already well recognised, his teaching could be exposed as needless.

At a genuinely spiritual level, his question, 'What must I do to inherit eternal life?' was a most important question and one which we each need to ask. 'How can I be right with God, be stirred to live a life that is pleasing to him here and now, and be freely pardoned and given life that not even death can snatch away?' But we will never tremble and ask that, until the Holy Spirit opens our eyes to see that our very breath is in the hand of Almighty God; that we are answerable to him and that we desperately do need to be right with him. Until then, we will give no thought to these things and, courting ultimate disaster, we will carry on living in God's world as if there were no God to whom we are accountable.

The underlying assumption of the lawyer and his fellow religious leaders was that, by 'religious observance', they could make themselves righteous. Their aim was to live a life that was so pleasing to God that they could make themselves acceptable before him and so 'earn' or 'achieve' eternal life. On this basis, they taught that eternal life was to be achieved by merit; by the detailed keeping of the Law as expanded and defined in their traditions.

Sadly, the question on the lips of the lawyer completely lost any spiritual value as it was asked, not for his own learning and eternal well-being, but, as Luke records, to test or tempt the Lord Jesus. In the same way, if we reduce serious spiritual questions to malicious or casual debating points, or handle the word of God without a humble respect for it, we must not be surprised if we forfeit any experience of the power of the gospel of God to help or rescue us.

The Lord Jesus replied, in effect, 'You are the specialist,' and invited the lawyer to answer his own question. Not by asking for his considered opinion, nor by asking for the teaching of his religious contemporaries, but by asking, 'In regard to this, what has the Lord God caused to be written?' If we would truly lay hold of eternal life according to God's word, and avoid a sea of competing human traditions and opinions, all claiming equal validity, this is the question we must ask. 'What has the Lord God himself caused to be written?' The Scriptures were written 'for our learning' so that by reading or hearing their message, we might lay hold of everlasting life.

Intellectually, the lawyer gave an excellent answer. He offered the two greatest principles of the Law which carry all the rest of the laws with them and put them in their rightful priority and place. The first great principle, from Deuteronomy, is to enthrone the Lord God, and not ourselves, in key position in our lives, submitting all to him: mind, heart and will – our decisions, our work and our career, our money and our leisure. The second, from Leviticus, is to look after those around us, as we naturally look after ourselves. It is a command to wish well to all, and ill to none and, like our Lord, to go about doing good not hurt, and finally to be as generous and forgiving of others as we are so naturally forgiving of ourselves.

The lawyer came to test and tempt, and yet what he said was excellent and our Lord acknowledged it, and indeed quoted the same two passages when he was later challenged to define the greatest commandment in the Law.

If we assume 'love for God' is an occasional nod in his direction, maybe on Sundays, and think of 'neighbour' as those nice people next door, it is not difficult to keep these principles. This was how the religious leaders worked. Their traditional teaching defined 'love towards God' as ritual observance of the law, and 'love towards neighbour' as showing love and concern only for their own favoured and selected people. The great principles, as God gave them in the Scriptures, had no such boundaries.

The challenge to the lawyer came in the next breath. It was not intellectual but personal. 'Do this and you will live,' a command to actually do it, not just to know the great principles but in practice to love the Lord God with all of his being and to love his neighbour, whoever that may be, in the way that he loved himself.

Not surprisingly, the lawyer did not like it. It was much too direct. He wanted to escape such a personal challenge, as many of us do. Like the lawyer, when our lives are put under the searchlight of God, we find that we all fall very far short. Only the perfect Son of God could, and actually did, live these principles to the full. The challenge to the lawyer, and to each one of us, should drive us to cry to the Lord God for mercy. The challenge to continuously and completely love God and neighbour plainly shows us that we can never merit eternal life; it is a gift given by the mercy, forgiveness and kindness of Almighty God.

Seeing that he might be forced to admit his failure, the lawyer swiftly changed the subject. 'But wishing to justify himself he asked, "Who is my neighbour?"' Look to your own heart. Do we not much prefer to justify ourselves than admit our own need of forgiveness?

Over the centuries, the religious leaders had worked on this, debating, 'Who should be pulled out of a ditch and who not?' They made their traditional definition of neighbour relatively neat, narrow and easy to keep. You only needed to regard as neighbour a fellow member of God's ancient people the Jews and even then not if he was a sinner or heretic. So, should you come across a Gentile on the point of death there was no obligation to help to save his life; it was expendable because he was not one of God's chosen ones. Here was a terrible, false conclusion derived from wonderful truth. It grew out of God's chosen people keeping holy and separate, but that did not lessen their responsibility to care for those about them who are also made in the image of God.

The parable – The response of Jesus to the question, 'Who is my neighbour?'
The Lord Jesus answered the lawyer's question, not with a list of those he must care about and those he could ignore, as the lawyer was expecting, but with a parable which turned the lawyer's eye from rules and regulations that would determine who should and who should not be loved, to an examination of his own heart and his own attitude. As Archbishop Trench observes, it is as if Jesus said to him, 'You ask, "Who is my neighbour?" I will show you a man who did not ask that question, then your own heart can judge which of you is closer to the heart of God.'

This is a perfect example of how a parable works. The lawyer came to examine Jesus, but found himself having to examine his own heart – and that by comparison with a Samaritan, a man he would, by nature and training, utterly despise and reject.

The scene could very easily be pictured by the lawyer. There were constant incidents on the road to Jericho, a notorious, bandit-ridden route. A traveller could be suddenly surrounded by a band of thugs, mugged, robbed, stripped, wounded and left for dead.

Nevertheless, this road from Jerusalem was used by the priests and Levites as they came on and off duty at the temple. Along came first a priest, then a Levite. These were men who taught others the great principles spelled out by the lawyer. Men who theoretically knew the principles very well and could have put them into practice by helping the wounded man – but, as the listening lawyer would expect, neither of them did so. Their traditional teaching excused them. Was he one of them? Was he a sinner? Stripped and unconscious, there was no telling.

The priest, a man of social standing, would hardly have been on foot or alone for the 17 mile, 3,000 ft descent through very dangerous territory. In a similar manner a priest's assistant, a Levite, also passed by. These first two men in the Lord's parable did not feel any need to get involved and could undoubtedly have supplied many good, practical and religious reasons why they should not. For example, the man was unknown, there were robbers about, they had their own business to attend to. And, as Kenneth Bailey points out, they must not defile themselves or they would be unable to perform their religious role and would alienate themselves from their supporting community of fellow clergy. Personally, ridding themselves of any ceremonial defilement would prove costly. However, their 'rule-book religion' had overturned the great principle. The great principle of loving your neighbour needs to govern lesser traditions, not the other way round – as it must for us. For example if our personal house rules state that we must not get our shoes muddy, that must not stop us from rescuing a child stuck in a mire if we are safely able to do so.

These two men, although very religious, had no heart for the man in trouble even when they could help. Here in the Lord's parable was a stinging reflection on the lawyer; an arrow to his heart as he was, of course, a member of the same clerical class. And maybe a challenge to ourselves; is there a unity and a continuity, between our 'religious life and words' and the way we actually treat people Monday to Saturday?

Alexander Mclaren points out that if the description of the two 'legally correct' but heartless religious leaders was offensive to the lawyer, how much more the next scene!

If there was one group of people the religious leaders absolutely despised, it was the Samaritans who had blended the true faith of Israel with their own local and historical beliefs. Yet, following the priest and the Levite, and to the horror and discomfort of the lawyer, here is a Samaritan pictured as 'a man after God's own heart'. When he saw the half-dead victim, he was moved to the very depth of his being with pity for this unknown man in such trouble. Unlike the self-consciously correct religious leaders, the Samaritan was filled with compassion for him, not just with kind words, but with practical, costly and time-consuming help. His own business had to wait while he attended to the needs of this stranger. He himself was a prime target for robbers, yet he stopped, cleaned and bound up the man's wounds, set him on his own beast and brought him to a place of safety. At the inn he personally cared for him – maybe of necessity, for inns were not always good places to be. When he left next morning, as if the man was his own son, the Samaritan paid for his care till the man was well enough to be on his way, making sure he was not trapped as a debtor for, having been robbed, he had no means to pay. Should his stay need to be longer there was the promise of settlement of any outstanding charges.

The conversation concluded and the parable applied
In the conversation that follows the parable, the Lord Jesus reshapes the lawyer's question, 'Who is my neighbour?' to, 'To whom am I to be neighbour?' and draws the answer to from the lawyer's own lips. To the question of our Lord, 'Who proved to be a neighbour?' he answers, somewhat uncomfortably and grudgingly, 'The one who showed mercy.' He could just not bring himself to say 'the Samaritan.' However, he had to accept the challenge to go and do likewise – even if that meant helping a despised Samaritan should he find one in desperate need.

The compassion pictured in the parable knows no bounds, it is not restricted by our 'already being very busy', or the cost, or the rules of 'our community'. Here is a foretaste of the kingdom of heaven, godly loving concern for one another, with every human barrier removed.

The lawyer, who, with his great knowledge, came to test the Lord Jesus Christ, finds himself tested – and learning from a despised Samaritan! Before the One with whom we have to deal, the pride of man is brought very low.

Pictures from the parable
We do not know to what extent the Lord intended to reveal his own heart and purpose to this unfriendly lawyer, who might nevertheless, in later years, reflect on the encounter. But we do know that Christian eyes throughout the centuries have seen, in the compassion and costly care freely given by the Good Samaritan, a picture of the Lord Jesus himself.

The Lord lived as he taught others to do, and so his own approach is often reflected in his parables. As, through this parable, he taught the lawyer compassion, so he showed compassion again and again throughout his earthly ministry. So we are justified in noting parallels between the compassion of the Samaritan and that of the Lord in order to stir us to gratitude for what he has done for us.

When, like the wounded victim on the road, we come to the end of our own self-help and, maybe to our great disappointment, find formal, legalistic religion an absolute failure, then and only then will we cast ourselves on the Living God. He sees us in our helpless extremity and has compassion on us. He personally rescues us. The rescue is very costly and all at his expense. His own dearly beloved Son laid down his life for us. Finally, taking us into his safe care, he continues to make provision for us and to care for us.

Reflections like these can cause us to be moved with wonder. Why did the very Son of God bother with me? Why did he not pass me by? Why did he choose me and with such costly love make me one of his precious rescued people, a child of the living God?

How can I love him enough in return? How can I serve him? How can I spend my remaining days poured out in gratitude to him?

How very different this is from the lawyer's route of detailed religious observance, believing he could earn the Lord God's favour and eternal life. He was able to quote the two great commandments, but at heart knew nothing of such love.

Leon Morris writes, 'This kind of love is our response to God's love for us, it is not the cause of his acceptance of us.'

Stirred from the heart by the Holy Spirit of God, here are the two great commandments quoted by the lawyer – to love the Lord God and to love your neighbour as yourself – being joyfully fulfilled from a deep and heartfelt sense of gratefulness. Love like this, when it touches a community, is surely a foretaste of the kingdom of heaven.

Heavenly Father, by your Holy Spirit set our hearts and minds and lives ablaze with love for you. Stir us with compassion; give us eyes to see, ears to hear and hearts to respond to the secret cries of those you would have us help. Cause your kingdom to come, your will to be done, beginning in our own hearts and lives.

Questions for reflection or discussion

1. Is it possible to be sincere and earnest in religious observance without having a humble love for the Lord God and other people?
2. Why do we need the Holy Spirit to open our eyes before we will genuinely ask the lawyer's question?
3. How can we discern true godliness from the great variety of opinions and church teachings around us?
4. Do we, like the lawyer, have limits to make these great principles of God's Law 'manageable'?
5. Are we willing to heed the direct challenges of Scripture?

6. To whom are we to be neighbours? Is that always going to be comfortable?

7. What would the world be like if the two principles the lawyer quoted were practised by all of us?

8. What glimpses of the Lord Jesus himself might you see in the parable of the Good Samaritan?

References

Written for our learning – Romans 15:4

Love toward God, Deuteronomy – 6:5

Love toward neighbour – Leviticus 19:18

The greatest commandment – Matthew 22:35-40, Mark 12:28-31

This people honours me – Isaiah 29:13

A man after God's own heart – 1 Samuel 13:14

The Friend at Midnight and the Good Gifts of a Father

Now Jesus was praying in a certain place, and when he finished, one of his disciples said to him, "Lord teach us to pray, as John taught his disciples." And he said to them, "When you pray, say: "Father, hallowed be your name. Your kingdom come. Give us each day our daily bread, and forgive us our sins, for we ourselves forgive everyone who is indebted to us. And lead us not into temptation."

And he said to them, "Which of you who has a friend will go to him at midnight and say to him, 'Friend lend me three loaves, for a friend of mine has arrived on a journey and I have nothing to set before him'; and he will answer from within, 'Do not bother me; the door is now shut, and my children are with me in bed. I cannot get up and give you anything'? I tell you, though he will not get up and give him anything because he is his friend, yet because of his impudence (his shameless persistence) he will rise and give him whatever he needs. And I tell you, ask, and it will be given to you; seek, and you will find; knock and it will be opened to you. For everyone who asks receives, and the one who seeks finds, and to the one who knocks it will be opened. What father among you, if his son asks for a fish, will instead of a fish give him a serpent; or if he asks for an egg, will give him a scorpion? If you then, who are evil, know how to give good gifts to your children, how much more will the heavenly Father give the Holy Spirit to those who ask him!"

Luke 11:1-13, English Standard Version

"Ask, and it will be given to you; seek, and you will find; knock and it will be opened to you. For everyone who asks receives, and the one who seeks finds, and to the one who knocks it will be opened. Or which one of you, if his son asks him for bread, will give him a stone? Or if he asks for a fish, will give him a serpent? If you then, who are evil, know how to give good gifts to your children, how much more will your Father who is in heaven give good things to those who ask him!"

Matthew 7:7-11, English Standard Version

The Friend at Midnight and the Good Gifts of a Father – the Lord's teaching on prayer

The setting of these parables
As a result of a disciple's request, Luke records that we are given what is often called the 'Lord's Prayer'. It is a pattern of prayer given for disciples individually and for disciples to pray together. The Lord had just spent time in prayer and so it was a natural question for one of the disciples to ask. The short parable of the friend at midnight is only recorded by Luke. It was given to the disciples as he privately taught them to pray.

Matthew records the Lord Jesus publicly teaching a fuller version of this great prayer to the disciples and to the listening crowd, in the setting of the Sermon on the Mount.

The prayer is in two parts. The first part is entirely centred on the Lord God, his glory and his purposes for the whole of the human race. We pray that he would cause his name to be universally honoured, that his kingly rule might be seen in practical outworking throughout the world, each of us playing our part and living according to his will; doing that which pleases him. Only after prayers like these, do we ask, in the second part, for his enabling and provision that we may joyfully live for him. We ask these things, not for our own comfort, but in order that we may be able to fulfil his purposes for our lives, and to do so as his forgiven and forgiving people, free from anxiety.

Alexander Maclaren, commenting on the Lord's Prayer, says, we may or may not recite it often, but we use it aright when it teaches us how to shape our lives. He also notes that in the prayer, the Father's glory takes first place and our needs come second, and comments, tellingly, how few of our prayers follow that pattern. The Lord's Prayer is not like so many of our self-centred prayers.

The Friend at Midnight

Immediately following his teaching of the prayer, Luke records the Lord giving these two short parables. They were given to spur disciples to persist in praying to our heavenly Father and not to give up easily. And they were given to teach us to pray for his good hand on our lives in all that we attempt to say and do.

The first parable is the vivid picture of a man hammering on his neighbour's door at midnight because he has no bread to set before his unexpected guest – a great lapse of hospitality in that culture. Eastern travellers often travelled in the evening in order to avoid the heat of the mid-day sun and so could easily arrive late and unexpectedly. Typically the houses were tiny, with the whole family living and sleeping in a single room. The settled household may even have included the family's domestic animals being kept safe in the house overnight. So it is easy to imagine the disturbance that would be caused by getting up in the dark, trying to step over sleeping bodies, opening the door and providing bread for the neighbour. The whole household would be awakened and thrown into commotion. No wonder the neighbour told his friend to go away! Nevertheless the man continued to knock on his friend's door, totally shameless in his urgent need to have bread to set before his guest. In the end, for the sake of peace and some sleep for the rest of the night, it was better to get up and give the man some bread, rather than let him continue hammering on the door.

The Lord was not teaching his disciples to be inconsiderate in making demands on friends. Nor was he teaching us to have a hard and uncaring attitude to neighbours in need, when, despite the inconvenience, we are able to help them. The Lord Jesus was simply holding up, as an example, the unrestrained boldness of the man in need, showing that this is the way disciples must learn to pray; urgently, really meaning business with the Lord God – exactly as he taught his disciples to pray: 'Father, cause your name to be held high, cause your kingdom to come, cause your will to be done throughout the world, in the way it is gladly and willingly done in heaven.' It really is as urgent as that; just like the man knocking on his friend's door at midnight.

Disciples must really mean business, put heart and mind in praying for, and pursuing, the honour of the name of the Lord God, the extending of his kingdom and the doing of his will – just as the first disciples learned from the Lord, and then spent the rest of their lives doing. If we really want to see what we are praying for fulfilled, we must also be doing all in our power to play our part in bringing it about. Matthew Henry challenges us, not to hold our peace before God, or give up, until the kingdom of God and his Son comes in all its fullness and in all its glory.

Campbell Morgan points out that this is a 'how much more' parable. If the sleeping neighbour will rise to give bread to his friend, how much more will the Lord God answer the earnest prayers of his children. If the shameless knocking of the friend can stir even a sleeping and very unwilling neighbour like this, how much more will the feeble, yet serious and persistent, prayers of his people be heard by a loving Father in heaven in whose hand are all our circumstances and who never slumbers or sleeps.

The Lord is teaching us to be as serious and persistent as this man in the parable, as we pray for the spiritual awakening of family members, friends and neighbours; to be bold as we 'hammer on the gates of heaven' or, as a former generation of godly people, alluding to Jacob, put it, as we 'wrestle with God'. Leon Morris comments that if we do not want what we plead for enough to be bold and persistent, we do not want it very much!

In praying for the awakening and revival of the church and the restoration of our land to godly ways, we do well to heed Calvin's words and be assured that the Lord will hear us '. . . if we persevere constantly in prayer and if our minds do not slacken through difficulty or delay.'

William Burns spent years earnestly praying for the kingdom of God to be established in China. It was not until towards the end of his life that the Lord God, in answer to those prayers, raised up the mightily used missionary to China, Hudson Taylor. We may see answers to our prayers long delayed, yet we are called, as were the first disciples, to be unashamedly 'bold and persistent'.

We have only applied the parable to the first section of the Lord's Prayer, but it also applies to the second section. By this parable disciples are taught to earnestly pray for all that we really need to live for the honour of our heavenly Father. We are taught to pray seriously and continuously for forgiveness and for a forgiving spirit toward those around us, for our Father's provision of our essential daily needs, for safety in a world of temptation and for deliverance from the malice and interference of the evil one and those under him.

Teaching in both parable and plain speech
That our heavenly Father welcomes such boldness in the prayerful requests we make, is spelled out plainly by our Lord, and recorded by Luke between the parables, 'And I tell you, ask, and it will be given to you; seek, and you will find; knock and it will be opened to you. For everyone who asks receives, and the one who seeks finds, and to the one who knocks it will be opened.'

Three clear instructions for disciples then and now: To ask, and go on asking. To seek and, like a treasure hunter, to go on seeking with ongoing effort and diligence. To knock, and to prevail in our knocking. We have the word of our Lord that those who do so will be heard, will find, and will be given.

Should this be taken as a guarantee that all our prayers will be answered as we would choose? Surely not, says Alexander Maclaren, in this world of bitter disappointments, baffled desires and frustrated quests! Yet we will be heard. However, we are invited to pray, not for ourselves and the fulfilment of our personal desires and comfort, but for the glory of his name. As the apostle James reminds us, too often we forget that and ask wrongly or mistakenly.

The Father's Good Gifts

'What father among you, if his son asks for a fish, will instead of a fish give him a serpent; or if he asks for an egg, will give him a scorpion?' Immediately, our Lord catches our imagination. Would any responsible father behave like this? If we, with all our failings, know how to give our children good things, and would never give them useless or dangerous things in place of the food they need, how much more can disciples depend on our heavenly Father to give us all that we really need.

Our heavenly Father is so much more than even the very best of human fathers. He is consistently providing all that is best for his children. The Lord God's steadfast loving care, his mercy towards his people, is one of the great themes of the Hebrew Bible, our Old Testament.

Matthew records the Lord telling a slightly different version of this parable beginning, 'Which one of you, if his son asks for bread, will give him a stone . . . ?' and concluding, '. . . how much more will your Father who is in heaven give good things to those who ask him!' We can each think of many 'good things' which, from our point of view, would be desirable! But our Lord had something greater in mind.

In Luke's gospel, the promise of the Lord Jesus is very specific, "How much more will the heavenly Father give the Holy Spirit to those who ask him!" The Lord Jesus is drawing attention to the one 'good thing' that is absolutely essential for our eternal well-being, and is essential, too, for our usefulness in our Lord's service here and now. It is not a prayer for comfort, but a prayer for the Lord God, by his Holy Spirit to take up residence and to glorify his name in and through our lives.

At the time, the disciples may not have fully understood what their Lord meant, for, as John makes plain in his gospel, the Holy Spirit had not yet been given, neither had the disciples been given the teaching they were to receive in the Upper Room. They had known something of the Holy Spirit with them, but, until later, knew nothing of the Holy Spirit in their lives and filling their lives, in the way they did at and after Pentecost.

Luke, who we believe wrote the Acts of the Apostles as well as the gospel bearing his name, would have been able to see the whole picture. He would have seen first-hand the mighty working of God by his Holy Spirit in the lives of the first disciples. From those passages in the book of Acts which make reference to 'we' – it also appears that Luke accompanied the apostle Paul on part of his final missionary journey. And so he would have witnessed the work of God the Holy Spirit in and through the life of the great apostle to the Gentiles.

An overall picture of the Lord God at work by his Holy Spirit

Luke's record of this parable with our Lord's promise of the Holy Spirit to those who ask the Father, is very challenging. We would perhaps do well to look at what lies behind the promise, by way of a brief survey of the nature and work of God the Holy Spirit.

From the very beginning, the Spirit was involved in bringing our whole world into being. Then, throughout the Old Testament, we read of the Holy Spirit moving the prophets of God to speak God's word, and giving individual people gifts and abilities to enable them to fulfil God's purposes. In New Testament times, the Holy Spirit was to bring to the disciples' minds all that Jesus had taught, and so cause the gospels to be written. His work in and through the lives of the apostles is recorded by Luke in the book of Acts.

Today the work of the Holy Spirit is most strikingly seen in times of revival, when the eyes of totally God-ignoring men and women are opened to see their plight before Almighty God, causing them to cry out to him for mercy, as they come to recognise that each one of us will be called to account for our failure to honour him. It is then the work of the Holy Spirit to open eyes to see the wonder of God's amnesty: his free forgiveness offered in and through the cross of his Son. This is the work the Holy Spirit did so dramatically as the apostle Peter preached on the Day of Pentecost and as the apostle Paul reached out to the Gentile world with the gospel.

The Holy Spirit and the individual child of God
In our day, the Holy Spirit begins his sovereign work in each of our lives by giving us an interest in, and then a hunger for the things of God. He shows us our desperate plight and draws us to long to know and be right with our heavenly Father. He brings to life the Bible and through its pages shows us who Jesus truly is, and what he has done for us. He enables us, individually, to put our trust in the Son of God who loved us and gave himself for us, and, as we do so, causes us to be born of the Spirit and so become a child of God. As with those who came to believe on the Day of Pentecost, it is the Holy Spirit who gives us an ongoing hunger for the apostles' teaching and a longing to put it into practice in our lives. He gives us a delight in the company of fellow believers and in opportunities to pray. We find that we love to be among God's called-out people.

Only when the Holy Spirit does his sovereign work, will we begin to discover the wonder of the Lord God's love, mercy and kindness towards us his wayward creatures. For it is the Holy Spirit who shows us the majesty of God and how desperately far we have fallen by failing to honour our Maker. It is then the Holy Spirit who opens our eyes to see and softens our proud hearts to be willing to accept the Lord God's provision for our forgiveness in and through the cross of his only Son.

The apostle Paul writes of the love of God flooding our hearts and lives. 'The love of God poured into our hearts by the Holy Spirit who is given us.' Here is an overwhelming and abiding awareness of the Lord God's mercy, patience, kindness and love towards us, totally unworthy as we discover ourselves to be.

Only when the Holy Spirit enables us to know for ourselves the immensity of God's love in giving his Son for our rescue, will we respond in grateful love to him from the heart, and only then will we truly love his Son, the Lord Jesus, who loved us and gave himself for our forgiveness.

As we discover our totally undeserving selves to be beloved of God and made his forgiven sons and daughters, it is the Holy Spirit who will begin to change our thinking and attitudes, prompting us to tell others of God's mercy and to be increasingly forgiving of those around us.

Then further, it is the Holy Spirit of God who opens our eyes to greatly value, learn from, and spiritually grow by the reading of the Scriptures. Until then, reading the Bible may be a religious duty or academic exercise, but when our prayers and our reading, and the prayers that spring from that reading, are in all in submission to the leading of the Holy Spirit, the word of God truly becomes a light to our path and a nourishing joy to our spirits.

What great things we miss, if we ignore or pass over our Lord's invitation to ask the Father for the Holy Spirit, and welcome him to do these things and so much more in and through our own lives.

The Holy Spirit and the people of God

Among God's people as a community, it is the Holy Spirit who, having opened our eyes to see who Jesus truly is and what he has done for us on the cross, moves among us to enable us to work together as a team as, with love, forgiveness and a common purpose, we reach out to those around us in compassion and concern for their spiritual and physical well-being. When it is real, outsiders recognise it immediately, 'God is with them.' 'God is among them.' 'See how these Christians love one another.'

The Holy Spirit active in our lives, individually and as a company of believers, is God's seal and mark of ownership of his people.

As we begin to live in obedience to our heavenly Father, the Holy Spirit equips us to bring honour to the Lord God, as he did the first disciples, in both natural and supernatural ways. Too often, this last mentioned work of the Holy Spirit can either be promoted out of all proportion to the rest of his sovereign work of making us God's holy people. Or it can be neglected, even shunned and denied, to our great loss.

Without the Holy Spirit actively at work in our lives we are left spiritually arid, 'dry as dust'. Sadly, you will find many an all but 'God-free' ministry and church, ably led and socially active but spiritually barren; unaware of any need for the 'felt presence of God' to be brooding over the people and the preacher.

On the other hand if the more dramatic work of the Holy Spirit in our lives is over-emphasised at the expense of the full Biblical picture of his wonderful work, we are, as John Newton puts it '. . . on enchanted ground, and exposed to all the illusions of imagination and enthusiasm.' We easily become prey to the latest exciting 'spiritual fashion', often 'highly spiritual' in our own eyes, and yet, like the Corinthian Christians, actually shallowly rooted in the truth of God's word, very open to being misled, and often very worldly in our attitudes and in the way we live. Like all that God gives us, his more dramatic gifts can be used for the glory of his name and the furtherance of his kingdom, or in some way used to feed our hunger for excitement or our own ego.

For our spiritual wellbeing, we need to remember to hold fast to the whole Biblical picture of the Holy Spirit's work in our lives, which is to bring glory to our heavenly Father. Then we will keep together a close attention to the word of God and a humble dependence on the help and leading of his Spirit. Matthew Henry suggests that disciples should not read a godly book, write a letter, or visit someone, without first bringing it to our heavenly Father and begging the Holy Spirit to go before us to open eyes, lead and guide.

It is, surely, for this great and total work of God that our Lord bids us to pray, as he promises, "How much more will the heavenly Father give the Holy Spirit to those who ask him!"

Heavenly Father, stir us to pray as earnestly and from the heart as our Lord Jesus taught us, as we pray for our world, for those around us and for ourselves. Give us a hunger to know you better, and for the Holy Spirit to touch and inhabit all we think and do and say, for the glory of your name.

Questions for reflection or discussion

1. Alexander Maclaren quoting from the King James' Version of the Bible, asks, "How many of our prayers are 'after this manner'?" – God centred and after the pattern of the Lord's Prayer?
2. Why do so many of our public and private prayers tend to be self-centred?
3. Have we known of people who have seriously 'hammered on the doors of heaven' or 'wrestled with God'? What do we know of such praying?

4. Many people live in God's world as if God did not exist. Have you seen someone turn from such a way of thinking and, under the hand of God by his Holy Spirit, become a believing and thoroughly new person?

5. To what extent have you experienced such a work of God? Can you see something of the evidences of the Holy Spirit working – often quietly – in your own life?

6. Have you known a church where outsiders have been attracted because they sensed a real work of God amongst his people?

(There is a sister book by the same author exploring the Lord's Prayer much more fully, *To Change the world for good . . . Exploring and Applying the Lord's Prayer*. For further details, see page 403)

References

Matthew's record of the Lord's Prayer – Matthew 6:7-15
Jacob wrestling with God – Genesis 32:24-28
Because we ask wrongly, or amiss – James, 4:3
The Lord God's steadfast loving care – e.g. Psalm 103:15-18
'. . . good things to those who ask . . .' – Matthew 7:11
Holy Spirit not yet given – John 7:37-39
The Upper Room teaching on the Holy Spirit – John 14:15-17 and 25, 15:26-27, 16:4-15
The Holy Spirit poured into our hearts, Romans 5:5

The Holy Spirit:
Involved from the beginning – Genesis 1:2
Moved the prophets to speak – e.g. 2Peter 1:20-21
Gave gifts and abilities – e.g. to the master craftsman Bezalel, Exodus 31:1-5
To bring to mind and instruct – John 14:25

Called to account – e.g. John the Baptist Luke 3:7, Peter at Pentecost Acts 2:36-40, Paul at Athens Acts 17:30-31

Open eyes to see the things of God – John 3:3

Born of the Spirit – John 3:5-7

Hunger for the Apostles' teaching – Acts 2:42

Love of God poured into our hearts – Romans 5:5

The Holy Spirit as God's seal and mark of ownership – Ephesians 1:13-14, Romans 8:9

Working together as a team; partners and co-workers – Philippians 1:27 and 2:1-5

'See how they love . . .' Tertullian, one of the early Church Fathers, noting what the local people were saying about the Christian community, wrote, '"Look," they say, "See how these Christians love one another," – for they themselves hate one another.'

The Rich Farmer or the Rich Fool

Someone in the crowd said to him, "Teacher, tell my brother to divide the inheritance with me." But he said to him, "Man, who made me a judge or arbitrator over you?" And he said to them, "Take care, and be on your guard against all covetousness, for one's life does not consist in the abundance of his possessions." And he told them a parable, saying, "The land of a rich man produced plentifully, and he thought to himself, 'What shall I do, for I have nowhere to store my crops?' And he said, 'I will do this: I will tear down my barns and build larger ones, and there I will store all my grain and my goods. And I will say to my soul, "Soul, you have ample goods laid up for many years; relax, eat, drink, be merry."' But God said to him, 'Fool! This night your soul is required of you, and the things you have prepared, whose will they be?' So is the one who lays up treasure for himself and is not rich toward God."

Luke 12:13-21, English Standard Version

The Rich Farmer; the Successful but Mistaken Man

The background to the parable
Why was the parable told? The Lord Jesus had just been speaking of very serious matters; of being dragged, on his account, before councils, of trusting the Holy Spirit to give inspired words, God's words, in such a situation. He had spoken some of the most solemn and terrifying words that ever passed his lips: that ongoing sinning against the Holy Spirit is the one unforgivable sin. Into such solemn matters, one of his hearers broke in, interrupted, to say, 'Take my side and tell my brother to divide the inheritance with me.' And Jesus responded,

'Man,' – by no means a warm and friendly response – 'who made me an arbitrator; a judge and divider of wealth?' Would he not arbitrate in such a situation? Would he not support the man's cause? Did he not care about injustice?

Yes, clearly, Jesus did care, but he went to the root of it. Addressing both the man and the crowd, he said, 'Be on your guard against all covetousness.' The real problem was not the division of the inheritance but the single-minded pursuit of this world's possessions. There are several Biblical words for covetousness, but the underlying word here is a grasping after property, money and 'things'. And such an all-consuming desire for this world's goods is a foe to be fought. Concerning money, the Romans had a proverb, 'Money is like sea water; the more you drink the thirstier you become.' 'Be on your guard,' said the Lord Jesus, 'against all covetousness,' you cannot own or buy life – and great possessions are not its measure.

An inheritance, under the blessing of God, can be a liberating joy. As Solomon put it, 'The Lord makes rich and adds no sorrow.' But without that blessing, great wealth, whether secured by our own straightforward endeavour, gained at the expense of others, or given to us as an inheritance, can be our undoing. It can enslave us – or even carry us to hell. Thirty gleaming pieces of silver – could love of money have been the bait with which Satan secured Judas the betrayer? There are strong hints in the Gospel of John that it could have been so. Beware.

Did this man, asking the Lord to secure his part of an inheritance, find himself with an inheritance that was the junior share of a partnership with an elder brother who was withholding his younger brother's share? Perhaps this was the very difficult situation that the prodigal son of our Lord's later parable was determined to avoid. If that was the case, no wonder the younger brother wanted the inheritance divided. To leave it undivided, as was the custom in those days, would come at great cost to himself. It could make him, in all but name, a slave to his elder brother. The elder brother would want to hold onto the total inheritance, for to divide it would weaken the overall estate, while the younger brother was determined to tear his portion away, no matter what damage that did to the whole estate. What a situation grasping covetousness creates!

Into that situation, the Lord Jesus spoke to the man, to the disciples, and to all who will hear, 'Take care, and be on your guard against all covetousness, for a one's life does not consist in the abundance of his possessions.'

Kenneth Bailey draws attention to the fact that by natural human selfishness we see an injustice only from our own perspective. We rarely attempt to see the whole picture by asking questions: How has this come about? What is the other party's perspective? Is reconciliation or restitution possible? And so we rarely seek a God-honouring solution. The demand is for justice from *my* perspective, in this case division of the inheritance.

Sometimes, when all proper and legal avenues have been pursued, there simply is no justice, no earthly possibility of reconciliation or godly harmony. The stark choice is then either, to live, and maybe die, consumed with a bitter determination to secure what we consider to be 'justice' – or, to let go a just claim and live at peace before God, recognising that ultimate justice is in his hands.

Look for yourself and see that, in our day, grasping for money, possessions and property – covetousness – is the root of so much sharp practice, so much misery, so much evil and strife in society – and, as in this case, in families.

And so to the parable itself

I want to follow Joseph Parker and look at it phrase by phrase to see where the farmer went wrong, and so learn from this man who was so successful – and yet before the Lord God was so mistaken; such a fool.

'The land of a rich man produced plentifully.' There is nothing dishonourable or dishonest mentioned about that, nor is it suggested that he became rich by exploiting those who worked for him. He clearly had good ground, had prepared it well, had sown good seed and as a result had prospered. That is wisdom, not foolishness. God bless him! Christians and Christian preachers in particular have a habit of verbally attacking the rich and successful. Rather, pray for wealthy and successful people, they are 'God's treasurers'. The rich person's responsibility before God, for the use of their wealth, is very great.

'. . . and he thought to himself, 'What shall I do, for I have nowhere to store my crops? . . . I will tear down my barns and build larger ones.' He is no fool here, he is to be commended. He faces the problem without delay or uncertainty. There is no sentimental clinging to the past, to the old barns which, maybe, a family member built. He wants to make the most of his, unacknowledged, God-given prosperity. The barns are too small and so no longer fit for purpose and must be replaced. Here is a forward-looking man of clear and decisive action, who, as a result of his success, is poised to take early retirement.

'And I will say to my soul, "Soul you have ample goods laid up for many years; relax, eat, drink, and be merry."' – Sadly, his wisdom has a very great defect. At heart he is totally self-centred: 'Relax,' reflecting his years of stress and toil building up his little empire. 'My soul' – yet our very breath is in the hand of God. Life itself is a trust from God, we never own it. At any time God can call us to give account of the one life he has entrusted to us. 'For many years' – a rich man may hire and fire men and service-providers at will – but 'years,' you cannot hire them! You cannot secure 'years' by contract or on leasehold! When God's final summons arrives you cannot defer it even for a moment let alone for 'many years.'

Whether we like it or not, both individually and nationally, our breath and all our circumstances are in the hand of Almighty God. He is Sovereign. He is Lord, and occasionally, perhaps to our discomfort, he reminds us of this.

How sad then, despite all his enviable worldly wealth and wisdom, to find no hint of gratitude to the Lord God who had so prospered him.

No awareness of the privileged opportunity he had to bring glory to God with his wealth. No awareness, either, of the needs of those around him; or even a hint of offering his skills in early retirement for the benefit of others. At root he is totally self indulgent; gathering all to himself and proposing to fill his life with ease, eating, drinking and making merry – totally unaware of either God or neighbour.

Note well the rich farmer's long deliberation with all his underlying implied assumptions: 'my skill, my good fortune, my crops, my goods, my happy problem of having so much, my life, my days, my happiness and my many years.' These are disastrously common assumptions. Do we not make them all the time?

Then, note well, the crushing brevity of the words of Almighty God, in whose hand and by whose gift the rich farmer had all these things. 'Fool! This night your soul is required of you.' What was his gathering of wealth all about, whose will it be? But he was doing so well, his barns were full, he had just conceived his new-barns project, he seemed to have secured for himself an enviable future to which to look forward. But God – 'Fool! This night . . .' See the foolishness of living in God's world without living for the glory of God. See the consequences of failing to love him, honour him, serve him and be ready for that summons.

'This night your soul is required of you.' It is a simple fact that not one of us is further than the squeal of a lorry's brakes, a few heartbeats missed, a few cells gone wildly wrong – from being in exactly this man's situation.

Laying up treasure for ourselves, or seeking first the kingdom of heaven?

At a funeral it was asked, 'What did he leave?' And the instant response: 'Everything.' So it was with this man, 'Everything.' 'So it is,' said our Lord, 'for the one who lays up treasure for himself and is not rich' – or 'enriching' as the active, Greek word has it – 'toward God.'

These are terrifying words for those who ignore God; for those who omit God from their thinking. Yet here is the unspoken, underlying assumption of society around us. It undergirds the whole thinking of modern, secular Western society. We are making the same error as this rich but foolish man; living as guests in God's world as if he did not exist and as if we were not accountable to him.

Our postmodern society is founded on an essentially self-centred, 'God-free' world view; that there is no need to live with reference to the Lord God. However, this is exactly what our Lord is warning about. It is the disastrous assumption made by the rich man of our Lord's parable. The word of God is consistent. The charge against the ancient Babylonian king, Belshazzar, on the night he was swept away, was just the same, 'The God in whose hand is your breath and all your ways' – your health, your great wealth and exalted position – 'you have not honoured.' Both the rich farmer in the parable and King Belshazzar, had been entrusted with so much, and yet a humble walk with the Lord God was totally absent. Our Lord's teaching by this parable is both highly relevant and terrifying.

These are disturbing words, too, for comfortable Western Christian disciples who have, in comparison with those in many other countries, such wealth. We are called to use it in ways that bring honour to our Father in heaven, that further his kingdom and that bring relief to those in genuine need.

The challenge of the parable is to be actively enriching toward God with life itself and with all that the Lord God entrusts to us. Alexander Maclaren puts it so clearly, 'To hold all as a trust from him, to use all with reference to him and for ends of which he approves.'

In conclusion

Why did the Lord Jesus tell this parable? To judge? To condemn? Thank God, no. The gospel of John makes it plain that he did not come to judge or to condemn. He told this parable to alert and warn his hearers then, and ourselves now, of the ease with which we can make the same disastrous mistake.

The parable was not given as a warning against unrighteousness, but against covetousness. In the words of Archbishop Trench, against '. . . that love of the world, which . . . takes all the affections of the heart from God, and robs divine things of all their interest. Against that men have to be continually warned . . .'

The parable was a call to Jesus' first hearers, and is a call to us all to examine before the Lord God our assumptions and our attitudes – and then to turn, repent and plead for forgiveness and a fresh new understanding. It is a call to use all the resources he has entrusted to us – money, home, influence, skill, opportunity, and wisdom – for his glory. Covetousness is a foe, and this is a call to recognise it; to take care and be on our guard against grasping, self-centred covetousness in all its forms and with all its subtlety. It is a call to recognise – despite appearances and the many social pressures placed on us by the expectations of colleagues, family and friends – that life does not consist in the abundance of our possessions.

Here is a call to walk humbly with the Lord God, loving justice, showing mercy and, as far as we can, living in godly harmony with those around us – joyfully acknowledging that every breath we take, every morning we rise, every skill, possession and opportunity we have, is a trust to be acknowledged as given by God, and to be used for his glory and for the wellbeing of those around us.

Heavenly Father, you know our strong, natural, self-centred, human desire to own yet more and more of this world's treasures and property. Stir our hearts to hear and heed the warnings of this parable. Help us to see that we do not 'own' life and that possessions are not its measure. Stir us to live in generous and godly harmony. Turn our hearts so that they are set where true joys and lasting treasures are to be found, so that we may use all you entrust to us to bring glory to your Holy Name.

Questions for reflection or discussion

1. Would we be embarrassed or horrified if others were aware of the thoughts that really occupy us as we apparently attend to the things of God?
2. Why is grasping for money, possessions and property the root of so much sharp practice, misery and family strife?
3. Can great wealth be a cause of a very great deal of distress? Why?
4. How can securing our rights and what we perceive as 'justice' blind us to the things that really matter; the things of eternity?
5. Do we sometimes need to let go a just claim, and leave the life-consuming pursuit of personal 'justice' with the Lord, with whom lies ultimate justice?
6. In wealth and plenty, how easy is it to forget the things this parable teaches?
7. In what ways would the parable challenge the 'accepted thinking' so persuasively and continuously presented to us by the media and the world around us?

And for ourselves
8. What assumptions are we personally making about our life and health and material possessions? How would this parable challenge us and teach us to view them?
9. How could I make better use of all that the Lord God has entrusted to me to bring glory to him and help forward his kingdom?

References

Solomon – Proverbs 10:22
Judas – John 12:4-6
Prodigal son – Luke 15:11-32
Godly harmony – Psalm 133
Ultimate justice – Romans 12:19
Breath and circumstances in the hand of God – Daniel 5:23
Not to judge – John 12:47
Not to condemn – John 3:17
Walk humbly – Micah 6:8

The Faithful Servants

"Fear not, little flock, for it is your Father's good pleasure to give you the kingdom. Sell your possessions, and give to the needy. Provide yourselves with moneybags that do not grow old, with a treasure in the heavens that does not fail, where no thief approaches and no moth destroys. For where your treasure is, there will your heart be also.

"Stay dressed for action and keep your lamps burning, and be like men who are waiting for their master to come home from the wedding feast, so that they may open the door to him at once when he comes and knocks. Blessed are those servants whom the master finds awake when he comes. Truly, I say to you, he will dress himself for service and have them recline at table, and he will come and serve them. If he comes in the second watch, or in the third, and finds them awake, blessed are those servants! But know this, that if the master of the house had known at what hour the thief was coming, he would not have left his house to be broken into. You also must be ready, for the Son of Man is coming at an hour you do not expect."

Peter said, "Lord, are you telling this parable for us or for all?" And the Lord said, "Who then is the faithful and wise manager, whom his master will set over his household, to give them their portion of food at the proper time? Blessed is that servant whom his master will find so doing when he comes. Truly, I say to you, he will set him over all his possessions. But if that servant says to himself, 'My master is delayed in coming,' and begins to beat the male and female servants, and to eat and drink and get drunk, the master of that servant will come on a day when he does not expect him and at an hour he does not know, and will cut him in pieces and put him with the unfaithful. And that servant who knew his master's will but did not get ready or act according to his will, will receive a severe beating. But the one who did not know, and did what deserved a beating, will receive a light beating. Everyone to whom much was given, of him much will be required, and from him to whom they entrusted much, they will demand the more.

Luke 12:32 to 48, English Standard Version

The Faithful Servants

The structure of the parable
There are three parts to the parable of the faithful servants. The first part is a challenge to all disciples to be faithfully about the Master's business. The second is also a call to faithfulness, but is particularly addressed to those who are called to lead God's people. And the third part, in graphic terms, warns of the consequences of unfaithfulness.

The gospel setting of this parable
By these pictures of servants awaiting the certain yet sudden and unannounced return of their master, the disciples were shown how they should be living. The Lord Jesus had just spoken of the danger of getting our priorities totally wrong – by setting our hearts on this world's pleasures and possessions, and forgetting the fact that our every breath and all our circumstances are in the hand of Almighty God.

By and large, rich men find that they never have enough. They always strive for more. Poor men, of course, find that they never have enough. But middle-income men also find that they never have enough! For this reason, the Lord Jesus taught disciples not to make the things of this life – food and drink, clothing, houses and so on – the heart and centre of their existence. Disciples are called to live lightly to this world's treasures, 'sell your possessions'; share their value with those in need; use them for the kingdom. He is not saying disciples should make themselves dependent paupers, scrounging off other people's goodness. Rather, he is saying, do not grasp to yourself and hoard possessions which could be used to help those in real need, or which could be used to bring honour to his name. Better by far to look to the honour of God, and use our wealth for the King and his glory. As the Lord taught, "Provide yourselves with moneybags (purses) that do not grow old, with a treasure in the heavens that does not fail, where no thief approaches and no moth destroys. For where your treasure is there will your heart be also."

This is the setting of the parable describing how disciples then, and now, should be living. Disciples are pilgrims on their way to being with their Lord; in parables like these, says John Calvin, our Lord has given us clear light, information, a map and compass.

"You also must be ready, for the Son of Man is coming at an hour you do not expect."

The challenge of the first part of the parable is to live like faithful servants; dressed for work with lamps burning and at all times ready for the return of their master.

In the parable, the master or lord of a great house will be returning from a wedding feast, maybe not until the early hours of the morning. His return is certain, yet will be sudden and unannounced. If the returning master finds the servants awake, ready and about his business, he will reward and honour them. The reward will be beyond this world's wildest dreams. He, the master, will sit them down and serve them, mere servants faithfully doing their duty. Here is an amazing picture of the kindness and generosity of our heavenly Master, given for the encouragement of disciples. To drive home the need for disciples to be constantly prepared, the Lord compares the suddenness of his own return, that of the Son of Man, with the equally sudden and unannounced 'visit' of a thief.

The parable was addressed to the disciples and to the crowd who had gathered to listen. But, for today's disciples who would learn how to live, it still holds true. The parable is a serious call for disciples to live lightly to this world's goods and possessions, and faithfully play our part in furthering the kingdom of heaven – and to do so in the light of the sudden and glorious return of the King, the Son of Man, the Lord Jesus Christ. The parable's challenge to be ready is coupled with a very strong and encouraging picture. Those who are found actually doing so, will be very greatly honoured by their Lord and Master.

A parable for the Lord's disciples or for all?
The second part of the parable follows a question. Peter asked, "Lord, are you telling this parable for us or for all?" And the Lord said, "Who then is the faithful and wise manager, whom his master will set over his household, to give them their portion of food at the proper time? Blessed is that servant whom his master will find so doing when he comes." Continuing with the same illustration of the returning master, our Lord speaks of a senior servant called to be the manager of his fellow servants, to faithfully oversee the household.

This part of the parable applied in the first instance to the disciples themselves, who were to become his witnesses and apostles and the pillars of the early church. It was a solemn call to faithfulness. It was as if he said, 'As the parable I have just told applies to all, how much more it applies to you, Peter, and these fellow disciples around you.' If the whole household is to watch, how much more the principal servants must lead the way by encouragement, exhortation and by the example of their own lives.

The scene is of a servant appointed to manage all the affairs of the house. In looking after his fellow servants, he will need to arrange for the supply of all their needs. He will need to give clear instructions and directions; sometimes there will be a need to challenge or correct, and in other circumstances a need to gently encourage, support or restore one or another of them. Here is the pattern set by the Lord himself, as throughout his earthly ministry he taught and looked after his disciples.

From the letters we have in the New Testament, it is clear that the apostles, including the later addition of Paul, proved to be 'faithful and wise managers' set over their Master's household. Looking after a number of churches, they wrote to encourage them, warn them of dangers, and where necessary to correct them. It is also clear that they were constantly seeking to prepare the 'household of God' for the Master's return.

Closely following the pattern of this parable, Peter wrote to encourage and strengthen the churches in the regions of Galatia and Cappadocia in what is now north-eastern Turkey. For his Master, the apostle Paul planted and cared for many churches. He prayed for the church in Thessalonica, 'Now may our God and Father himself, and our Lord Jesus, direct our way to you, and may the Lord make you increase and abound in love for one another and for all, as we do for you, so that he may establish your hearts blameless in holiness before our God and Father, at the coming of our Lord Jesus with all his saints.' Paul's great concern for well-being of the church in Thessalonica, and his longing that they might be 'a household prepared for the Master's return' show clearly as he writes such words of encouragement to them.

Blessed is that servant whom his master will find so doing
Although this was clearly addressed to the disciples, it echoes down the centuries to each one of us in whatever situation of authority the Lord has put us: mothers and fathers with the responsibility of rearing godly youngsters, Bible class leaders, Sunday school and youth leaders, ministers and church leaders. J.C. Ryle makes it clear that it would also include those servants of the Lord placed in positions of responsibility and authority in the state and in national church affairs.

The parable is a call to be a faithful servant of the Lord in whatever situation the Lord has put us, and the most solemn call to faithfulness if he has put us in a position of leadership. Paul the apostle clearly understood this as he describes himself as a willing slave of the Lord Jesus Christ – everything else, his birthright, status and attainments being 'dung' in comparison with knowing and serving his Master.

J. C. Ryle also draws attention to the importance of the expression 'finds his servant so doing.' Not just knowing what we should be doing as servants, or discussing it, or intending to do it but actually and actively doing it.

The practical outworking of the parable
For the servant in the parable, should his master's absence be short, it would mean arranging for the household to be ready and awaiting the master's return. If the absence was to be longer, he would need to attend faithfully to the day by day running of the house and to making sure that everything was kept in good order. This was the task entrusted to him.

If we count ourselves servants of the Lord Jesus, how do we measure against his parable? Is our heart holding fast and growing in love and devotion to our Master? Springing from that love, are we keeping the charge he has given us? Are we seeking to manage our own family and household in a God-honouring way? If we are called to look after fellow disciples, are we determined to be fair and faithful in whatever situation the Lord has put us?

Together with our fellow disciples, are we encouraging one another to be salt and light in society; playing our part to hold back ungodly corruption, decay and pollution? Are we shedding godly light and perspective in our everyday discussions and meetings with our work or leisure colleagues? We have also been called to proclaim the gospel and to make disciples of all nations with the aim of increasing the household of God. Are we 'so doing'? There is great joy and glorious gain for those about their Master's business and eagerly awaiting his return.

The Parable of the Faithful Servants – continued

The third part of the parable contains the Lord's three warnings of the consequences of unfaithfulness. Be prepared, for the warnings do not sit comfortably with our tender modern feelings!

'But if that servant says to himself, 'My master is delayed in coming,' and begins to beat the male and female servants, and to eat and drink and get drunk, the master of that servant will come on a day when he does not expect him and at an hour he does not know, and will cut him in pieces and put him with the unfaithful. And that servant who knew his master's will but did not get ready or act according to his will, will receive a severe beating. But the one who did not know, and did what deserved a beating, will receive a light beating. Everyone to whom much was given, of him much will be required, and from him to whom they entrusted much, they will demand the more.'

But if that servant says to himself, 'My master is delayed in coming.'
This part of the parable describes in horrifyingly graphic terms the terrible and most severe judgement that will fall on those who enjoy the privileges of high position but misuse those privileges, and fail in their responsibility before the Master. The servant, who had been appointed by his master as manager, is described as taking advantage of his master's delay, getting drunk and mistreating his fellow servants. "But if that servant says to himself, 'My master is delayed in coming,' and begins to beat the male and female servants, and to eat and drink and get drunk . . ."

The unfaithful servant, who had greatly abused the trust his master had placed in him, is given the most severe punishment. This is the first and most serious level of unfaithfulness and carried the greatest penalty.

The Lord's picture of the punishment is terrible indeed; ". . . the master of that servant will come on a day when he does not expect him and at an hour he does not know, and will cut him in pieces and put him with the unfaithful." In the ancient world, the penalty for unfaithfulness among slaves and servants was very severe. It had to be, in order to serve as an example and a warning to others.

If 'cut him in pieces' is not literal, but a picture of terrible punishment, a very severe beating or whipping could indeed cut into the flesh and tear it – 'cut you to pieces,' – though you might survive. The words '. . . and put him with the unfaithful,' would then mean the imprisonment of the servant with other unfaithful servants. But, if 'cut to pieces' (the word in the original means to cut in two) indicates that the unfaithful servant would be put to death, then the words '. . . and put him with the unfaithful,' mean that, after death, his body would be put in a common grave or pit with other unfaithful servants of his master, who had received the same penalty, and ultimately might refer to Hades, the place of the unfaithful dead.

The significance of this part of the parable is that those to whom the Lord God entrusts the care of his chosen people, must note well the severe judgement that will be given to those who abuse that trust.'

If, as the Lord went on to warn, punishment awaits servants who by idleness or mistake are not about their master's business, how much more is dreadfully severe punishment deserved by those in senior positions who choose to ignore or even despise the Lord and his word and abuse the trust placed in them.

The South African pastor Norval Geldenhuys comments, 'For those servants of Christ who labour faithfully and devotedly in his service, every moment expecting the coming of their Lord and joyfully looking forward to it, the second coming of Jesus will be a matter of the greatest joy and of the most glorious gain. But for those who doubt his promises and who live in selfishness, imperiousness and worldly-mindedness, the second coming will be fraught with terror and irrevocable loss.'

A second and third level of unfaithfulness and of punishment
'And that servant who knew his master's will but did not get ready or act according to his will, will receive a severe beating.' Here is a servant who had been given a trust by his master but who, for one reason or another, simply does not fulfil it. Will his master smile on him? Clearly he will not. Perhaps the servant was lazy and idle, or maybe he spent his time pursuing his own concerns and interests rather than those of his master, or perhaps he was just very busy with many other smaller matters that seemed urgent and necessary at the time. In one way or another he failed to do his master's will and failed to prepare for his master's return. He, too, had to bear the consequences of his failure, a severe beating. From the parable such a servant of God in the Lord's household, will also be called to account and punished appropriately.

The third and final level of failure and of consequent judgement that Jesus portrayed in the parable was for those who 'did not know'. 'But the one who did not know, and did what deserved a beating, will receive a light beating.' There may be reasons why less than faithful behaviour could, at least in part, be excused. The Lord Jesus allows for that, the punishment is just, for those unaware 'a lighter whipping' or 'a light beating'.

On the master's return, here is the dreadful discovery made by a servant who, perhaps by his own failure to find out, or by the failure of the senior servant to tell him, was never aware of what the master required of him.

It is salutary to ask, how many well-intended and good people will recoil in horror, on the last day when the Master returns, with these words on their lips, we 'did not know'?

How did the apostles warn of the seriousness of these things in the early church?

As already noted, the apostles wrote to encourage believers in their care. But very closely related to this part of the parable concerning the failure of a trusted leading servant, Peter found it necessary to warn church leaders to 'shepherd the flock of God that is among you, exercising oversight, not under compulsion, but willingly, as God would have you; not for shameful gain, but eagerly, not domineering over those in your charge, but being examples to the flock'. In the second letter bearing his name, there are warnings about 'false teachers' and 'scoffers' who would question or deny the return of the Master.

In the Corinthian church, Paul had to stand against self-appointed and smooth-speaking 'super-apostles' who were 'false apostles, deceitful workmen, disguising themselves as apostles of Christ'. He also warned that such people were taking advantage of them, 'For you gladly bear with fools, being wise yourselves! For you bear it if someone makes slaves of you, or devours you, or takes advantage of you...'

The apostle John warns believers against even greeting or eating with those who bring another teaching and deny the deity of our Lord. 'Watch yourselves, so that you may not lose what we have worked for, but may win a full reward.'

Is this a word for ourselves?

In our own day, these are very real and urgent warnings. How many church and denominational leaders would play down or deny the reality of our Lord's deity? How many would question the possibility and serious consequences of his return? How many, in high position, will be found at the last to have actually been indulging themselves, as they pursued their career and enjoyed power and prestige? Even more dreadfully, when the secrets of all hearts are disclosed, how many will be found to have taken advantage of, or disheartened true and faithful servants of the Lord?

A Christian husband and wife, Sunday School leaders, were invited to lunch with a visiting and very senior churchman. But the man ate and drank perhaps too freely, and when the couple shared the wonderful way God was working among the young people, he showed no interest whatever; he completely brushed them aside. Rather than encourage them, he crushed and disheartened them. You can see that when the Master returns, this parable gives me reason to quake should I be found to have treated the fellow servants of my Master in such a way.

Extreme, you may say. Maybe, but with a steady income, a comfortable house to live in and a privileged position in society, how easy it is for those called to be overseers in the Master's household to let things slip. We can so easily assume that it is natural and right for us to lord it over others and indulge ourselves. As J.C.Ryle again makes clear, it is not just ministers of religion and church leaders who are in great danger but those in society in any position of trust under the Lord God, in politics, education, commerce etc.

The world about us, our own fallen nature, and the evil one, will all contrive to persuade us: "He has not returned. Perhaps we are mistaken. He may never return – at the very least there is no urgency. There is no immediate need to worry about 'a calling to account', so I can carry on doing as I choose."

From the parable, firstly, it is clear that any call to leadership among the people of God carries with it a very great weight of responsibility to do so faithfully. The parable plainly shows our need to keep constantly before us the fear of God, and our accountability before him. The apostle Paul displays just such an awareness of the seriousness of his calling as he writes, 'Therefore, knowing the fear of the Lord, we persuade others.' Or, in the arresting words of the older translations, 'Therefore, knowing the terror of the Lord, we persuade men . . .'

Secondly, the Lord's parable alerts us to the great danger of being so occupied with apparently urgent and pressing matters that take up so much of our time that we fail to seek and do the Master's will or prepare for his return.

A great many church leaders ably keep the church organisation humming; busy, enjoyable, financially viable and in good repair . . . flowers, garden parties, concerts, cleaning, fund raising . . . but have little awareness of a household ready for the Master's return, of the priority of doing our Master's will and preparing the household of God for the return of the King. That priority implies putting our best efforts into developing a people growing in godliness; a people busy about their Master's business. In practice that means growing a people who are well grounded in the word of God, supporting and encouraging one another as they reach out with the gospel of God to those around them both near and far, making and growing other disciples, watching, praying, and eagerly awaiting their Master's return.

Thirdly, how many church leaders, how many leaders in society, how many good and enthusiastic people in our churches and chapels, will echo the words 'we did not know'? 'We have never taken to heart the seriousness of parables like these.' 'Nobody told us.' 'Nobody showed us.' 'We did not realise.' 'We did not know.'

We are each responsible for finding out what the will of the Lord is, and doing it. His word is open and plain, and other people's opinions and teachings will not shield us from the all-seeing judgement of Almighty God. We are each answerable to him. As John Calvin points out, ignorance will not excuse us.

A very great responsibility
The parable concludes with a very solemn charge reflecting the tremendous privilege of any kind of Christian service in church or in society, especially that of leadership, 'Everyone to whom much is giv-

en, of him much will be required.' Here is the recurring theme of the great responsibility before the Lord God to be faithful. The challenge is to stand firm in the faith, growing in love and devotion, and to use all our God-given skills and abilities, training and opportunities with a single eye to the Master's honour; a household prepared for his return. Here is the challenge not to abuse, or fail to use, the gifts and graces, the privileges and opportunities he has entrusted to us.

Let Matthew Henry have the last word. To church leaders he says, 'To be unaware of the solemnity of our holy calling and to take our eye off the return of the Master is the root of the failure and weakness of the church.'

This parable in its three parts is not a parable for our comfort, but, in the original sense of that word, it was told for our strengthening and for our strong encouragement.

In summary, in whatever situation our Lord has placed us, the parable challenges us to be servants of God, faithfully about our Master's business, preparing and keeping ready for the certain, sudden and unannounced return of the Son of Man, the Master of the house, the Lord Jesus Christ, the King of kings and Lord of lords.

Heavenly Father, stir us to humble ourselves and pray for the mercy offered in your Son, the Lord Jesus. And, by your grace, awaken us to the joyful and solemn reality of his return in glory at any time. By your grace enable us to be faithful servants. Keep us alert, about your business, just, generous, kind, making disciples, encouraging and building up one another and, as the great day approaches, watching and ready.

Questions for reflection or discussion

1. How can we, personally, be on guard so as to avoid making the things of this world the point and purpose of life?

2. How did the ministry of Paul the apostle measure up to the teaching of this parable?
3. How was the teaching of the Lord Jesus reflected in his own life?
4. Can I see ways to encourage my fellow disciples?
5. Can I see ways I must avoid, in order not to discourage my fellow disciples?
6. What implications does this parable have for disciples in high office in society?
7. What implications does the parable have for our church or chapel, both for its leaders and for its people – that is, each one of us?

... and questions for personal reflection
1. How faithful am I as a servant?
2. How ready am I for the Master's return? Is there something I should be doing that I am knowingly not doing? Are there other particular things I should be doing?

References

In whose hand is your breath and all your circumstances – Daniel 5:23
Pilgrims on their way to be with the Lord – Philippians 1:21-24
Paul's prayer for the church in Thessalonica – 1Thessalonians 3:11-13
Status and attainments being 'dung' in comparison with knowing his Master – Philippians 3: 8-9
Not domineering or 'lording it' over those in your charge – 1 Peter 5:2-3
False teachers and scoffers – 2 Peter 2:1 and 3:3
Self-appointed and smooth-speaking 'super-apostles' – 2 Corinthians 11:5
Deceitful workmen, disguising themselves as apostles of Christ – 2 Corinthians 11:13

People who would take advantage of the people of God – 2 Corinthians 11:19-21.

Watch yourselves . . . do not receive him – 2 John vs. 7-10

Therefore, knowing the terror of the Lord – 2 Corinthians 5:11

The Barren Fig Tree

At least three times the Lord Jesus taught his disciples and the crowds using the fig tree as his illustration or parable.

The parable of the *barren fig tree*, found only in the Gospel of Luke, is a call to repentance and fruitfulness. The incident of the *withered fig tree* recorded in Mark's gospel gives our Lord the opportunity to challenge the disciples to faith. Finally, the parable of *the fig tree and all the trees coming into leaf* is recorded in each of the first three gospels and is a challenge to disciples to be watchful and ready for their Lord's return.

We look here at the parable of the barren fig tree, the verses leading up to the parable, and the parable itself.

He also said to the crowds, "When you see a cloud rising in the west, you say at once, 'A shower is coming.' And so it happens. And when you see the south wind blowing, you say, 'There will be scorching heat,' and it happens. You hypocrites! You know how to interpret the appearance of the earth and sky, but why do you not know how to interpret the present time?

"And why do you not judge for yourselves what is right? As you go with your accuser before the magistrate, make an effort to settle with him on the way, lest he drag you to the judge, and the judge hand you over to the officer, and the officer put you in prison. I tell you, you will never get out until you have paid the very last penny."

There were some present at that very time who told him about the Galileans whose blood Pilate had mingled with their sacrifices. And he answered them, "Do you think that these Galileans were worse sinners than all the other Galileans, because they suffered in this way? No, I tell you; but unless you repent, you will all likewise perish. Or those eighteen on whom the tower in Siloam fell and killed them: do you think that they were worse offenders than all the others who lived in Jerusalem? No, I tell you; but unless you repent, you will all likewise perish."

And he told this parable: "A man had a fig tree planted in his vineyard, and he came seeking fruit on it and found none. And he said to the vinedresser, 'Look, for three years now I have come seeking fruit on this fig tree, and I find none. Cut it down. Why should it use up the ground?' And he answered him, 'Sir, let it alone this year also, until I dig around it and put on manure. Then if it should bear fruit next year, well and good; but if not, you can cut it down.'"

Luke 12:54 – 13:9, English Standard Version

The Barren Fig Tree

The difficult verses leading up to the parable
From verse 54 of chapter 12, Luke records the Lord's teaching directed to the great crowds who flocked to him. Each of the brief sections is an aspect of his great call to repentance before Almighty God, our ultimate Judge.

Jesus began with the weather – always at the forefront of our minds! His hearers were well able to see that if the wind was blowing from the West, over the Mediterranean, it would bring rain, but if it was blowing from the South, over the deserts, the weather would be hot and dry. Yet they could not see the historic times in which they were living. Blind, deaf and dumb people were being healed, spiritually imprisoned people were being released and poor people were having good news proclaimed to them. But they could not see, or would not see, that here, standing before them, was the fulfilment of the promise of God given by the prophets; the long promised Son of David, the Anointed One of God, their long sought Messiah. Neither could they see that his presence among them marked the approach of the Day of the Lord; the judgement of Almighty God. Judgement that would begin with the rebellious house of Israel, as Rome crushed Jerusalem and dispersed the Jews among the nations, and that will finally fall on the whole unbelieving world.

The second scene is that of a debtor having to go to court. His case is hopeless; he will lose the case and then be thrown into jail until the debt is fully paid. His plight is desperate. His only hope is to settle with the man to whom he owes so much before it gets to court. Here is our Lord's brief yet vivid picture of his hearers' – and of our – standing before Almighty God. Hence the wisdom of pleading for mercy now before it is too late.

There was no television, radio or newspaper in our Lord's day, so every fresh event caused a buzz by word of mouth. 'Have you heard...' and, of course, an opinion added. Referring to two horrible pieces of current news involving sudden deaths, Jesus gave a repeated warning that, unless his hearers repented, a similar, terrible fate awaited them, '. . . you will all likewise perish.' Each disaster is not just a fresh piece of news to talk about, but a 'wake-up call', a warning of the urgent need to repent.

Although some commentators separate the parable of the fig tree from the teaching that Luke has recorded just before it, it seems that the parable of the barren fig tree fills out this call for repentance.

The owner of the vineyard was acting with absolute justice in sweeping away the fruitless tree he had planted. The parable is not the pretty story we might have liked, but a solemn warning to nations, to churches as well as to individuals, that unless we repent and prove fruitful before him we 'will likewise perish'.

The details of the parable itself

The fig tree of Jesus' parable was a choice tree actively planted in the owner's vineyard. It was not a wayside, 'self set' tree growing from a pip casually dropped along some public way.

The owner naturally expected fruit and gave the tree three years beyond normal fruit-bearing age in which to prove itself. However, there was still no evidence of fruit. For some reason it seems that it was not going to prove a fruitful tree, and so the most appropriate thing to do was to get rid of it. In the old words, it was 'cumbering the ground'; the tree was only using up space, water and nutrients, and so preventing the planting of more useful things.

Although judgement was richly deserved, 'Look, for three years now I have come seeking fruit on this fig tree, and I find none. Cut it down. Why should it use up the ground?' The vinedresser pleads for the owner to give the fig tree one more opportunity. He does not plead for the fig tree to be kept forever, but simply for one last chance to bear fruit before the owner cuts it down. 'Sir, let it alone this year also, until I dig around it and put on manure. Then if it should bear fruit next year, well and good; but if not, you can cut it down.' The vinedresser undertakes to give the tree the best possible opportunity to bear fruit. By 'digging around it' he may well have intended to prune its roots, for perhaps the tree had grown too lush and comfortable to fruit. It is well known that fig tree roots need to be constrained in some way to encourage fruitfulness. So digging around it would be a 'wake-up' call to fruitfulness; a fruitfulness strongly encouraged and enabled by the manure placed over the remaining roots.

Is there any significance in the little detail of who will cut down the tree if it fails yet again? The owner said, 'Cut it down.' The vinedresser, pleading for one more year concludes, 'Then if it should bear fruit next year, well and good; but if not, you can cut it down.' Scholars debate, but ultimately it is the owner's decision either way and it would fall to the vinedresser to put the decision into practice. Eastern owners do not personally 'cut down' or probably more accurately 'dig up' trees!

Like so many of his other parables, Jesus leaves the parable open ended. We do not know whether the owner granted the vinedresser's request, or whether or not the tree responded with fruitfulness. However, it is clear that even if, in mercy, the owner agrees to one more chance, a 'stay of execution', he will not tolerate for ever a fruitless tree 'using up the ground' in his vineyard.

The great principles of the parable
Like his first hearers, we love the parables, they are such vivid stories. However, as with so many of his stories, this parable carries a lesson that we do not readily receive or even wish to hear. The Lord Jesus had just warned his hearers that unless they repented, turned, believed and proved fruitful before the Lord God, they would perish. Here, in this parable, he shows the Lord God's absolute right as creator and owner, to see what proves to be fruitful and to remove anything that proves to be unfruitful.

In the parable there is justice, but it is justice tempered with mercy. Our natural human response is to presume on God's patience; to go on doing as we please, assuming that he will always be forgiving. However, in mercy he may give us further opportunities to prove fruitful but, ultimately, he will not give us a 'free pardon' for fruitlessness. God is merciful and very patient, but in his world he retains the ultimate right to remove anything that proves useless before him. The terrifying truth is that it is possible to escape all the dangers of life and die comfortably in great old age – and yet perish. Why? Because we 'live and move and have our being' in God's 'vineyard', and yet it is too easy to fail to bring honour to his name, and so prove to be 'fruitless' before him.

In order to prove fruitful, the repentance Jesus is calling for is no mere nominal repentance or a repeated form of words, 'I repent of my sins,' but something much deeper. As he demonstrated in the parable of the Pharisee and the tax gatherer and in his encounter with Zacchaeus, he was calling for a cry from the heart, real business with God which results in a total change of attitude. It means an active turning from all the self-centred thinking and behaviour that had gone before – and a determination from now on to live to please and serve the Living God; to be humbly useful before him.

How did the parable apply to Jesus' hearers?
The parable is primarily addressed to the people of Israel and its religious leaders. By and large Israel was continuing to make the greatest error we humans can make. They were living in God's world as if there were no God. Despite the outward appearance of being very religious, inwardly, the religious leaders were very far from 'doing justice, loving mercy and walking humbly with the Lord God'. They were ignoring, or narrowly reinterpreting, his commands and holy ways in order to fit their own ways and opinions. In failing to truly honour the Lord God, it is no surprise to find that they also refused to recognise and honour his Son, the Messiah.

The failure of God's ancient people, the nation of Israel, was no new phenomenon. God's people were the chosen 'planting of the Lord' in his favoured vineyard. Time and again he looked for fruit; sending his spokesmen, the prophets, to call the nation to repentance, to turn and to produce the fruits of godliness, righteousness and mercy. Although, under godly kings, there were short times of reform, there was little or no deep change or lasting fruit.

For example, in the years before Israel was swept into exile, Isaiah had called for repentance and warned of the judgement of God falling on fruitless Israel in very similar terms. Singing it as a love song, Isaiah speaks of Israel, as a beloved vineyard planted with choice vines on a very fertile hillside, walled and looked after – yet producing only wild, useless grapes. Like the house of Israel, it was a vineyard fit only for destruction; its walls broken down and its vines trampled.

However, despite God's many warnings, and the presence now of their Messiah – God amongst them – the nation had not changed; it remained fruitless. In the light of Jesus' teaching, given immediately before it, surely this parable of the fruitless fig tree must be seen as a warning that, unless the people and their leaders repented, they were destined, like Isaiah's vineyard, to be trampled down in judgement – as indeed they were, first by the Romans in AD 70, and then by the Gentile nations for nearly 2000 years.

Israel justly deserved to be totally cut off, and yet here in this parable is mercy; 'one more year', one more chance, a merciful stay of just judgement – yet notice it is only a 'year of grace' and not a free pardon. The people of Israel have been given further opportunity to produce the fruits of repentance and faith; first, during our Lord's ministry, and then, secondly, under the Holy Spirit empowered ministry of Peter and the apostles from Pentecost onwards. In that time many did, indeed, repent and believe. Even now, as they are re-gathering in Israel, the Lord is giving further opportunity, often through the witness of the Christian church, where it is offered, not in arrogance, but in love and true humility.

How does the parable apply to our nation?
As the days of the 'year of grace' tick by, the day of God's final judgement draws closer. In the West, and in particular throughout the English speaking world, whole nations have been so favoured with gospel preaching that, over the centuries, godly thinking and godly ways have permeated the whole of our society. This has been reflected in godly laws and stable government, in mutual trust and in law-abiding citizens, in law, education, medicine, art and science and in the care of the more vulnerable in society.

However, like a widely rooted and well nourished fig tree, have we grown so 'lush and comfortable' that we no longer have any desire to bear godly fruit? Postmodern, humanist and secular thinking strongly press us to 'live in God's world as if there were no God'. Having flourished under the good hand of God, we now prefer to pursue our own way, ignoring the One whose favour has been on us, actively cutting the Lord God completely out of our public life and thinking. Can we, who have been so favoured with the gospel, expect to escape with fruitlessness? With an unwillingness to humble ourselves and turn from our ungodly ways and pray, can we expect to escape the just judgement of Almighty God? From this parable, we have no grounds to think so.

If the Lord is looking for fruit nationally, what of the church and of ourselves as individuals?
How often has the Lord looked for fruit in our churches? In our day, the traditional churches are typically full of ceremonial religion and of social activity, but so often short of spiritual fruitfulness before the Lord. They offer uplifting music and a source of friendship – but it is salutary to ask if even regular church-attending people are being shown the great need to be put right with God. Do they hear the good news that they can be 'ransomed, healed, restored, forgiven' by God? Are our people seriously warned of the judgement to come and called to repentance before God and faith in his Son?

J.C. Ryle asks, pointedly, if many of our churches and their leaders are very much like this fig tree, 'cumbering the ground' and so taking up the space and opportunity for godly ministry that others could use more fruitfully before the Lord?

At a personal level, Matthew Henry asks, equally uncomfortably, 'How many times through the years has the Lord looked on our lives for fruit and found none?' Will our Lord be patient forever? Like the fruitless tree in the vineyard it is easy to enjoy Christian privileges and do nothing for the honour of our Lord. So we might ask, are we actively seeking to grow in understanding and faith? Are we playing our part in encouraging one another to walk with the Lord Jesus in simple, humble trust and obedience? As the Lord gives us opportunity, are we willing to advance the kingdom of God in any way we can, to share the gospel message, and to be salt and light in a decaying society?

We may not be called to preach before thousands! But, like the lady with her precious jar of ointment, we are all called to do what we can, to do it while we can and to do it for the Lord.

Christian churches are not called to be like a coach or railway train with a driver and many passengers, but more like a local football team with a common aim, and with every person on the field playing their part.

In our churches will there be found a holy people, humbly 'about the Master's business'; a people prepared for our Lord and Master's sudden return in glory and in judgement?

The challenge of our Lord's picture of the vinedresser and his request

1. The vinedresser's relationship with the owner of the vineyard

The vinedresser was not only able and willing to make such a bold request, he also offered to do the necessary work. There was no hint of sullen slavishness or of doing the bare minimum of work. There was, clearly, a very happy and productive relationship between the owner of the vineyard and his man on the site. The vinedresser recognised that the owner's decision was final and that he was merely a servant, and yet the relationship between them was such that he could make this request and offer to dig around the tree and fertilize it during the year-long experiment.

If the fruitless fig tree is a picture of unrepentant Israel, who is on record in Scripture pleading for the nation to be spared?

Moses, with whom God spoke face to face, pleaded with the Lord to spare the people of Israel. They had been miraculously rescued from oppression in Egypt, but now, because of their blatant, God-provoking idolatry in creating and worshipping a golden calf as '. . . the gods who brought them out of Egypt,' justice demanded that they be totally destroyed.

Daniel and later Nehemiah both acknowledged their personal failures and the godlessness of the people of Israel, and pleaded with the Lord for mercy.

Each of these men walked very closely with the Lord God and like the vinedresser they were able to boldly cry to their Lord to hold back his hand of judgement. They were also more than willing to play their part. Surely this in itself is a spiritual challenge to each one of us.

Could this parable also be mirroring the Lord Jesus himself? His own walk with Father could not have been closer and his whole aim was to do his Father's will. Was he reflecting 'a conversation in heaven'? Isaiah speaks of the suffering servant of the Lord interceding for transgressors. The Lord Jesus did not come to condemn, to judge or destroy, but to rescue and save. The Lord Jesus' ministry and, subsequently, that of his chosen apostles gave the house of Israel opportunity to turn back to the Lord God, to repent and be fruitful.

2. What the vinedresser asked for and what he did not ask for

The vinedresser only asked for 'a stay of judgement' – one more year for the tree to prove whether it could be fruitful and worthy of its place in the vineyard. He did not ask for a fruitless tree to be spared indefinitely.

In his day, Matthew Henry urged ministers and church leaders to pray earnestly for the people entrusted to their care, that like this fruitless fig tree, they might be given more time and every opportunity to repent. How many of us, as John Calvin points out, have cause to thank the Lord God for his patience with us! When justice was well deserved, he gave us time and opportunity – under one form of godly influence or another, perhaps by reading the Bible or other godly books, by hearing faithful preaching, or by the encouragement of friends – to turn, to believe and to begin to bear spiritual fruit.

What an encouragement this is to pray to the Lord for members of our own family who have yet to believe. Not just to plead that the Lord God would cause them to flourish, but that he would make himself known to them; that they might come to trust in the Son of God, and so become his ransomed people, living fruitfully to the praise of his greatness and glory.

3. The willingness of the vinedresser to play his part

If the owner granted what he was asking for, the vinedresser was willing to do everything he could to enable the tree to be fruitful. He offered to dig around it and to put manure over the remaining roots in order to give the tree every encouragement to bear fruit.

Matthew Henry asks, again uncomfortably, 'If we pray for others and yet do nothing that we could do to help them to faith and fruitfulness before the Lord, are we not mocking the Lord God?' The challenge the vinedresser puts before us is to pray for those around us – and help them, speak with them and share with them 'the manure of loving kindness and a word in season'. Those delightfully quaint words have within them the seeds of both genuine friendship and godly faithfulness.

How can we encourage those for whom we pray and help them in some way to find for themselves the wonder, liberty and joy of being a forgiven and fruitful child of God? It may be an invitation to hear a speaker; it could be a book or video or just mixing with truly Christian people or, most likely, a mixture of all these things. If our small effort bears fruit, all heaven and the Christian servant alike will rejoice. If not, the Lord God's justice and final judgement still stands.

For our strong encouragement to follow the vinedresser's example in pleading with the Lord and doing all we can, we read in Peter's second letter that the Lord God is patient toward us; it is not the will of God that anyone should perish but that all may come to repentance.

Lord, in your mercy, give your ancient people Israel ,the Jewish people, 'one more year' that they might turn and be exceedingly fruitful before you, as is your great purpose for them.

In your mercy, give your often sleeping, over-comfortable Christian church 'one more year' that we might turn and be fruitful before you, as is your purpose for us.

Father, thank you that your terrible final judgement is tempered with mercy; you have given us 'days of grace' in which we have every opportunity to repent; turn and become fruitful, believing, willing servants of yours. Thank you for the Scriptures that that 'trim our roots' and plainly display how far short we have fallen; and that call us to repentance, and point us to your provision of forgiveness in the cross of your Son, the Lord Jesus. Thank you that they then go on to teach us how, empowered by your Holy Spirit, we can, in love toward you and our neighbours, live fruitful lives before you.

Questions for reflection or discussion

1. From Jesus' words in the verses leading up to the parable and the parable itself, if we live in God's world as if there were no God and so prove fruitless before him, what prospect lies before us?
2. As he did with the Jewish nation, does the Lord God still look for the fruits of godliness, righteousness and justice? Have there been times of national fruitfulness in our own society? What of our own time?
3. In what ways would modern society have us 'cut God completely out of our thinking'?
4. Do we have cause to thank the Lord God for his patience toward us?
5. Do we have any heart to intercede for our nation and our leaders, and for other nations and their leaders in these momentous days?

6. Have we cause to thank the Lord God for those who interceded for us?

7. Can we think of any particular things that have encouraged us to true repentance and perhaps the beginnings of fruitfulness?

8. In a hostile world, how can we encourage one another to pray and offer 'the manure of loving kindness and a word in season' to those around us?

References

Pharisee and the tax gatherer – Luke 18:10ff

Zacchaeus – Luke 19:1-10

'Doing justice, loving mercy and walking humbly' – Micah 6:8

'The planting of the Lord' – Isaiah 61:3

A beloved vineyard, yet wild, useless grapes – Isaiah 5:1-7

Moses – Exodus 32:7-13; Face to face – Exodus 33:11

Nehemiah – Nehemiah 1:5-11

Daniel – Daniel 9:16-20

To do his Father's will – John 4:34 and 6:38

'Interceding for transgressors' – Isaiah 53:12

Not to judge but to save – John 3:17, John 12:47

'Do what we can' – Mark 14:8

'Not the will of God . . .' – 2 Peter 3:9

'Ransomed, healed, restored, forgiven – a line from the hymn *Praise, my soul, the King of heaven* by Henry Francis Lyte 1793-1847

The Mustard Seed or the Mustard Tree

He said therefore, "What is the kingdom of God like? And to what shall I compare it? It is like a grain of mustard seed that a man took and sowed in his garden, and it grew and became a tree, and the birds of the air made nests in its branches." And again he said, "To what shall I compare the kingdom of God? It is like leaven that a woman took and hid in three measures of flour, until it was all leavened."

Luke 13:18-21, English Standard Version

He put another parable before them, saying, "The kingdom of heaven is like a grain of mustard seed that a man took and sowed in his field. It is the smallest of all seeds, but when it has grown it is larger than all the garden plants and becomes a tree, so that the birds of the air come and make nests in its branches."

He told them another parable. "The kingdom of heaven is like leaven that a woman took and hid in three measures of flour, till it was all leavened."

Matthew 13:31-33, English Standard Version

And he said, "The kingdom of God is as if a man should scatter seed on the ground. He sleeps and rises night and day, and the seed sprouts and grows; he knows not how. The earth produces by itself, first the blade, then the ear, then the full grain in the ear. But when the grain is ripe, at once he puts in the sickle, because the harvest has come."

And he said, "With what can we compare the kingdom of God, or what parable shall we use for it? It is like a grain of mustard seed, which, when sown on the ground, is the smallest of all the seeds on earth, yet when it is sown it grows up and becomes larger than all the garden plants and puts out large branches, so that the birds of the air can make nests in its shade." With many such parables he spoke the word to them, as they were able to hear it. He did not speak to them without a parable, but privately to his own disciples he explained everything.

Mark 4:26-34, English Standard Version

The Mustard Seed

Introduction
The parable of the mustard seed is found in each of the first three gospels. Matthew describes the seed being planted in a field, Mark in the ground and Luke in a garden – the different places accurately reflecting the original Greek. Matthew and Luke set the parable with the parable of the woman hiding a small amount of leaven (dough containing live yeast) in a large amount of flour to cause all of it to rise. In Mark's gospel the parable follows that of the seed growing quietly without any attention from the man who sowed it. Matthew and Mark note that Jesus drew attention to the smallness of the mustard seed. 'As small as a grain of mustard', was almost certainly a proverbial saying.

The plainest application of the parables
If the seed sown and growing steadily produces a harvest, the mustard seed produces a very large plant, and the small amount of yeast digests and works its way through all of the flour, then, surely, all three parables are parables of growth. It is the kind of growth that, from a small beginning, quietly continues until it yields a very significant result; a harvest, a tree, or a batch of risen bread. We have an English proverb to the same effect, 'Great oaks from little acorns grow.' From a little acorn to a tender plant and then, almost unnoticed, it grows year by year till it becomes a broad-spreading and well-rooted tree. As C.H. Dodd observes, these three parables should not be separated, or over-

interpreted, but taken together as illustrating the remarkable growth of the kingdom of God. From such a small and apparently insignificant beginning the kingdom will, over the course of time, become mighty and far reaching.

Such an understanding is in accord with the vision given to the prophet Ezekiel, who, when looking forward to the promised kingdom of the Messiah, spoke of God taking the topmost sprig of a cedar tree and planting it on the mountains of Israel. He spoke of God causing it to grow to become a mighty tree in whose branches the birds found shelter as did the animals beneath. The little cedar cutting became a tree which dwarfed all other trees, as the kingdom of God under Messiah's reign will dwarf all other kingdoms and empires.

None of this will surprise or offend us as modern people with the hindsight of twenty centuries of Christian history. The Lord's pictures exactly fit the growth of the worldwide company of God's people. However, these parables were completely new thinking to those who first heard them, they were counter-cultural and shocking. Certainly, our Lord's hearers were longing for the Messiah's majestic rule. However, the all-pervading yearning and hope of the oppressed people of Israel, in our Lord's day, as the yoke of Rome lay heavy upon them, was of a powerful military kingdom that would overthrow their Roman conquerors and restore the nation of Israel to the power, wealth and world position it enjoyed under King David and his son Solomon.

This kind of expectation can be seen as the disciples asked the Lord Jesus, 'Will you at this time, restore Israel?' It also underlies James and John's longing to be in positions of power in his kingdom, and the shattered hope of Cleopas and his fellow disciple as they walked back from Jerusalem to Emmaus after the crucifixion, saying to the risen, but unrecognised, Lord Jesus, "But we had hoped that he was the one to redeem Israel."

These three parables speak of the very different kind of growth of the kingdom of God. Not growth that is sudden, decisive and won by military conquest and the overthrow of all enemies, but a kingdom that grows quietly and steadily without any of these things. Each of these parables teaches that the kingdom of God will come '. . . not by might, nor by power' but by the Spirit of God. It will be entirely different from this world's 'proud empires'.

Like the growth of the crop, the tree and the leaven, the growth of the kingdom of God will be almost unannounced. Nevertheless, eventually, like the leaven, it will permeate every nation on earth; like the tree, it will fulfil God's purposes when full grown; and like the growing grain it will be ready for God's final harvest. Such an apparently insignificant sowing would produce a world-wide people of God, watching, waiting and ready for the return of God's anointed King.

The Lord was challenging and correcting the mistaken nationalistic thinking of his hearers, and drawing attention to the ultimately dramatic and yet almost unnoticed growth of the kingdom of God, beginning with the days he spent among them, until the day of his final return as King of kings and Lord of lords.

Is there a warning here for us, in our day?
We view the ancient, nationalistic misunderstanding of the nature of the kingdom of God, with the benefit of the Gospel teaching of the New Testament as well as 2,000 years of history. But it is challenging to ask, could such a misunderstanding be paralleled by some of our current Western expectations? We, too, are creatures of our age; do we have widely held, yet mistaken assumptions?

The New Testament writers clearly saw new disciples as a people chosen, adopted, redeemed and wonderfully caught up in the great purposes of Almighty God. At great personal cost, the apostles focused on building up the body of disciples so that, as fellow labourers, believers could each play a God-given part in warning people of the judgement to come, in spreading the gospel of forgiveness and in encouraging fellow disciples. They were fulfilling the Lord's commission and so preparing for the Master's return, both in glory and in judgement.

We live in a time when society has moved its focus from each of us playing our part in the whole community, to each of us pursuing our individual rights and self-fulfilment. The great danger for us is that we import this thinking into our Christian lives and churches.

If we do, we could find ourselves assuming that the kingdom of God is here for our personal protection, comfort and encouragement. However, like Jesus' hearers, we will have put our hope and trust in an understanding that is mistaken.

In our churches, we delight to meet and assure one another that God loves us and is 'here to bless us'. But, unlike the New Testament church, tend not to see ourselves as called to be a team of God's servants with a very great task to fulfil. We may delight in his promises, but pass lightly over his commandments. We will be more enthusiastic to be 'blessed' in all that we are doing, than to be challenged to turn from any ungodly ways, stirred by a clearer vision of the mighty purposes of God and better equipped to spend our lives in his service. Many of our modern 'worship songs' and even our prayers quite often have ourselves and our own wellbeing at the centre, rather than the Lord God and our lives bringing glory to his name.

The parable of the mustard seed sharply challenged the expectation of the Lord Jesus' disciples and their fellow hearers. It completely overturned their hope of military and national supremacy. In our day, the Lord's words are a challenge to each one of us to examine our own assumptions concerning the kingdom of God.

How does the kingdom of God grow?

Immediately following the parable of the mustard seed, Mark records that the Lord taught the great crowds only in parables – which he explained privately to his disciples. However, the gospel writers have not recorded the Lord's explanation of this parable, or told us much about the context in which it was taught.

So the question arises, should we simply take the parable of the mustard seed as an illustration of dramatic and yet quiet and gradual growth? Or might we usefully look more closely at the man, the seed, the growing seedling and the ultimate tree? Similarly, is the reference to the birds nesting in the branches simply an indication of the size to which the tree grows or could these be identified with particular aspects of the kingdom of God? So, we could ask:

'Who can sow the kingdom of God?'
This must be the Lord God himself: God the Father in overall, sovereign control. God the Son, as he sowed both his God-centred way of living and his teaching, in the lives of those first disciples. And God the Holy Spirit, as he opens eyes to see the kingdom of God, and as he sows a hunger for the things of God in the hearts of men and women – both then and in our day.

We might also ask, 'What field, ground or garden had the Lord God been preparing for the sowing of his kingdom?'
The Scriptures show us that for centuries, by prophet, priest and king, the Lord God had been preparing his ancient people, Israel – the Jewish nation. From Abraham onwards, they were his chosen people, a people through whom he would fulfil his purposes and on whom he set his love – not due to any merit of their own, but by God's sovereign choice. It was through the Lord God's ancient people, the children of Abraham, that the nations would be blessed. Much later, full of the Holy Spirit of God, John the Baptist declared that God's chosen mo-

ment to begin to fulfil his purpose had arrived. By divine appointment, John prepared the way and called the people of Israel to repent and to be ready.

'As he sowed the kingdom of God, who or what did the Lord God sow; who or what was his grain of mustard seed?'

'In the fullness of time, God sent forth his son, born of a woman, born under the law to redeem those under the law . . .' writes the apostle Paul, referring to the Jewish people. As the Lord Jesus healed the sick, raised the dead, gave sight to the blind, set captives free and proclaimed good news to the poor, Isaiah's words of prophecy concerning the signs of the coming of the Messiah, God's anointed King, were fulfilled. As he taught, he declared that by his very presence among them, the kingdom of God had come. Here is the mustard seed; here is the seed of the kingdom of God, the long promised Messiah; God himself among his people, as both the sower and the seed.

And yet, to the world, he was just a baby boy, born in turbulent times, who escaped a massacre. He was just an irregular rabbi, an itinerant preacher sowing his life and teaching in the hearts and minds of a dozen unlearned and ignorant men in a backwater of the great Roman Empire. His trial and sentence to death was just one more miscarriage of justice; one more crucifixion among so many which took place to keep the conquered people, and especially the slaves, under subjection. Each of these things was apparently quite insignificant. And yet God was sowing his kingdom; a kingdom hidden from those who consider themselves the great and the wise, but a kingdom that would grow until the great day dawns when 'every knee bows . . . and every tongue confesses that Jesus Christ is Lord to the glory of God the Father.'

'How did the Lord God continue to grow his kingdom after the resurrection of Jesus?'

Jesus left a seedling church, a sapling mustard tree; a little group of disciples who, typical of seedlings, were very vulnerable and unsure. They were frightened, confused, and tempted to return to fishing. However, they were charged to wait in Jerusalem for the promise of the Holy Spirit. At the feast of Pentecost, devout Jewish people from many different nations were gathered in Jerusalem and, in their own native languages, heard these same disciples, now filled with the Holy Spirit, boldly telling out the mighty works of God.

The Lord God had long before promised, by his prophet Zechariah, that he would pour out a spirit of compassion and supplication on his ancient people as they looked on the one they had pierced, and cause them to 'mourn for him, as one mourns for an only child, and weep bitterly over him, as one weeps over a firstborn.' He had also promised, 'on that day', to open a fountain of forgiveness and cleansing for the house of Israel; the Jewish people.

On the Day of Pentecost, as the devout men of Israel listened to Peter's God-owned declaration concerning the Messiah, identifying him with the Jesus they had put to death, they were deeply moved, 'cut to the heart', by the Holy Spirit. Crying out, 'What must we do?' three thousand of them turned in repentance and faith and were baptised. They found the promised fountain of forgiveness and cleansing in the name of Yeshua, Jesus, their crucified Messiah. Under the Spirit of God, the kingdom of God, the mustard tree, grew strongly that day. From then on, 'the Lord added daily to his church those who were being saved.'

As we consider these things, we must not overlook the fact that the Lord God's kingdom, his mustard tree, was very clearly primarily among his ancient people, the Jews. 'He came to his own people . . .' writes the apostle John. Jesus came, as he declared, '. . . to the lost sheep of the house of Israel.' It is for this reason that the non-Jewish person seeking help for her sick daughter could initially be given such an astonishing reply, 'It is not right to give the children's bread to the dogs.'

At this point it would be easy to conclude that the kingdom of God, his mustard tree, was to be composed of those members of the house of Israel who believed: those who believed then, those who, through the running centuries, came to believe – and those of the Jewish people who in our day believe on their crucified Messiah, Yeshua, the Lord Jesus.

But was the kingdom to be restricted to the people of Israel? Some Jewish believers certainly thought it was. However, it is the Lord God who plants and is growing his kingdom. 'For my thoughts are not your thoughts, neither are your ways my ways, declares the Lord. For as the heavens are higher than the earth, so are my ways higher than your ways and my thoughts than your thoughts.'

Heavenly Father, this parable challenged the religious and socially accepted thinking of our Lord's hearers. In the light of your word, awaken us to examine equally mistaken comforting assumptions of our own, of our denomination or church, and of society around us in our times.

Questions for reflection or discussion

1. Why do you think the Roman occupation caused the people to understand the Scriptures in the way they did?
2. In our day, to what extent have we brought into our own Christian thinking, and into many of our churches, the 'my personal fulfilment, satisfaction and comfort' thinking of modern Western society?
3. How can our personal circumstances affect our understanding of the purposes of God? In times of personal peace and plenty we may re-

joice that our breath and all our circumstances are in the hand of the Lord. Could we also do so in times of difficulty, sickness or sorrow?

4. Are you aware of other areas in which we could be misunderstanding the ways of God in our day? For example, it is very widely believed that all baptised people are secure members of the kingdom of heaven, but in the light of the words of our Lord, can that be so?

5. In what ways could we do better at building the kingdom, proclaiming the gospel and countering society's self-centred culture?

6. Can the thrilling way in which the Lord God began to grow his 'mustard tree' be an encouragement to us?

Footnote

A minor difficulty

Matthew and Mark record Jesus referring to the mustard seed as being, 'the smallest of all the seeds'. There are plenty of seeds no larger than dust, but in the Middle East, mustard was the smallest seed generally sown as an annual crop. It rapidly grew to be the largest of annual plants, over two metres high, and birds could easily settle and roost in it.

If the underlying word, which literally means 'tenting', implied not only settling and roosting but also 'nesting', how could mustard, grown fresh from seed each season, be large and available long enough for nesting? For this reason, a number of other, more substantial, plants that could have been known as mustard have been suggested. They include trees such as the bay tree or the toothbrush tree, each of whose peppery leaves are used in food. (The second one, *Salvadora persica*, gets its fascinating English name because the benefit to teeth and gums from chewing its twigs has been recognised for thousands of years.)

References

The mustard tree – Matthew 13:31-32, Mark 4:30-32, Luke 13:18-19
Cedar tree – Ezekiel 17:22-24
Restore Israel? – Acts 1:6
Positions of power – Mark 10:35-37
Cleopas – Luke 24:21
Not by might, nor by power – Zechariah 4:6
Explained privately – Mark 4:33-34
King of kings and Lord of Lords – Revelation 19:16
Only in parables – Mark 4:33-34
Not due to any merit of their own – Deuteronomy 7:6-7
The nations would be blessed – Genesis 12:3 and 18:18
John the Baptist, 'repent' – Matthew. 3:2
In the fullness of time – Galatians 4:4
Good news to the poor – Luke 4:17-18 and 7:20-23
Long promised Messiah – Isaiah 7:14, 9:6-7 and Micah 5:2
The kingdom of God among them – Luke 17:21
Escaped a massacre – Matthew 2:7-13
Every knee bows – Philippians 2:10
Tempted to return to fishing – John 21:3
Charged to wait in Jerusalem – Acts 1:3-5
Day of Pentecost – Acts 2:1-47, particularly verses 37, 38 and 47
Zechariah – Zechariah 12:10 and 13:1
His own people – John 1:11-12
Lost sheep of the house of Israel – Matthew 15:24
Not right to take the children's bread – Mark 7:27, Matthew 15:26
My thoughts are not your thoughts – Isaiah 55:8-9

The Parable of the Mustard Seed – part 2

From 'Jerusalem . . . to the end of the earth'

Following the stoning of Stephen, the Jewish believers were persecuted and scattered from Jerusalem far and wide. They preached the gospel wherever they went. Philip preached to the Samaritans and, by divine appointment, shared the same gospel with the Ethiopian eunuch. Although it ran counter to all his Jewish background, by a dramatic vision it was made plain to Peter that the approaching invitation, to preach to the Roman soldier, Cornelius, and his household, was of God. Obeying the vision, Peter brought the gospel to these non-Jewish people and saw for himself the unmistakable signs of the coming of the kingdom of God.

Some of the believers preached the gospel to the Greek-speaking people of Antioch amongst whom, again, God did a mighty work – so much so that Barnabas was sent from Jerusalem to see if it was genuine. He found it to be clearly a work of grace; the kingdom of God truly planted among Gentile people.

Barnabas needed help to tend and teach this new and God-owned branch of the growing mustard tree. He brought Paul from Tarsus and they laboured together until that church, where believers were first called 'Christians', found itself called of God to send first Paul and Barnabas, and then Paul and Silas, as missionaries throughout the Roman empire. Within a few years there were many Gentile branches of God's mustard tree, nurtured and defended from error, taught and looked after by the apostles.

Those of us who are Gentile (non-Jewish) Christians can be in danger of overlooking the great contribution of these Jewish people. We owe so much to those faithful members of the Jewish believing church who shared the gospel, and who nurtured those whom the Lord called to himself from among the non-Jewish people. In doing so, they planted the seed for the Lord God's great harvest among the nations.

Pick up a New Testament and see how much of it has come to us by the labours of men such as the apostles Peter and Paul. Read the Acts and the Epistles and see what it cost these early, Jewish members of God's mustard tree to bring the gospel to the Gentile world.

Here is clear and undeniable proof that the Messiah is indeed, as Simeon had said, '. . . the glory of your people Israel', but, by the grace of God, he is also '. . . a light for revelation to the Gentiles.'

How is the Lord God sowing and growing his mustard tree today?
The Lord Jesus himself was constantly sowing the seed of the kingdom of God in the lives of those with whom he spoke and those he healed and helped. He knew all about each one of them. He opened the eyes of Nathanael simply by addressing him as '. . . an Israelite without guile,' and of the Samaritan woman by telling her that she '. . . had had five husbands and that the man she now lived with was not her husband.' As a result of those words she, and later the whole Samaritan village, believed him to be the true Messiah.

These are New Testament accounts of small and apparently insignificant seeds of the kingdom of God that our Lord sowed in the minds and hearts of individual people. This is still the principal way in which the Lord God grows his kingdom. It may be just a phrase or a few words read in a hymn or a tract, in a book or in the Bible. It could be the God-owned words of a faithful preacher, writer, broadcaster or public speaker. We could be stirred by the care or kindness with which we have been treated. In such apparently insignificant ways the Lord God sows the seed of the kingdom in our hearts and minds. The thoughts and questions arising from such an encounter challenge and disturb us. We find that we are hungry to discover more, and God begins to open our eyes to see the kingdom of heaven. Slowly we discover from the New Testament, as did John Newton, that we have been completely unaware of our true and desperate situation before Almighty God, and then go on to discover, with wonder, the way of forgiveness and cleansing that he has provided for us in his Son, known to those of us who are Gentiles as the Lord Jesus.

Here is yet another sharp and personal challenge presented by the parable. Has the Lord God sown the seed of his kingdom in our hearts and lives? Do you count yourself eternally grateful for that gospel warning, phrase or word that the Lord God first planted in your heart? A word that so challenged and stirred you that you had to ask, seek, enquire, step forward, pray, or as in times of revival, cry out to the Lord – until the kingdom of God began to take root in your life. If it was genuine and has been nurtured by prayerful reading of the Scriptures and the encouragement of fellow believers, it will be like the seed growing or like the yeast at work bringing the whole of life under the saving rule and kingship of the Lord God. Little by little, as we grow in understanding, love of Scripture and of the ways of God, it will lift heavenward our attitudes and priorities, our aims and concerns, our use of time and money, our career and our friendships.

Under the hand of God, we may grow into a godly 'bush in the garden of our own home', as did Susannah Wesley faithfully bringing up her many children, or we may grow into a mighty 'tree in the field of God's world', as did her sons, John and Charles Wesley and their contemporary George Whitefield.

Here is God's powerful and yet secret work of the gospel seed; the life-changing presence of the kingdom of God within us.

Where are we today? How greatly has the mustard tree grown?
The kingdom of God, the mustard tree, continues grow. There are genuine believers to be found on every continent. In some situations the mustard tree is growing fast. In other places it is static, declining or actively being squeezed out or suppressed. Many times, the Lord Jesus directly and by parable warned of tribulation and, by the parable of the widow and the judge, urged disciples to hold fast, watch, pray and await the vindication of God. He made plain how hard it might be-

come by the sombre addition, 'Nevertheless, when the Son of man comes, will he find faith on earth?'

What a great challenge this is to every current member of the kingdom of God, each one of us in our own sphere – are we able to encourage one another to hold fast and to uphold and promote godly ways in a hostile world? Are our own family, and the people around us, benefitting from our godly fair-mindedness, patience, kindness and mercy; are they able to safely shelter in our branches? Are we willing to play our part to the glory of God?

Here lies the great work of the whole people of God – the 'mustard tree' that is his church. Certainly it is called to be a place of refuge, safety and mutual encouragement for disciples, but also to be a witness to the world. Each of us is called to reach out by our lives and by our words to those around us with the gospel, and then encourage them to grow in grace and in knowledge and understanding of the ways of God and in humble obedience to his Son.

Just like the grain of mustard seed when it has been sown, the kingdom of God, faithfully lived and proclaimed, has a dynamic and a power of its own – the power of God. Pray, therefore, that the Lord God would restore and revitalise his church. Pray that he would stir, thrill and revive his people and so enable us to live as vigorous branches of the mustard tree in our own day and society. Pray that he would fill each true member of his kingdom afresh with his Holy Spirit. And that he would stir up that 'first love' for his risen, reigning and soon returning Son who loved us and gave himself for us.

Where will it end?

What a thrilling prophetic picture this parable gives us of God first sowing and then growing his kingdom!

The Lord God sent his one and only Son to live among his ancient people the Jews, to help, to heal, to teach – and finally to lay down his life on the cross in order to fulfil his Father's purpose of establishing the kingdom.

The Lord God continued to grow his kingdom, first in the lives of the disciples, and then – after Jesus' resurrection and ascension, and the sending of the Holy Spirit on the day of Pentecost – among Jewish and non-Jewish people throughout the Roman Empire. Finally the branches of God's 'mustard tree' would, and indeed have, spread throughout the world.

Looking to the future, in the light of Ezekiel's prophecy concerning the cedar tree, the parable gives us a glimpse of the day when the purposes of God for his kingdom will be fulfilled. The day is coming when everything will be placed under the rule and authority of his beloved and anointed Son, the Messiah.

The apostle John's vision in the book of Revelation is of a people ransomed, from every language and tribe and nation by the sacrificial death of the Lamb of God – the cross of the Lord Jesus. And so it will be when our Lord returns. But before that time, the apostle Paul speaks of a great turning among God's ancient people. No wonder Paul spoke with such excitement as he wrote of the day when all Israel will be saved as being '. . . life from the dead.'

Heavenly Father, by your grace and forgiveness, cause each one of us, by repentance and by faith in your Son, the Lord Jesus, to be a living part of your mustard tree. Fill us with gratitude and joy, and stir us to be truly caught up in your purposes and actively part of your worldwide kingdom, your mustard tree.

Questions for reflection or discussion

1. How great is the debt we owe to the faithful Jewish believers of the New Testament church?
2. Do we pray and care as we might for the current generation of Jewish people, both those gathered in Israel and those scattered throughout the nations? Why do we have good reason to do so?
3. Can you look back on the first small seeds of the kingdom of God sown in your own life?
4. In what ways can we better encourage the growth of the seed of the kingdom of God in our own lives, and in the lives of those around us?
5. Have you known people whose genuine Christian faith has been a shelter and encouragement to you? Can we offer the same to those around us?
6. Do we reach out to our fellow men and women as the early church did? What would help us to do better?
7. Can you think of countries where the gospel mustard tree is growing with great vigour; where it is dormant; where it seems to be dying; where it is threatened with extinction? What are the reasons for this?
8. Do we care as we ought for our fellow Christians facing great tribulations? How can we do better?

References

From 'Jerusalem . . . to the end of the earth' – Acts 1:8
The stoning of Stephen – Acts 7:54-60
Philip, the Samaritans and the Ethiopian – Acts 8:4-5, 26-39
Cornelius – Acts 10
The church at Antioch – Acts 11:19-26
Simeon – Luke 2:32
An Israelite without guile – John 1:47-48
Five husbands – John 4:16-18 and v. 39
Tribulation – John 16:33 see also Acts 14:22

Will he find faith on earth, the widow and the judge – Luke 18:8
The love you had at first (first love) – Revelation 2:4
Loved us and gave himself for us – Galatians 2:20
The Day of Pentecost – Acts 2:1-47
The cedar tree – Ezekiel 17:22-24
All authority – Matthew 28:18 see also Philippians 2:9-11
Ransomed from every tribe – Revelation 5:9
Life from the dead . . . all Israel saved – Romans 11:15 and 26

The Parable of the Mustard Seed – part 3

An optional section for those wishing to explore some of the other interpretations of the birds settling in the branches

J.C. Ryle, quoting John Chrysostom, advises, 'It is not right to search curiously, and word for word, into all things in a parable: but when we have learned the object for which it was composed, we are to reap this, and not to busy ourselves about anything further.' There is one great teaching in all three of these parables, and that is the way the Lord God is growing his kingdom. Maybe we should be content to lay hold of that, and stirred to play our part in it.

The Lord Jesus describes the mustard tree growing to such a size that the birds shelter or nest in its branches. He certainly did so to indicate the vigour of the growth and the great size to which it would grow. He may have intended to convey nothing more than that. However fertile minds have interpreted the reference to the birds settling in the branches much further.

For those who wish to explore this and make their own judgement, here are some of the interpretations of the significance of the birds nesting in the branches. Some of them are clearly open to question, others contain useful challenges and warnings for both individual disciples and for the people of God as a whole.

The birds settling in the branches could represent the Gentiles lodging in the branches of God's Jewish mustard tree.
From the earliest days, Gentile believers have been seen by some people as mere birds settling in the Jewish mustard tree, but not really part of it. Many of the earliest Jewish believers would only accept Gentile believers – who they recognised as being true believers – if they submitted to becoming fully Jewish. They regarded the Gentile believers

as people benefitting from the Jewish mustard tree but not actually Jewish and therefore not actually part of the tree themselves.

At the Council of Jerusalem, described in Acts chapter 15, the apostle Paul, with Barnabas, vigorously defended these non-Jewish believers from this kind of thinking and from those Jewish believers who would have them submit to the Jewish rites and customs. As the apostle Paul later wrote his letter to the Romans, he described Gentile believers as being 'grafted in' – different but absolutely part of the kingdom of God. The suggestion that believers from the nations are mere 'lodgers' in the kingdom of God, does not sit well with the apostle's picture of the Jewish church as an olive tree with Gentile branches grafted in.

From the apostle Paul's convincing defence in Jerusalem, and from his letter, the birds sheltering in the branches really cannot represent believing Gentile people.

The Lord God's ultimate purpose, as the epistle to the Ephesians makes plain, is to put all things under Christ, Jew and Gentile alike. When that day dawns all believers will be one body and all believers will have benefitted from those early Jewish believers who, led by the apostles, brought the gospel to their own people and then, as the Lord God scattered them, to the Gentile world.

The birds settling in the branches could be a picture of evil infesting the whole body of Christian believers

There are positive benefits of 'birds' being able to settle in the branches of God's mustard tree, his people. But there is also a negative side, for birds can cause considerable damage to a tree; for example, some, like bullfinches, strip a tree of the flower buds and others, like pigeons, of the young fruits.

May I invite you to explore another very widely held and respected, but I believe mistaken, understanding of the birds nesting in the branches.

If you note that in the gospels of Matthew and Luke the parable of the mustard tree is paired with the parable of the leaven, you may come to see them both either as parables of growth – or as parables of evil. The basis for this second understanding is that the birds eating the seed on the pathway in the parable of the sower, are clearly identified by our Lord as representing the devil. 'Then the devil comes and snatches away the word.' Add to this our Lord's warning to his disciples about 'the leaven of the Pharisees' and the apostle Paul's reference to 'the leaven of malice and wickedness' and you have the beginning of a collection of verses that may lead you to understand that, in the parable of the mustard seed, our Lord is teaching that, as the kingdom of God grows, it will become riddled with hypocrisy, malice and wickedness and its branches will become infested with devils. Certainly, historically there are elements of truth to be found in such an understanding. However, is this really what the Lord was teaching at the time? Could I be coming to the parable and making it fit an idea that I have brought to it?

Surely, a safer approach is to let the whole Bible speak for itself. Birds are by no means always a picture of evil. For example the Lord challenged his disciples to learn from the birds, which 'neither sow, nor reap, nor gather into barns' and yet are fed. Our Lord is simply drawing attention to the way the birds are fed. If our heavenly Father feeds them, cannot disciples trust him to provide for their needs also? Or again, the Lord speaks of gathering the people of Jerusalem '. . . as a hen gathers her chicks under her wings.' The Psalmist speaks many times of hiding, sheltering or taking refuge and of rejoicing 'under your wings' – but neither the Lord nor the Psalmist are speaking of the devil! On each occasion, we must allow the setting to show us how the illustration is being used.

The birds settling in the branches could be a picture of societies and nations sheltering and benefitting from the godly ways of the believing people of God

Ezekiel and Daniel speak of rulers of huge empires as great trees with smaller nations as birds sheltering in their branches. Can nations and societies benefit from the godliness of life of members of the kingdom of God? Can believing people bring enormous benefits to society as a whole? It is the calling of God's people to be salt and light in society; to work for justice and mercy, respect, and a forgiving attitude – and to demonstrate these things in their own lives and attitudes. Because of this, the kingdom of heaven, outwardly expressed in the sincere, godly living of its members, will permeate, form and reform the whole of a society; over the years it will transform a nation.

One African president commented on his experience in his own country, 'You can always tell the areas where the Christians are – it is safe to travel.' In that remark, he gave a perfect illustration of the birds being able to roost safely in the branches of the kingdom of God – honesty and respect for other people and their property, is one of the benefits of the kingdom of God to society as a whole.

In Britain 'godly natural justice', the honest dealing based on trust, a willingness to work for the common good and a willingness to be forgiving of others, are all things that flow from the true godliness of sufficient numbers of its citizens. Over many centuries, such godly ways gave this country a parliamentary system and a system of justice, education and honest trading that have been the envy of the world. These are benefits that flow from godliness, and without godliness they very soon evaporate. Sadly this is something not generally appreciated by the secular governments of our own day. Indeed, ungodly folk are determinedly tearing down our rich Christian heritage; ripping the branches from the tree and would be altogether rid of the kingdom of God and of all godly influence in school, work place, legal justice and the public sphere.

The birds in the branches could be a picture of individual people, who have not yet come to believe, sheltering among God's people

Another, and challenging, understanding of the reference to the birds settling in the branches is that the Lord Jesus intended to alert his hearers to the terrible possibility of being associated with the kingdom of God, rather than being a vital part of it – of being present among the people of God without being one of them.

We could usefully ask, who 'flocked' to our Lord in the time of his ministry, and who has 'settled in the branches' of the kingdom of God through the running centuries?

Great crowds of ordinary people came to hear the Lord Jesus and followed him from place to place. The sick and suffering, the oppressed and disabled also flocked to him with their relatives. So did the despised tax gatherers and sinners. Clearly some, like the tax collector Zacchaeus, truly became members of the kingdom of God – 'salvation came to his house.' However, the vast majority of those who flocked to him – although they loved his teaching and many were helped and healed by him – went on their way fundamentally unchanged. Could such people be described as 'birds'? They had rested or roosted for a spell in the branches and benefitted from doing it. But they did so without ever becoming part of the kingdom of God; truly part of God's mustard tree. As our Lord said of the towns around Galilee, that had seen so much of his teaching and healing ministry, they failed to repent; failed to receive and believe in him and so, in practice, rejected both him and the Lord God who sent him.

In our own day, thousands of us who attend our chapels and churches do so for a whole variety of reasons, often without any sense of spiritual hunger or need. We may have the great benefit of a lifelong habit of church-going or find ourselves attracted by the music, be it ancient or modern, or by an appreciation of the orderliness of things done well. We may be attracted by the sense of being in the presence of holy things or drawn by a particularly gifted preacher. We may 'roost' in the church because we value the company of the people who go there; perhaps because of their generosity in a time of need, or hoping to find true friendship and sympathy, a marriage partner – or even a career or good business contacts. These are all real benefits offered by roosting in the Lord God's 'mustard tree'. However, being part of even the most dynamic of churches does not actually, of itself, mean that we have humbled ourselves before Almighty God and submitted to his Son the Lord Jesus Christ and so really become a member of the kingdom of God.

At a far more serious level, from church history it is clear that some able and well-meaning people who 'settle' in the church can cause serious damage to those who are truly part of Christ's mustard tree. For, if such people, 'birds,' who are not actually part of God's kingdom, consider themselves so comfortable and settled that they begin to assume positions of leadership among God's people, then his people are in great trouble. God's true people will be led further and further from the root and stem. They will be persuaded that there is no need for a close personal bond of repentance towards God and faith in his anointed Son, the Lord Jesus, or need of a humble, willing obedience to his teaching and to that of his chosen apostles. These 'birds' will offer another gospel, one far less demanding and more suited to their considered opinions, the world around them and their way of life. They will also appoint like-minded 'birds' to positions of authority, and be inclined to exclude those who do not share their views.

We will look further at these things as we come to explore the second of this pair of parables, the parable of the leaven.

A personal look at the birds settling among the branches of the people of God
The Lord, alone, knows who are his and knows the secrets of our hearts. Yet, there is a challenge here for each one of us. There is a time to humbly and prayerfully examine ourselves, asking for the Holy Spirit's enlightening to show us, in the light of Scripture, our own true

standing before Almighty God. Are we truly members of the kingdom of God or are we only 'members of the church'; 'birds' roosting in the branches? Surely, it is an alarming thought that it is possible to be merely 'a bird' even as a church dignitary or a minister; a horrifying possibility that we can be 'a bird' as a respected church officer or as one of those who are active members and regularly attend.

After a visiting speaker had shown a video and spoken in a Christian home for older people, an elderly resident spoke privately to him and said, 'I love it here and they all think I'm a truly believing Christian, but I know that I'm not, can you help me?' The Holy Spirit had shown that man that he needed to be a member of the kingdom of God, not just a 'bird' roosting in its branches. And the speaker was able to lead him to the mercy of God and to true faith in the One who told this parable.

Heavenly Father, by the Holy Spirit, open our eyes and ears to heed the warnings of these understandings of the birds settling in the mustard tree. Enable us to humbly examine our own hearts and underlying assumptions before you and in the light of your word, lest, before you and too late, we find ourselves to have been birds, passengers or lodgers – enjoying the external benefits of the kingdom of God, but not actually members of it.

By your grace and forgiveness, cause us to be vitally connected by repentance and by faith in your Son, the Lord Jesus Christ. Full of gratitude and joy, may we be truly caught up in your purposes and actively part of your world-wide kingdom, your mustard tree.

Questions for reflection or discussion

1. How can we be spiritually open to let Scripture speak for itself rather than making it fit the ideas we bring to it?

2. What important benefits do you see flowing from true godliness in society?

3. Over the years, what benefits has Christian influence brought to our nation?

4. What is happening to our Christian heritage in our day?

5. Is it possible to merely 'roost' in today's church?

6. Can you perhaps see a time in your life when, like the elderly man, you came to recognise that you were just 'roosting'?

7. Are you increasingly aware of a vital link and humble dependence on the Lord Jesus himself, in John Newton's words, as 'Shepherd, Shield and Saviour'?

References

Council of Jerusalem – Acts 15:1-32

The olive tree with branches grafted in – Romans 11:24

To put all things under Christ, Jew and Gentile alike – Ephesians 1:10 and 22-23

The birds in the parable of the sower – Luke 8:5 and 12

The leaven of the Pharisees – Luke 12:1

Leaven of malice and wickedness – 1 Corinthians 5:8

Neither sow nor reap – Matthew 6:26

As a hen gathers her chicks – Matthew 23:37, Luke 13:34

Rejoicing under your wings – Psalms 17:8, 36:7, 57:1, 61:4, 91:4

Empires sheltering birds – Ezekiel 31:2-9 of Egypt and Pharaoh,
        – Daniel 4:20-22 of Nebuchadnezzar

Salt and light – Matthew 5:13&14

Zacchaeus – Luke 19:1-10

Capernaum, Chorazin and Bethsaida, the towns around Galilee, failed to repent – Luke 10:13-16

The Lord, alone, knows who are his – Matthew 7:21-23

The Leaven

He said therefore, "What is the kingdom of God like? And to what shall I compare it? It is like a grain of mustard seed that a man took and sowed in his garden, and it grew and became a tree, and the birds of the air made nests in its branches." And again he said, "To what shall I compare the kingdom of God? It is like leaven that a woman took and hid in three measures of flour, until it was all leavened."

Luke 13:18-21, English Standard Version

He told them another parable. "The kingdom of heaven is like leaven that a woman took and hid in three measures of flour, till it was all leavened."

Matthew 13:33, English Standard Version

The Leaven Hidden in a Large Quantity of Meal

Introduction
"What is the kingdom of God like?" Like the similar questions that Jesus asked before the parable of the growing grain and the parable of the mustard seed, Jesus' questions arrest the attention of his hearers and invite their involvement, 'Yes, what is it like? – I want to know.'

Jesus answered his own question by comparing the kingdom of God with the scattered seeds of grain growing and producing a harvest, the mustard seed growing into a plant large enough for birds to settle in, and the leaven 'hidden' in the meal.

As we come to explore the parable of the leaven, we find a sharp division of interpretation. Most commentators see the parable as one of a group of parables illustrating the growth of the kingdom of God.

142 · EXPLORING AND APPLYING THE PARABLES...

However, others believe that by way of these parables, Jesus was giving a strong warning of the danger of the gradual development of evil among the people of God. For either interpretation, the tiny amount of yeast totally changing the nature of a very large amount of flour is a perfect picture.

May I invite you to explore each of these two quite different understandings in turn?

Understanding this parable as a parable of growth

Classical interpreters like John Calvin and Matthew Henry, and more modern ones like William Barclay and C.H. Dodd, see this parable of the leaven as a picture of the vigorous and all pervading growth of the kingdom of God.

This would seem to be the most straightforward understanding of the whole group of parables: the growing grain, recorded only by Mark, the mustard seed and the leaven. From a very small beginning each develops to yield a very significant result – a harvest, a tree and a large batch of bread.

Leaven was a piece of uncooked dough that had been kept from a previous baking. It contained live yeast, and salt to pause the fermentation process until it was wanted for use. The woman 'hid' her leaven by mixing it, with water, into three measures of meal. The water, diluting the salt, sets the yeast free to quietly multiply and work its way through the meal. After a time it will totally modify the whole great batch of meal. Three measures was the amount typically used when baking for a large and gathered family – it was a small sack-full of perhaps 25kg.

Our Lord's use of leaven as a picture of the spreading of the kingdom of God
The parable of the leaven gives a fresh view of the way the kingdom of God was to grow. Unlike mustard, yeast is not a plant grown from a

single seed, but individual cells that remain independent of one another. Yet together, they permeate and totally change the meal. The cells divide and multiply and spread through the meal, digesting and changing it cell by cell and little by little.

This is the second of our Lord's amazingly instructive pictures of the growth of the kingdom of God. All that he has shown us by the picture of the mustard seed is true of his believing people, but here his kingdom is viewed from another angle. We are many distinct individuals, yet we each have our personal part to play in permeating this world for the glory of God.

One by one we are 'born anew' and become a member of the kingdom of God, and then our calling is to multiply and to bring glory to our heavenly Father. We are to do so by our care and concern for those around us, by the way we live, by a godly word from ourselves, and by our taking of God-given opportunities to bring those around us under the sound of God's gospel. As we do these things we will permeate and change society around us. Like the yeast, we will each be playing our part as the Lord 'adds to his church those who are being saved' and so causes his kingdom to grow.

Sometimes we call little groups of believing people meeting together to pray, search the Scriptures and encourage one another, 'cells'. And such cells are not there to be closed, inward-looking, permanent and comfortable; they are there to support and encourage one another as we permeate society around us. Like leaven, they are meant to be alive, changing, dividing and forming new cells in fresh areas.

The same applies to churches, which are only large 'cells'. Is it our fear, or the friendly comfortable atmosphere of like-minded people, that stops the dynamic growth and multiplying of so many of our churches? Too often we shut ourselves away and have little or no 'fermenting', life-changing, community-changing effect. We may seem 'very nice people', but in other respects are all but irrelevant to the unbelieving world in which we have been 'hidden'. That is hardly like yeast in its almost unstoppable permeation of the whole great mass of meal.

The challenge of the parable for ourselves and for today's church

As individuals and as a church, we would do well to constantly keep in mind the vision given to us in this parable of the leaven – the active, cellular permeation of the 'whole batch' of society around us. To do so, we need, as with the growing mustard tree, to be rooted and grounded in the Lord Jesus, day by day dependent on him and nourished by his word, as it is recorded by his chosen apostles and as it is applied to our hearts by the Holy Spirit.

Here is a dynamic picture of the growth of the kingdom of God. It grows all but unnoticed within the lives of those who believe. It grows as those who believe reach out to those around them. It grows in and through groups of believers pulling together as a team. Through such groups it grows in a society, in a nation and throughout the nations of the world. Each of us has a part to play in the kingdom of God in whatever calling or position in society the Lord God has placed us. Like the yeast, the growth of the kingdom is quiet. It is often resisted, belittled and ignored yet, empowered by the Holy Spirit of God, mighty in the change it produces.

This is exactly how the New Testament church spread so rapidly throughout the Roman Empire. The first generation of believers were scattered from Jerusalem by persecution. They carried the gospel to wherever they could safely settle, and more and more little groups of believers were formed. We have a record of such a group in Antioch where the believers shared the gospel with their Greek neighbours. Barnabas was sent to that group and with Paul built up the new-born church. Led by the Holy Spirit, the Antioch church prayerfully sent Paul and Barnabas, and later Paul and Silas, to plant and establish other churches.

Conclusion

Bread-making took place in every household. As he taught the parable of the leaven, Jesus used, what was to his crowds of hearers, this very familiar picture of yeast multiplying and working its way through a whole batch of meal. He used it as a picture of the permeating and spreading of the kingdom of God. We can see the parable working out in practice. The kingdom grows within us, as we gradually bring each part of our lives into submission to our Lord. It grows through us, as we reach out to others. Like the leaven, the kingdom of God multiplies one by one, group by group, and church by church, until whole communities, societies and nations are permeated and changed.

As we seek to understand the parable of the leaven, it seems wiser, and is definitely safer not to go beyond this simple picture of the multiplication and growth of the kingdom of God in, among, and through believing people. With the blessing of the Holy Spirit, growth like this leads to the ongoing growth of godliness and godly ways throughout the whole of society around them.

Heavenly Father, please stir us and open our eyes to catch the dynamic and wonderful vision of our part in your growing kingdom, so clearly depicted by your Son, the Lord Jesus, in this brief parable of the leaven.

Questions for discussion or reflection

1. Can you see something of the out-working of our Lord's use of the illustration of leaven:

    In your own life?
    In the life of the local church?

2. What can we learn from these two parables?

The parable of the mustard tree – growing as a single body and able to shelter the birds?

The parable of the leaven – nimble, multiplying, permeating and spreading through society?

References

Growing grain – Mark 4:26-29

Born anew – John 3:3

The Lord added . . . those who were being saved – Acts 2:47

The church at Antioch sending out Paul and Barnabas and later Paul and Silas – Acts11:19-26 and 13:1-3, and Acts 15:36-41

The Parable of the Leaven – part 2

Taken with the other parables in the group, I remain convinced, with the main body of commentators, that at this point Jesus is using the very familiar yeast-driven rising of bread as an arresting and positive illustration – as he says, as a parable of the kingdom of God. However, we need to be aware of another, very different, interpretation of the parable.

Understanding this parable as a parable of the spreading of evil

Our Lord's use of leaven as a picture of evil
Without question, Jesus did sometimes compare the working of leaven through a batch of flour with the way evil can spread. He privately warned the disciples, "Watch and beware of the leaven of the Pharisees and Sadducees," – meaning their teaching. He did so again as he warned them, "Beware of the leaven of the Pharisees, which is hypocrisy."

On this foundation, together with many other biblical references to leaven used to illustrate the of the spread of evil, commentators and interpreters such G. Campbell Morgan, G.H. Lang, and the contributors to the New Bible Commentary, strongly argue that the parable of the leaven is a warning to the disciples of the possibility of the spread of evil among them.

For this reason, we explore in turn the particular evils of which Jesus warned; the evil of hypocrisy and the evil of teaching based on human opinion.

The leaven of hypocrisy
Our Lord warned the disciples, "Beware of the leaven of the Pharisees, which is hypocrisy." The Pharisees were seriously devoted religious leaders, and yet as our Lord said of them, although they honoured God

with their lips, their hearts were far from him. They were very able administrators, managers and teachers. However, in any humble, obedient and personal sense, they were strangers to the Lord God, the One they claimed to honour and in whose name they claimed to speak.

The word hypocrite was not necessarily a slur on a person's character, as we use the word today. The Pharisees could be described as hypocrites because, both in the original meaning of the Greek word and in the original sense of our English word, they were 'acting a part' – speaking, teaching and occupying a position – but ultimately, strangers to the heart and ways of God.

Hypocrisy, in the original sense of the word, is an evil which has dogged the church throughout its history. Only when the secrets of all hearts are known, will it be made terrifyingly plain just how many religious leaders and office-holders in Christ's visible church have been actually 'acting a part'. They are often the most decent and upright of people who are sincerely and faithfully serving the church in a great variety of ways, and yet remain quite unaware of the need of forgiveness by the Lord God and a humble submission to, and trust in, the Son of God. Of these, warned the Lord Jesus, he may have to say, "... I never knew you ..."

There may even be those who, like some of the Sadducees and Pharisees, are in positions of leadership, and yet who, beneath a highly respected religious exterior, are actually ungodly at heart, and perhaps secretly or even flagrantly ungodly in lifestyle.

From our Lord's warning, it becomes clear that Christians, and Christian leaders in particular, need to be not just 'able people fulfilling a role' but to be genuinely godly; living in trust and obedience to the Lord in every aspect of our lives.

The leaven of teaching based on human thinking and opinion
The Pharisees and Sadducees were outwardly very religious and yet lacked the inward marks of an obedient, child-like trust and vital walk with the Lord God.

Holding fast to their position in society as trusted leaders and guardians of Israel's historic faith, the Sadducees had reduced true faith to near unbelief, with an outward religious display.

The Pharisees, on the other hand, replaced vital and obedient faith with the keeping of their inherited rules and traditions. In the words of our Lord, '. . . for the sake of your tradition you have made void the word of God . . . teaching as doctrines the commandments of men.' In one way or the other, both Sadducees and Pharisees were giving teaching that was misleading.

As J.C. Ryle comments, this particular evil of misleading teaching has been used by the evil one again and again throughout church history, either 'to bleed the gospel to death by subtraction from its truths,' or 'to stifle the gospel by heaping on traditions.'

Attractive human teaching that subtracts from the teaching of our Lord and his apostles has unsettled believers and, just like leaven, permeated the church and put it into ferment and turmoil many times over the centuries. Athanasius (c. 296-373) found himself having to stand 'against the world' in order to uphold the apostles' witness to the Son of God being truly God amongst us in human form. All but alone, Athanasius stood against the increasingly widely accepted, but unbiblical, teaching of Arius that our Lord '. . . was not God by nature, but a changeable human creature.'

The apostles Peter and Paul had to defend the Gentile believers in Antioch against some Jewish believers who would have stifled the gospel by imposing Jewish traditions on those Gentiles whom God had clearly chosen. They were misleadingly teaching, 'Unless you are circumcised according to the custom of Moses, you cannot be saved,' and insisting, 'It is necessary to circumcise them and to order them to keep the law of Moses.'

Just as the yeast can permeate and change a large batch of meal for good, as in the making of bread – the teaching of religious leaders who are at heart strangers to the ways of God, can infiltrate the people of

God, and end up having a controlling influence over them. Church history confirms this understanding of the spread of false teaching and of this kind of hypocrisy, again and again.

Are these warnings of relevance to Christians today?
As J.C. Ryle makes plain, successors to the Sadducees and Pharisees are to be found among God's people in every generation, often in very influential teaching positions.

Some, like the Sadducees, are all but humanists. Their teaching and writing betrays the fact that they are scarcely believers in the apostles' witness to the Lord Jesus at all. They often undermine and question every aspect of the apostolic faith – of such teachers and their teachings, warned our Lord, disciples need to beware.

Others, like the Pharisees, would replace the simplicity of faith with dearly held customs, rituals and traditions; traditions that would all but obscure and over-ride the simple trust and obedience to the Lord God and his Son taught by the apostles – of such teachers and teachings, warned our Lord, let disciples beware.

Christianity 'adjusted' to conform to modern thinking
Like the leaven of the Pharisees and Sadducees, the teaching of many scholars and church leaders in our own day puts aside much of the teaching of our Lord and his chosen apostles, regarding it as no longer tenable, or no longer relevant to the age in which we live.

Such teaching typically brings into question our Lord's deity and the gospel record of his words, and also questions the teaching of the apostles concerning both doctrine and practical godly living. Our humble submission to our Lord and his word is discredited, and 'the obedience of faith', as the apostle Paul describes it, is discarded as 'simplistic'.

Such a 'new theology' will inevitably lead to a 'new morality,' and each will inevitably undermine biblical faith and true godly living.

Like the leaven hidden in the meal by the woman, teaching that attempts to bring the apostles' teaching into line with the world's current thinking, often begins 'hidden away' in the high academic circles of the church, particularly in ministers' training schemes and theological colleges. However, before too long, like leaven, such teaching will quietly permeate and change the whole thinking, character, nature and direction of the church.

Writing of his concern for the church of the 1800s, J. C. Ryle comments of false teachings, 'Like leaven, they might seem a small thing compared to the whole body of truth; like leaven, once admitted, they would work secretly and noiselessly; like leaven, they would gradually change the whole character of the religion with which they were mixed.'

Has such 'leaven' permeated our churches?
In our churches, have we been, and could we be, preaching what the apostle Paul described as 'another gospel'?

We can so easily build a faith based on our own opinion of how the Lord God should be regarded and of how God should behave toward us. However, such a man-made faith held personally and presented to others will be very different from the gospel recorded in the New Testament.

Biblical faith declares that we are accountable before God, and so calls us to live every part of our lives in a way that honours him. In contrast, a faith built on human reason and current opinion would, because of its human roots, naturally teach that 'God is love' and will in no sense call us to account. Such a faith allows us complete freedom of choice to live as we will. This fits very comfortably into the free choice, all-tolerant, repentance-free thinking of our day, and so is widely taught and accepted in our churches as the truth.

The man of the world sees straight away that such an undemanding faith, though fine for those 'religiously inclined', has absolutely no bearing on real life. It can safely be ignored. And so he discounts both it and the church which has so sadly failed to be a faithful herald of God.

A perceptive warning from the last century

Writing about our Lord's warning concerning the leaven of the Pharisees and the Sadducees, G. Campbell Morgan asks: 'Is it not true at this present moment, the church's power to bring the world under conviction concerning the Kingdom of God is feeble because of her complicity with evil things? She is still weakened by the leaven of hypocrisy, which is profession without possession; by the leaven of rationalism, which is denial of the supernatural; by the leaven of materialism, which is the adoption of the world's standpoints and principles . . . and is it not true that not least among the leavening influences at work is that weak toleration of evil, and false pity for the wrong-doer which allows him to stay within her borders, making her incapable of speaking with authority to those in rebellion against the Kingdom of God?'

Biblical faith is so very different

Unlike a faith we construct, New Testament faith is rugged, robust, challenging and straightforward. Our Lord and his apostles constantly warned of the coming judgement of God. Wherever they went they called men and women to repent and believe, because the Lord God is holy and just, and will call each one of us to account for the one life he has entrusted to us. As they warned of judgement to come, they also proclaimed God's wonderful mercy towards those who humbly turn to him, acknowledging their failure to honour him. They made plain the Lord God's merciful provision of a way of forgiveness for those who turn from God-displeasing ways. His provision is that we submit to his chosen, risen and anointed Son who loved us and gave his life for us.

Let the apostles speak for themselves. In Peter's words to those gathered in the house of Cornelius, "And he commanded us to preach to the people, and to testify that he is the one appointed by God to be judge of the living and the dead. To him all the prophets bear witness that everyone who believes in him receives forgiveness of sins through his name." It is clear, as the apostle John writes, that to those who turn and believe on his Son, the Lord God grants everlasting life; he spares them and forgives them. 'For God so loved the world, that he gave his only Son, that whoever believes in him should not perish but have eternal life.'

A strong warning for modern disciples of the Lord Jesus
From time to time we will find ourselves being led by those who will be found at the last to have been 'acting a part'; at rock bottom, strangers to the One in whose service they have been publicly honoured and probably funded.

If that is the case, we will find ourselves reading or listening to teaching that would lead us into a comfortable 'By-Path Meadow' of human, Christian-sounding, and yet less than faithful teaching. Teaching that would, over time, cause us to slip and wander away from the simplicity, trust, submission, obedience and the joy of the true faith as it was taught by the apostles.

For us, forgiveness, peace with God must not rest on a comfortable feeling or 'the church's assurance'. Nor must our ongoing growth in faith and usefulness before the Lord be dependent on the teachings of others.

We need to hear faithful preaching and to read godly books, but we should not depend on being entirely fed by other fallible human beings, no matter how exalted they may be. We would do well to learn to daily and prayerfully feed ourselves on the words of our Lord and his appointed apostles and prophets. As John Newton puts it, '. . . the chief and grand means of edification, without which all other helps will disappoint us, and prove like clouds without water, are the Bible and prayer, the word of grace and the throne of grace.' Only by the prayerful reading of Scripture will we be strong enough and mature enough to discern the dangers about which our Lord gave such strong warnings to his disciples. In order to be able to stand, we really do need to personally and actively fasten on 'the belt of truth'.

Luke records that as the apostle Paul said farewell to the leaders of the church at Ephesus, he said, "And now I commend you to God and to the word of his grace, which is able to build you up and give you the inheritance among all those who are God's holy people."

A reason to question this understanding of the parable as a picture of the spread of evil

Both Luke and Matthew record that Jesus began this parable of the leaven by saying, "To what shall I compare the kingdom of God (or the kingdom of heaven)? It is like leaven that a woman took and hid..." He did not begin by saying, "To what shall I compare the spread of evil among disciples? It is like leaven that a woman took and hid . . ."

Although, as he warned the disciples concerning the Pharisees and Sadducees, our Lord was using leaven as a picture of the spreading influence of evil, at the beginning of this parable he makes it very clear that he is speaking of the kingdom of God.

On two separate occasions Jesus warned the disciples about the 'leaven' of the religious leaders. Jesus gave this warning *privately* to his disciples. The question must be asked, have we assumed that as he taught the parable of the leaven *publicly* to the great crowds who followed him, he was giving the same warning to them?

As Arthur Carr readily admits, all through the Scriptures leaven is used to illustrate the working and contagious nature of evil – 'Except in this one parable.' Could it be that Jesus used leaven in this unusual and arresting way in the parable to stir the interest of his hearers and make them think? – It would be yet another of the surprises to be found in so many of his parables.

Overall conclusion to the parable of the leaven

From the first understanding of it as a parable of growth, we can be greatly encouraged – even in the face of determined opposition and scorn – for it is the Lord God who is growing his kingdom. The great privilege of true children of God is to be caught up in the marvellous and mighty purposes of God, and our calling is to play our part, no matter how small and insignificant that may appear.

From the second understanding of it as a parable of evil, we are warned to walk warily in this fallen world and to heed our Lord's warning to his disciples, to 'watch out' for and to 'beware' of those whose lifestyle or teaching – spoken or written – would undermine the word of God; the truth taught in the Scriptures.

Heavenly Father, help us to be discerning, to walk warily and to examine and guard our own hearts lest we wander or are led astray.

By your grace enable us to hold fast to the truth of your word as it is brought to us by your chosen prophets and apostles, and stir and encourage us to play our full part, as through your believing people you cause your kingdom to grow.

Footnote

What might a 'modernised' gospel look like in a local church?

By no means all, yet many of our local churches have been permeated with the kind of leaven of which our Lord warned. For those with ears to hear, what follows is offered to help us if we wish to reflect on our own local situation.

Our Lord and his apostles proclaimed a robust and challenging gospel. They called their hearers to 'repent and believe'; to turn from ungodly ways and accept the Lord God's provision for our forgiveness; to believe on his Son, his anointed One, who, by his cross and death in our place, loved us and gave himself for us to make possible that forgiveness.

I remain convinced that the gospel, as proclaimed by the apostles, remains the Lord God's powerful way of rescuing those who accept and believe it. In the apostle Paul's words, 'I am not ashamed of the gospel, for it is the power of God for salvation to everyone who believes . . .'

The way in which the gospel is presented needs to be accessible and appropriate to the people to whom we are speaking, but the gospel itself, as the apostle Paul makes plain, must not be altered or modified to please us or our hearers, but faithfully presented in all its fullness, majesty and glory.

However, many preachers and church leaders see the apostles' teaching as being too harsh and unpalatable for this generation, and therefore unacceptable to them. If we share this opinion, we will be inclined to construct what we consider to be 'a faith for today's world'. With the biblical gospel 'softened' and 'modernised' for today's hearers, the local church might begin to look like this:

Our church will be essentially a place to meet one another and enjoy one another's company in a Christian setting. It would easily welcome new people into a warm, friendly and supportive community.

The church will often teach and preach on the mercy, patience and steadfast love of the Lord, but not on his awesome holiness and justice. Its emphasis would be that God loves each one of us; the whole world. However, it would hold back from teaching that each one of us will one day be called to give an account to the Lord God for the way in which we have each lived our life. Although corporate and general prayers of repentance may well be said, these would almost certainly fail to alert our people to a personal need to urgently turn to the Lord God in repentance and faith.

A modernised church would probably pass rather lightly over Good Friday, perhaps regarding it as the quiet and subdued prelude to contrast with the glory of Easter. But in preaching and teaching it would not emphasise the central message of the gospel, that the Son of God came ". . . to give his life as a ransom for many." – the one and only sacrifice that can put us right with God.

We would make much of the celebration of Easter and the resurrection, bringing a message of hope for our hearers. However, we would be very unlikely to teach and proclaim the resurrection of our Lord in the way the apostle Peter did in the house of Cornelius, and as Paul did at Athens; as the strongest and most urgent call for us to turn from our ungodly ways and seek the Lord God's mercy and forgiveness. Paul proclaimed the resurrection as the proof of God's command to 'all people everywhere to repent, because he has fixed a day on which he will judge the world in righteousness by a man whom he has appointed; and of this he has given assurance to all by raising him from the dead.'

We might enjoy the candles of Advent as the days draw in, and we look forward to the appearing, the 'advent', of our Lord. We would look forward to the birth of our Lord in Bethlehem. But far less attention would be drawn to the challenge of his 'second advent'; we would not boldly proclaim the need for each one of us to be ready for the Lord Jesus' return, – this time not in great humility but in great glory and majesty as King of kings and as Lord and as Judge.

We would keep and promote the well-attended Christmas services, with their scenes of the Bethlehem birth of the babe laid in a manger, the visits of the shepherds and of the wise men. However, we would hesitate to proclaim, as the prophets, the angels and the apostles did, that the 'child given', the 'son born' is the 'Saviour who is Christ the

Lord', 'the Son of God', the one and only Saviour, and the One to whom every knee must one day bow.

As a focus for the local community, the church would certainly have much to commend it. No matter what our chosen lifestyle may be, the church would be a very open and welcoming place to attend; there would be no fear of meeting with uncomfortable challenges. It would be full of grace; however, it would also be somewhat lacking in truth. On each occasion we would have kept the outward form and ceremonies, and yet all but emptied them of much of the true, and humanly less comfortable, teaching of Scripture. Like each of the seven churches of Revelation, it would fall far short of what it could be, and should be, before God and his risen, glorified and soon returning Son.

But for the amazing and overruling grace of God, how could we honestly expect the Holy Spirit to put his seal on our 'modernised' church's message and bring people to a genuine, and perhaps personally costly, repentance, and well-founded faith?

Questions for discussion or reflection

Understanding this parable as a parable of the spreading of evil
1. With regard to the human wisdom and tradition being taught in many of our churches, are we as discerning as the Lord Jesus warned we should be?
2. How can we grow in our faith and in godly understanding and lifestyle, and so not be carried along by the dangers of which our Lord warned?
3. The noble Berean believers searched the Scriptures to see if the apostle Paul's teaching was in accord with it. (Acts 17:11) Could and should we do the same in our day?

Two further notes

1. By-Path Meadow
(From *The Pilgrim's Progress* by John Bunyan.)
'Now a little before them there was on the left hand of the road, a meadow, and a stile to go over into it, and that meadow is called By-Path Meadow. Then said Christian to his fellow, 'If this meadow lieth along by our wayside, let's go over into it.' Then he went to the stile to see, and behold a path lay along by the way on the other side of the fence. ''Tis according to my wish,' said Christian, 'here is easiest going; come, good Hopeful, and let us go over.'

Hopeful: 'But how if this path should lead us out of the way?''

2. Parables with a past, present and future application
As C.H. Dodd points out, the parables of the seed growing secretly, the mustard seed, and the hidden leaven each have these three aspects. Looking to the past, the Lord God's first clear planting of the seed, or hiding of the leaven, was the call of Abraham with the promise that he would be the literal and the spiritual father of God's called-out people.

At the time the Lord Jesus was speaking, Jesus himself was the seed sown and the leaven of the kingdom of God, 'hidden' in the nation of Israel.

The future aspect lies in the growth of the kingdom of God through the centuries and throughout the world.

As with so many of his parables, though hidden below the surface, our Lord himself is at the heart and centre. He is the focal point of all that is implied by the parable and of all that flows from it.

References

The leaven of the Pharisees and Sadducees, their teaching – Matthew 16:6 and 12
The leaven of the Pharisees, which is hypocrisy – Luke 12:1
I never knew you – Matthew 7:23

Made void the word of God – Matthew 15:6
Honoured God with their lips – Matthew 15:8
Teaching as doctrines the commandments of men – Matthew 15:9
It is necessary to ... order them to keep the law of Moses – Acts 15:1-5
The obedience of faith – Romans 1:5
What the apostle Paul described as 'another gospel' – Galatians 1:8-9
Repent and believe – for example Mark 1:15, Acts 17:30-31 and 20:21
Peter speaking to the household of Cornelius – Acts 10:42-43
Those who turn and believe – John 3:16
Fasten on the belt of truth – Ephesians 6:14
Paul's farewell to the Ephesian church leaders – Acts 20:32

Footnote references
Cross and death, in our place – Isaiah 53:4-6
Loved us and gave himself for us – Galatians 2:20
Not ashamed of the gospel – Romans 1:16
Gospel itself must not be altered – Galatians 1:8-9
Gave his life a ransom – Mark 10:45
Peter in the house of Cornelius – Acts 10:34-44
Paul at Athens – Acts 17:30-34
Advent, 'Be ye also ready' – Luke 12:40
Child is given, a son is born – Isaiah 9:6
Saviour, who is Christ the Lord – Luke 2:11
Son of God – Luke 1:35 and John 20:31
One and only Saviour – John 14:6 and Acts 4:12
To whom every knee must one day bow – Philippians 2:10
The churches of Revelation – Revelation chapters 1-3
The call of Abraham – Genesis 12:1-3

The Narrow Door that will be Closed

He went on his way through towns and villages, teaching and journeying towards Jerusalem. And someone said to him, "Lord, will those who are saved be few?" And he said to them, "Strive to enter through the narrow door. For many, I tell you, will seek to enter and will not be able. When once the master of the house has risen and shut the door, and you begin to stand outside and to knock at the door, saying, 'Lord, open to us,' then he will answer you, 'I do not know where you come from.' Then you will begin to say, 'We ate and drank in your presence, and you taught in our streets.' But he will say. 'I tell you, I do not know where you come from. Depart from me, all you workers of evil!' In that place there will be weeping and gnashing of teeth, when you see Abraham and Isaac and Jacob and all the prophets in the kingdom of God but you yourselves cast out. And people will come from east and west, and from north and south, and recline at table in the kingdom of God. And behold, some are last who will be first, and some are first who will be last."

Luke 13:22-30, English Standard Version

The Narrow Door that will be Closed

In Luke chapter nine we read of Jesus setting his face to go to Jerusalem, here Luke records the beginning of the second stage of his long journey. As he walked with his disciples and those who joined them, Jesus paused and taught in each of the towns and villages through which he passed.

The parable of the narrow door tends to be over-shadowed by the better known teaching of the broad way and the narrow way, recorded by Matthew as part of the Sermon on the Mount, 'Enter by the narrow gate. For the gate is wide and the way is easy that leads to destruction, and those who enter by it are many. For the gate is narrow and the way is hard that leads to life, and those who find it are few.'

Although the opening words are very similar – especially as some of the ancient manuscripts have the word translated 'gate' in both – the teaching is distinct. Comparing the broad way and its wide gate with the narrow way and its narrow gate, our Lord is contrasting the two pathways and their final destinations. He emphasises the ease and the popularity of the broad way, as opposed to the difficulties and the loneliness of the way that leads to life.

In the parable of the narrow door the Lord Jesus is urging those with ears to hear, to strive, to make every effort to enter the narrow door before it is closed and they are too late – for then, '. . . many will seek to enter and will not be able.'

It is to our loss if we overlook the less well known parable of the narrow but open door, only recorded by Luke.

As John Calvin has done, may I invite you to consider each of the parts of the parable in turn.

Someone said to him, "Lord, will those who are saved be few?"
We do not know who the questioner was.

Was it trick question? For if Jesus answered, "A great many," he would be judged to be too liberal and if he answered, "Yes, very few," he would be judged as too strict. On either count, his teaching could be dismissed.

Was it a lawyer testing his orthodoxy? Did Jesus share the view of the scribes and Pharisees that only the most careful of law-keeping Jews would be saved? Or would he hold that the whole nation of Israel would be saved? Would he also affirm their view that Gentiles were to be excluded from the kingdom of God, and so, for the people of the surrounding nations, there could be no hope of being saved?

Was it a genuine question? Perhaps the questioner noted that out of all Israel, God's chosen heirs of life, relatively few were seriously following the Lord Jesus? It is as if the questioner asked, 'Out of all Israel, will we alone be saved?'

As a genuine question, it is worth seriously pursuing. Why were so few saved when Noah was building his ark, and by doing so was warning those around him of the flood to come? Why was no one willing to heed God's message and leave the city of Sodom? Even Lot lingered, and his closest family had to be dragged away to be saved from destruction. Why was the gospel, proclaimed by the Lord from heaven, the Messiah, generally unheeded by God's chosen people? Why is the same gospel of repentance towards Almighty God and faith in his Son so widely despised, rejected and ignored in our own day?

And he said to them, "Strive to enter through the narrow door."
The Lord did not directly answer the question, "Lord, will those who are saved be few?" or speak to the questioner in person. He spoke to the whole company of people following him, challenging them not to be influenced by what 'everybody else is doing', but to look to themselves and make certain of their own place in the kingdom of God. The challenge our Lord gave his hearers was to strive, the Greek literally means 'to agonize' – to earnestly seek to enter by the narrow door of the kingdom of God while the opportunity is there; while the invitation is still offered and the door still open.

This was made more difficult by the scribes and Pharisees who refused to recognise and accept the Lord Jesus as God's anointed one, the Messiah. Using their position as the religious leaders, they also put great pressure on the ordinary people to follow their example and refuse to acknowledge him. Nevertheless, as is made plain elsewhere in the New Testament, the One who was walking and teaching among them was, and is, both the door and the ultimate door-keeper of the kingdom of God. And to those who did recognise and receive him, he gave the right to be the sons and the daughters of God, citizens of the kingdom.

Whether we are religious leaders or ordinary people, like Jesus' first hearers, we need to examine our own standing before God and, despite the frowns and displeasure of family, friends, work colleagues and society, personally 'strive to enter by the narrow door.'

For many, I tell you, will seek to enter and will not be able
The Pharisees assumed that, as their aim was to be righteous in every detail of the law, they were certainly members of the kingdom of God and would be honoured guests at the final feast at the end of the age. They were so confident of this that they judged other people's state of righteousness by the measure of their own lives. This way of comparing others with themselves was dramatically portrayed by our Lord in the parable of the Pharisee and the tax collector:

'He also told this parable to some who trusted that they were righteous, and treated others with contempt. "Two men went up to the temple to pray, one a Pharisee and the other a tax collector. The Pharisee standing by himself, prayed thus: 'God, I thank you that I am not as other men, extortioners, unjust, adulterers, or even like this tax collector. I fast twice a week; I give tithes of all that I get.' But the tax collector, standing far off, would not even lift up his eyes to heaven, but beat his breast, saying, 'God be merciful to me, a sinner!' I tell you this man went down to his house justified, rather than the other."'

As it was for the chosen people of Israel and for the religious leaders in particular, it is very easy for church-going people, keeping company with like-minded people, to flatter ourselves that we are assured of a place in the kingdom of God. Comforted by one another, we can all but sleep-walk into being shut out at the last; abandoning ourselves to the anguish of a lost eternity. Here is a warning to be discerning and not be misled. Only those who strive to enter by the narrow door will find they have a place at the final banquet.

Understandably, the Pharisees did not like what they were hearing. By careful law-keeping, they had all but climbed to the top of the ladder of self-justification before Almighty God – only to be told that it was a fruitless quest. Justification before God is not something we can achieve by our own doing; it is the gift of God to those who recognise and submit to his chosen One, the Messiah.

As a monk, Martin Luther was considered to very godly, and yet he knew himself not to be at peace with God. It was not until he was studying Paul's epistle to the Romans that he discovered that justification, our being put right with God, comes by faith; it is not earned by ritual acts of penance as he had been taught. Salvation is given by faith in the One who told this parable. He, the Son of God, alone is the door. He, alone, can give citizenship of the kingdom of God.

Like the Pharisees who were seriously trying to be right with God, but attempting to do so by their own route, we can be seriously seeking heaven as our final resting place, but doing so by a way of our own choosing; a way that will, in the end, fail to deliver its promise. Like Martin Luther, we too need consciences 'captive to the word of God' rather than captive to the teachings or generally held views of our Christian companions, be they cathedral, church or chapel – no matter how greatly acclaimed those who would teach us may be.

If we will not take notice of our Lord's warning, persisting in our own comfortable religious traditions and unwilling to humble ourselves and enter the kingdom of God by the narrow door that he alone holds open to us, we may in the end find ourselves among those weeping bitterly and shut out.

When once the master of the house has risen and shut the door
As Jesus tells the parable, and as he goes on to apply it to his hearers with regard to entering the kingdom of God, it becomes clear that he is the keeper of the door. The Son of God, the one relating this parable, in whose presence the people of the towns and villages of Judea ate

and drank and who taught in their streets, is the One who judges who may enter the kingdom of God.

The narrow door by which to enter the kingdom of God is still open. These are still 'days of grace'. The invitation is wide open; 'whoever will' may enter. But, as Jesus warned, the Master of the house has chosen an hour and a day when the door will be closed. The Lord was giving a clear warning, to the religious leaders, the crowd following him and to all who will hear, that for our eternal well-being, and despite many objections and difficulties, we must each enter the kingdom of God now, while we still have opportunity to do so. Today is the 'day of salvation', tomorrow may be too late.

John Newton, the author of the hymn *Amazing Grace*, quotes freely from the New Testament as he writes: "Now is the acceptable time, the day of salvation. Now, if you will seek the Lord, he will be found of you. Now, if you pray for grace and truth, he will answer you. But 'when once the Master of the house shall arise, and' – with his own sovereign authoritative hand – 'shall shut the door' of his mercy, it will then be in vain, and too late, to say, 'Lord, Lord, open to us!'"

"We ate and drank in your presence, and you taught in our streets." But he will say, "I tell you, I do not know where you come from. Depart from me, all you workers of evil!"

By way of the parable, the Lord Jesus was speaking very directly to his hearers and challenging them to recognise who he truly is. He was warning them that their eternal destiny, their inclusion as guests in the feast of the kingdom of God, or their exclusion from it, depends on their submission to him and his words.

Only of Emmanuel, God among us, could it be written, '. . . the Word became flesh and dwelt among us, and we have seen his glory, glory as of the only Son from the Father . . .' and only of him, could it be said by the people of Israel, 'We ate and drank in your presence, and you taught in our streets.'

The people of Israel had the great privilege of hearing and seeing the Messiah, the Son of God, teaching in their streets. They looked and yet failed to perceive, they heard him but failed to understand. For so many, there was no life-changing encounter. They never knew him, and he never knew them. After Jesus had taught them and passed on to another village, life just carried on as it always had. It was as if they had never seen him or heard him teach in their streets.

For Zacchaeus it was so different, he welcomed our Lord, turned, repented and clearly demonstrated by his totally changed attitude to money that 'salvation had come to his house,' he had become a true 'son of Abraham.'

'Depart from me, all you workers of evil!' The words sound very harsh to our ears, addressed as they are to all those who are not known to him. And yet, either we are the Lord's people; members the kingdom of God and with lives dedicated to doing his will – or we are, in a great variety of ways, living for ourselves. It is those of us living for ourselves, having never seriously admitted the need to humbly seek forgiveness and trust and obey him, that Jesus sums up in the all embracing term 'workers of evil.'

In a comparable passage in Matthew's gospel, Jesus said, "Not everyone who says to me, 'Lord, Lord', will enter the kingdom of heaven. On that day many will say to me, 'Lord, Lord, did we not prophesy in your name, and cast out demons in your name, and do many mighty works in your name?' And I will declare to them, 'I never knew you; depart from me, you workers of lawlessness.'"

We can be born in a Christian country, have very godly family members, have been baptised into the church and even be those who regularly attend a church and are active members of it, and yet somehow, despite all these excellent religious things, fail to be aware of the 'one thing needful'. Could we be so occupied with making music, committee membership, or the practical tasks that have to be done to keep the church running smoothly, that we fail to personally strive, by a thoughtful and humble hearing and reading of the word of God, to discover who Jesus really is, and what he has done for us? Recognising who he truly is will lead us to echo prayers like the one uttered by the tax-collector of our Lord's parable, 'God be merciful to me, a sinner.' (Luke 18:13)

Abraham and Isaac and Jacob and all the prophets in the kingdom of God, but you yourselves cast out

The scribes and Pharisees were the acknowledged students of the writings of Moses and the prophets. Keeping company with their fellow religious leaders, who had strayed from the word of God, and perhaps conscious of their position in society, they had failed to learn from the faith and costly obedience of Abraham, and had not taken to heart the warnings and the promises of God given through the mouths of the prophets. They were totally unprepared for the 'Day of the Lord'; the day when the door is no longer open, when judgement falls and our fate is sealed.

Like them, we can so easily presume that our involvement and familiarity with church activities will carry us safely through to a seat at the heavenly banquet. But will they? – any more than, 'We ate and drank in your presence, and you taught in our streets'? Will we hear our Lord's terrible words, 'I never knew you' or 'I do not know where you come from'?

John Newton reminds us of the solemnities of that great day, when the Judge shall appear, the books are opened, and all mankind is summoned to his tribunal. He urges us to seize the present opportunity to seek the Lord God's face, to tremble and bow before him, 'while he is seated on a throne of grace, while the door of mercy stands open.'

And people will come from east and west, and from north and south, and recline at table in the kingdom of God

As the Lord Jesus applies his teaching directly to his hearers, it becomes clear that he is speaking of the great banquet that will be given in his honour at the end of the age, the banquet that the apostle John

THE NARROW DOOR · 169

describes as 'the marriage supper of the Lamb.' This great and final feast in the Messiah's honour is a major Biblical picture of the kingdom of God.

To help us to understand the thinking of the scribes and Pharisees, Kenneth Bailey explains that 700 years earlier, Isaiah had given a moving prophesy of this banquet, describing God-fearing Jews and Gentiles coming together to feast at the Lord God's invitation. However, the later Aramaic very free 'translations,' such as the Talmud, turned Isaiah's words on their head. They modified Isaiah's prophecy to describe God gathering the Gentiles to a great feast in order to shame them and secure their end. This was the understanding held by the scribes and Pharisees of Jesus' time. They had come to see themselves as the exclusive heirs of the kingdom of God, with the people of the nations around them to be despised and seen as of no value to God or to them, mere 'non-people'.

Holding to such an understanding, Jesus' words must have come as an absolute shock. Here were the peoples of the nations pictured as the honoured guests at the feast, reclining with Abraham and Isaac and Jacob and all the prophets in the kingdom of God – but they themselves cast out.

The door of the kingdom of God was the very opposite of what they had come to believe. A place at the Messiah's banquet was not to be secured by meticulous law-keeping. It was not theirs by nationality and birthright. It was open to all – including those from the surrounding nations, and indeed from the whole world – who would humble themselves before God, and pass through the narrow door.

And behold, some are last who will be first, and some are first who will be last

The gospel writers record Jesus using these words on at least four occasions, using them to emphasise different points. Here Jesus uses them to puncture the misplaced confidence of his hearers. They had come to assume that they alone, the sons and daughters of Abraham, the chosen people of God, must have a reserved and secure place in the great feast of the kingdom of God.

Jesus was warning them that the people of the nations they so despised will gladly take their places, while they, in their proud assumption of superiority and their rejection of God's Messiah, together with their unwillingness to humble themselves, will find themselves totally excluded. He paints a picture of the great feast taking place while they are shut out in the darkness. The door of opportunity has been closed. Having failed to recognise and receive their own Messiah, they will find themselves outside in dark and soul-searching wretchedness.

Will there be few?
In the Sermon on the Mount, the Lord Jesus draws attention to the large number who enter through the broad gate and walk the broad and easy path, and the few who enter through the narrow gate and follow that difficult path to life. 'Enter by the narrow gate. For the gate is wide and the way is easy that leads to destruction, and those who enter by it are many. For the gate is narrow and the way is hard that leads to life, and those who find it are few.'

From those lines it is reasonable to conclude that there will be few who enter by the narrow door; relatively few who will be saved and made true members of the kingdom of God. But, if the invitation is wide open and all is prepared, why should this be?

A few verses further on in the chapter containing the parable of the narrow door, the Lord answered the question as he responded to some Pharisees who warned him that Herod wanted to kill him, 'O Jerusalem, Jerusalem, the city that kills the prophets and stones those who are sent to it! How often would I have gathered your children together as a hen gathers her brood under her wings, and you would not!'

'And you would not,' 'You were not willing,' and similar expressions are a very sad commentary on human nature, but they are found frequently throughout the Bible. They reflect our fallen, human unwillingness to submit to the Lord God, his word, his ways and his rule.

Was it for nothing that the psalmist warned, 'Today, if you hear his voice, harden not your hearts . . .'? Only the Holy Spirit of God can warm and turn our stubborn and rebellious hearts, for by nature we will heed neither the Lord's warnings nor his invitations. As our Lord said of Jerusalem, could he also say of our nation, our church, and of so many of us, personally, "How often would I have gathered you . . . and you would not!"?

The parable of the open door leaves each one of us with the challenge the Lord presented to his original hearers. Will we, in our generation, like so many of our Lord's hearers, brush aside the God-given invitation to humble ourselves and enter through the narrow door? Will we leave it too late, and so to our endless regret find ourselves excluded from the kingdom of God?

Or, Jew and Gentile, from east and west, north and south, will we, in repentance before God and faith in his glorious Son, strive to enter the narrow door, while that door of mercy is open and the invitation offered to all?

The door is narrow, to pass through it demands a genuine humbling of ourselves before the Lord God and an acceptance of the one who taught in Israel's streets for who he truly is, the chosen and anointed Son of God, Emmanuel, God among us, the Messiah, 'the Lamb of God who takes away the sin of the world,' and the 'Saviour who is Christ the Lord.'

John Newton must have the final word, 'If these things be so, how much are they to be pitied, who hear of them without being affected or influenced by them! . . . As yet there is room. Strive to enter while the gate of mercy remains open.'

O Lord have mercy on us. Soften hardened hearts, unstop unhearing ears and open eyes blinded by pride, by modern technology, by the opinions of the media and the ungodliness of the age in which we live. By your grace, may we seek first your kingdom, and entering by the door made open by your Son, become truly members of it.

Questions for reflection or discussion

1. Is it hard to stand alone and not do what 'everybody else' is doing? Why is this so hard?
2. How easy is it for us, like the Pharisees, to judge others by their outward standards of dress, manners or religious practices?
3. Can we mistakenly reassure ourselves and one another of our place in the kingdom of God, without ever personally entering the narrow door?
4. The Pharisees were attempting to secure a place at the final feast by careful law-keeping. Why were they not pleased to hear what Jesus was saying?
5. Is it possible that we, too, could be seeking to be members of the kingdom of God on the basis of our religious practices and goodness – rather than by the narrow door of a personal prayer for mercy and a simple trust in, and obedience to, the One who told this parable?
6. Why does Jesus' description of the master of the house closing the door, put a note of urgency on the whole matter of our own entering through the narrow door and on our urging of others to do the same?
7. The door is narrow. To enter it requires an acceptance of who the Lord Jesus truly is and a humbling of ourselves before the Lord God. Why will there be few who enter?
8. 'And behold, some are last who will be first, and some are first who will be last.' What kind of uncomfortable surprises might there be on the last day?

References

Set his face to go to Jerusalem – Luke 9:5
Enter by the narrow gate – Matthew 7:13&14
Noah – Genesis 6:9 and following
Lot – Genesis 19:15 and following
Pressure on ordinary people – For example, John 9:18-23 and 32-34

Jesus the door and door-keeper of the kingdom of God – Implied in this parable and made plain in, for example, John 10:9, John 14:6, Romans 5:1&2
Sons and daughters of God – John 1:12
The Pharisee and the tax collector – Luke 18:9-14
Gift of God – Ephesians 2:8-9
Whoever will (the one who earnestly desires) – Revelation 22:17
Today is the day of salvation – 2 Corinthians 6:2
The Word became flesh – John 1:14
They looked and failed to perceive, they heard yet failed to understand – Matthew 13:14-17
Zacchaeus – Luke 19:5-6
Workers of lawlessness – Matt 7:21-23
One thing needful – Luke 10:42
The Day of the Lord – 1Thessalonians 5:1-11
The books opened – Daniel 7:10, Revelation 20:12
The marriage supper of the Lamb – Revelation 19:9
The Lord's great banquet – Isaiah 25:6-9
Some are last who will be first – Matthew 19:30 & 20:16, Mark 10:31, Luke 13:30
Broad and narrow gate – Matthew 7:13-14

But you would not – Luke 13:34 see also Isaiah 30:15-16 and Jeremiah 6:16-19 Most explicitly, Zechariah 7:8-12

Emmanuel – Matthew 1:18-25
Messiah (the Christ) – Matthew 16:13-17
Harden not your hearts – Psalm 95:7&8
Lamb of God – John 1:29 and 35
Saviour – Luke 2:10&11

The Wedding Feast and the Great Banquet

One Sabbath, when he went to dine at the house of a ruler of the Pharisees, they were watching him carefully. And behold, there was a man before him who had dropsy. And Jesus responded to the lawyers and Pharisees, saying, "Is it lawful to heal on the Sabbath, or not?" But they remained silent. Then he took him and healed him and sent him away. And he said to them, "Which of you, having a son or an ox that has fallen into a well on a Sabbath day, will not immediately pull him out?" And they could not reply to these things.

Now he told a parable to those who were invited, when he noticed how they chose the places of honour, saying to them, "When you are invited by someone to a wedding feast, do not sit down in a place of honour, lest someone more distinguished than you be invited by him, and he who invited you both will come and say to you, 'Give your place to this person,' and then you will begin with shame to take the lowest place. But when you are invited, go and sit in the lowest place, so that when your host comes he may say to you, 'Friend, move up higher.' Then you will be honoured in the presence of all who sit at table with you. For everyone who exalts himself will be humbled, and he who humbles himself will be exalted."

He said also to the man who had invited him, "When you give a dinner or a banquet, do not invite your friends or your brothers or your relatives or rich neighbours, lest they also invite you in return and you be repaid. But when you give a feast, invite the poor, the crippled, the lame, the blind, and you will be blessed, because they cannot repay you. For you will be repaid at the resurrection of the just."

When one of those who reclined at table with him heard these things, he said to him, "Blessed is everyone who will eat bread in the kingdom of God!" But he said to him, "A man once gave a great banquet and invited many. And at the time for the banquet he sent his servant to say to those who had been invited, 'Come, for everything is now ready.' But they all alike began to make excuses. The first said to him, 'I have bought a field, and I must go out and see it. Please have me excused.' And another said, 'I have bought five yoke of oxen, and I go to examine them. Please have me excused.' And another said, 'I have married a wife, and therefore I cannot come.' So the servant came and reported these things to his master. Then the master of the house became angry and said to his servant, 'Go out quickly to the streets and lanes of the city, and bring in the poor and crippled and blind and lame.' And the servant said, 'Sir, what you commanded has been done, and still there is room.' And the master said to the servant, 'Go out to the highways and hedges and compel people to come in, that my house may be filled. For I tell you, none of those men who were invited shall taste my banquet.'"

Luke 14:1-24, English Standard Version

The Wedding Feast and the Great Banquet

May I invite you to look at the setting, the content, the challenge to Lord's hearers and to us, and finally at other relevant scriptures and gospel insights.

First, the context or setting
There is a similar parable of a great banquet in chapter 22 of Matthew's gospel, where the scene is of a king giving a marriage feast for his son. The thrust of the two parables is the same; the great danger of contempt for the one who gives the invitation and the terrible loss if it

is refused or ignored. Yet the setting and details are so very different that it seems best to regard them quite separately.

Matthew is recording Jesus' response to a challenge by the chief priests and elders of the people in the temple in Jerusalem. He answers them by telling a whole series of very serious parables, enabling them, if they would, to see the terrible mistake they were making. This took place in the final days of our Lord's ministry. In Luke's Gospel, the setting is much earlier in his ministry, at a dinner party; so the whole setting in Luke is a conversation during a meal.

Luke records that the Lord Jesus had been invited to eat at a Pharisee's house and he accepted. Kenneth Bailey explains that this may well not have been the friendly gesture we might assume. It was typical of the custom of the time. 'A travelling rabbi/preacher passes through a local village. The religious leaders invite the village guest to a meal during which they investigate his political and religious views.' So the presence of the man with dropsy and the exclamation, "Blessed is everyone who will eat bread in the kingdom of God!" may not be part of a gentle conversation, but deliberately there to provoke him and to test his doctrine.

It is worth noting that the Lord was willing to spend time speaking with those who were hostile to him, as well as keeping the more comfortable company of his own disciples and those who genuinely welcomed him, such as the poor and needy. There are several other occasions when we read that he was invited to eat in a Pharisee's house. He did not hesitate to do so, even though the reception was usually very testing and hostile, as it was on this occasion.

Immediately, this is a challenge to us not to keep company only with fellow believers, but to be willing to go wherever we can be ambassadors for the Lord God – but to do so warily! Why warily? Do note that telling comment 'they were watching him carefully' or, 'and they watched him'. Was it a friendly glance? Not at all! They had invited Jesus and were assembled to trip him up and trap him and watch carefully what he would do when put in a tricky situation – and ourselves? Jesus warned, 'The servant is not above his master.' The unbe- unbelieving world is still 'watching' and doing so critically, and I would confess to have been put in such a situation and caught many a time!

They placed a man before the Lord with dropsy; literally a man 'full of water'. He was in the last stages of a terrible illness involving liver, heart and kidney failure. The day they had chosen to put him before the Lord was the Sabbath. Would he break their traditional law and heal a man in such dire straits on the Sabbath? There was no Law of Moses against doing so. But, over the years, the scribes and Pharisees had added elaborate Sabbath codes of practice. A chapter earlier we read of a synagogue leader saying, 'There are six days for work; come on those days and be healed, and not on the Sabbath day.'

However, as the Lord pointed out, the Pharisees themselves were well able to lay aside their own code of practice – if keeping it threatened their own wallet or family life! For example, should their own son, donkey or ox fall into a pit or a well on the Sabbath they would not hesitate to 'break the law' and organise a rescue operation.

Our Lord swept their religious rules aside, clearly demonstrating that what really matters is loving and serving the Lord God and really caring about those around us. In our own day, we too need to beware of man-made rules and traditions that stop us freely living for God. We must never let the keeping of our rules and traditions take the place of true godliness of living.

The wedding feast

As the guests arrived for this meal, our Lord noted how they aimed for the seats that would give them the greatest recognition and honour among their companions, or the greatest opportunity to gain the ear of someone who was in a position to do them a favour. It was as if they were all trying to obtain a seat at the top table of a modern wedding reception!

The warning against such self-centred grasping came from the lips of 'One greater than Solomon', but the principle had been spelled out in Solomon's proverbs centuries earlier, 'It is better to be told, "Come up here," than to be put lower in the presence of the prince.'

However, this is exactly how the religious leaders were consistently behaving. They hungered for 'the best seat in the synagogues and salutations in the market place.' And this is how the world operates in our own day. We see it as people promote themselves and scheme to out-wit and out-manoeuvre others to secure power or position.

What can we learn from the Lord's parable? Surely it is that, for the man of God, there is no need to do these things. God our heavenly Father is the Master of the Feast. The prophet Micah teaches us that as we seek to display justice and mercy in our own lives and promote them in our society, we are 'to walk humbly' with the Lord. And Peter urges his readers: 'Humble yourselves under the mighty hand of God, that in due time he may exalt you.' We are each called to walk humbly before God, as we play our God-given part in this world – be that sweeping a floor or publicly addressing thousands.

At a very practical level, that means that in taking the lead at home or in wider society there is no need to be pushing and grasping or to secure it by underhand means. It is far better achieved by consistent, godly integrity of the kind displayed by both Joseph and Daniel in the Old Testament. Each of these men, under the hand of God, rose to be prime minister. Perhaps this humility before God was most strikingly displayed by the future king David, who even when he had opportunity to be rid of murderous Saul, refused to kill God's chosen king. This kind of humility before the Lord does not destroy godly ambition to be the most useful we can be before him. But it does bring great peace and contentment if it is clearly the Lord God who puts us in a high position, or who chooses not to do so. He is the Master of the Feast.

The link between the parables
As the meal and conversation proceeded, Jesus said to the man who had invited him, "When you give a dinner or a banquet, do not invite your friends or your brothers or your relatives or rich neighbours, lest they also invite you in return and you be repaid. But when you give a feast, invite the poor, the crippled, the lame, the blind, and you will be blessed, because they cannot repay you. For you will be repaid at the resurrection of the just."

The man with dropsy was, clearly, not an invited guest. He was just 'of use' and so – having served his purpose of being a 'test case' concerning healing on the Sabbath – he left the meal. Jesus took him, healed him and sent him on his way. In another of our Lord's parables, the rich man 'who dined sumptuously every day', simply didn't notice the poor man, Lazarus, at his gate, he was just part of the street scene. In the same way, the scribes and Pharisees dined with one another but, in the main, despised and totally ignored the needy.

Can we not, unwittingly, do something similar – only invite friends and family, or work colleagues and valuable contacts? We are not called to neglect them, but not to forget, for example, those who live alone or the student whose home is far away and who cannot possibly invite us back, or repay us in any way. We are called to invite them out of love for God and love for our neighbour. Our homes and meal tables can be a God-given opportunity from the Lord to be used for his glory.

There really is heaven to be gained, and treasure before God, too. Here is reference to the resurrection; the life to come, 'For you will be repaid at the resurrection of the just.' Can you imagine anything more greatly to be treasured than our Lord's words, 'Well done good and faithful servant . . . Enter into the joy of your Lord'? The challenge to the true disciple is to use every opportunity we have, to bring glory to the Lord God.

Questions for discussion or personal reflection

1. Can you think of instances where people were 'watching' you to test the reality and consistency of your faith? Have you experienced tests and traps set like the one described here?
2. How can we be better equipped to face the types of traps the Pharisees were setting?
3. Can we, like the Pharisees, have long-standing habits or traditions that hinder us from living or speaking freely and whole heartedly for the Lord God?
4. Like the men at the wedding feast, do we find it necessary to be promoting ourselves, or are we willing to live humbly before Almighty God?
5. What attitudes do we need to repent of, and what attitudes do we need to pray for, in order to be consistently just in our dealings with those around us, and to 'love mercy and to walk humbly before our God'?
6. Is it part of our thinking to include those who are alone, or in difficulty, or who cannot possibly repay us any kindness shown to them?
7. What steps can we take to support the genuinely poor and needy in our community, in our country, and in our world?

References

Parable of the marriage feast – Matthew 22:2-14
Watch or trap him – Luke 7:36, 11:37 and 20:20 – Mark 3:1-2 where it is clearly stated that it was to trap him.
The servant is not above his master – Luke 6:40
Healing, but not on the Sabbath – Luke 13:14
One greater than Solomon – Luke 11:31
Come up here – Proverbs 25:6, 7
The best seat – Luke 11:43
Walk humbly – Micah 6:8

Humble yourselves – 1 Pet. 5:5, 6
Joseph – Genesis chapters 39-41,
Daniel – Daniel chapter 6
David and Saul – 1 Samuel 24 and 26:6-25
Who dined sumptuously every day – Luke 16:19-20
Well done good and faithful servant . . . – Matthew 25:21

The Great Banquet

A 'heavenly thought' but a terrible assumption
'When one of those who reclined at table with him heard these things, he said to him, "Blessed is everyone who will eat bread in the kingdom of God!"'

A guest at the meal, perhaps to deflect the uncomfortable personal challenge of the Lord's words and move the conversation forward, uttered this pious-sounding statement. 'Blessed is everyone who will eat bread in the kingdom of God!' Of course, this is a wonderful truth; none are more to be envied than those who have a God-given place in the kingdom of heaven. We might expect Jesus to commend him and offer an equally 'heavenly-minded' reply. Did he? No, he did not! He challenged the underlying assumption. For the speaker naturally assumed that he and his fellow diners would be there – but would they?

The scribes and Pharisees were testing Jesus, provoking him to tell them his views on who would be at that great final banquet. As Kenneth Bailey points out, they would have been well satisfied to hear him say that only by perfect law-keeping will we be counted to be worthy to be there. But he did not say that.

Jesus' response was to tell the parable of the great banquet. As the custom was, the guests were invited some time in advance, then a second invitation was given when all was prepared. The guests were greatly honoured to be given an invitation to such a banquet. They were reminded when all was ready. But they did not come; 'they all alike began to make excuses.'

The first excused himself as he had just bought a field and so, by implication, made it plain that the pursuit of his future wealth was more important to him than honouring the host and taking his place at the banquet. The second excused himself by saying that he had just bought five pairs of oxen and needed to examine them to make sure they were sound beasts. Here is the day by day pursuit of regular business. He considered that far more important to him than taking his place of honour at the great banquet. And finally, the third had just married a wife and so, of course, must be excused. There is provision in the Law of Moses for a newly married man to be free of his duty to serve in the army for a year, so as to happily spend time with the wife he has taken. However, could such a provision be reasonably stretched to excuse this man, at the last minute, from the short time it would take to attend such an important banquet? It was clearly right for him to honour his wife and fulfil a whole variety of domestic duties, but to use them to excuse himself from the banquet was to scorn the giver of the feast and his invitation.

These men were each honoured with an invitation. They were each reminded. But none of them came. Maybe they were just preoccupied with the day to day business of life and saw this as a higher priority than attending the feast. But by failing to come they showed contempt for the one who gave the feast and his invitation. No wonder they called down the anger and judgement of the master of the feast; 'For I tell you, none of those men who were invited shall taste my banquet.'

How tellingly this applied to the Hebrew people and particularly to their religious leaders, some of whom were gathered round this table. They had been invited by the prophets to watch with expectancy for the coming of God's salvation; to watch for the appearing of the promised Messiah. They were invited again by that herald of God, John the Baptist who, most plainly, witnessed to the Lord Jesus, 'Behold the

Lamb of God, who takes away the sin of the world,' and '. . . this is the Son of God.' But they would have none of it. 'He came to his own people,' writes the apostle John, 'but his own people would not receive him . . .' Note the words of our Lord's parable, 'None of those men who were invited shall taste my banquet.' What a terrible judgement when we stop to reflect that the Lord Jesus was speaking of the kingdom of heaven.

But are the Lord God's purposes frustrated by the indifference and contempt of men?
To continue with the quotation from the apostle John, 'But to those who received him, who believed on his name, he gave the power to become the children of God.' 'But . . .' – what a glorious word that is in this verse! The invitation was offered first to God's chosen people and their leaders. Their scornful rejection of it is pictured here in this parable, where the master of the feast says, 'Go out quickly to the streets and lanes of the city, and bring in the poor and crippled and blind and lame.'

The religious leaders of God's Israel rejected the One who was, and still is – as Simeon prophesied concerning him – Israel's glory, God's Messiah, the Lord Jesus. However, the ordinary people, the despised poor, heard him gladly. The tax-gatherers and sinners drew near him. Those in deep trouble flocked to him. The Lord God's feast will be filled!

But still there was room. 'And the master said to the servant, "Go out to the highways and hedges and compel people to come in, that my house may be filled."'

After the stoning of Stephen, ongoing persecution scattered the Jewish believers from Jerusalem. As they were forced to leave they carried the gospel invitation wherever they went. Philip brought it to the Samaritans, and then shared it with the official from Ethiopia. Peter was called to speak to the household of Cornelius, and the Lord God brought about a clear and miraculous sign; the whole household was filled with the Holy Spirit and began praising God. The Jewish believers who came with Peter were astounded, because the gift of the Holy Spirit had been poured out even on the Gentiles; those they regarded as 'no people'; nothing, worthless, mere 'hedge-dwellers'.

Paul and Barnabas were set apart to bring the invitation to the people of God's Israel scattered throughout the Roman Empire. But in Acts 13 we read of them being reviled by the Jewish leaders. Paul said to them, 'It was necessary that the word of God should be spoken first to you. Since you thrust it from you, and judge yourselves unworthy of eternal life . . . we turn to the Gentiles.'

It was just as Jesus warned those present at the table of the Pharisee, none of the contemptuous, invited guests would taste the banquet – but those from the highways and hedges would gladly take their place. Jesus had earlier given a very plain warning to the religious leaders; 'There you will weep and gnash your teeth, when you see Abraham and Isaac and Jacob and all the prophets in the kingdom of God, and you yourselves thrust out. And men will come from east and west and from north and south, and sit at table in the kingdom of God.' Matthew records Jesus delivering a terrible warning to the whole nation. Jesus warned them that because of their rejection of it, 'The kingdom will be taken away from you and given to a nation producing the fruits of it.'

God's chosen, Hebrew people stubbornly 'excuse themselves', while those they have regarded for centuries as 'non-people', the Gentiles, accept the invitation and crowd in – right down to ourselves. What a wonderfully merciful heavenly Father to invite us! Here we are, men and women and young people 'from the nations'; people outside the family of his chosen people, mere 'hedge-dwellers'. And yet, through no merit or deserving of our own, chosen and gathered at the express invitation of God. What a privilege!

Through the faithful ministry of the servants of God, we find ourselves, like the early Ephesian Christians before us, chosen and adopted as the sons and daughters of God, redeemed by the precious blood of the Son of God, called to live daily to the praise of his glory and destined to be with him forever. We, mere outsiders gathered from 'the highways and hedges', find ourselves, by the grace of God, destined to be seated at the greatest of all banquets; the banquet the apostle John describes as 'the Marriage Supper of the Lamb'.

An incredible invitation – but not to be taken for granted
But could this parable also be seen as a very solemn wake-up call to the formerly Christian nations of the West? In our headlong pursuit of secularism with its rejection of God and his word, are we repeating the terrible error made by the Jewish religious leaders in our Lord's day? Will we, like these religious leaders gathered in the house of the Pharisee, ignore and treat with contempt the fact that we have been so singularly favoured of God over these last centuries.

Our history shows us the fruit of godliness – a whole society built on trust, leading to integrity in politics and business, and a legal framework and education system that have been the envy of the world.

Will we in our generation turn our back on both God and his gracious invitation? Will we thrust aside our Christian heritage, excluding godly belief and practice from government and public life, from our laws, from education and medicine and from our home life? If we pursue godless ways, can we expect to see the Lord God's continued hand of protection and favour on us? To our great loss and their great gain, should we not rather expect to see the kingdom of God taken from us and given to 'another nation showing the fruits of it'?

The Pharisees were particularly careful to keep the Sabbath. For ourselves, it is possible to keep a formal Sunday morning hour for God. But then for the rest of the day and the rest of the week, like the men invited to the banquet described in the parable, excuse ourselves from godly ways. Like them, our minds and lives can be all but totally absorbed in securing our future wealth, or be immersed in the constant and demanding busy-ness of this world, or be just completely taken up with domestic duties.

Richard Baxter, preaching on the refusal and excuses of the invited guests, exclaimed, 'Good Lord! What dung is it that men make so much of, while they set so light by everlasting glory! What toys are they that they are daily taking up with, while matters of life and death are neglected!'

'Compel them to come in'?
Forced conversions, such as conversions on pain of death, are a great misunderstanding and a very dark blot on the history of the Christian church – and compulsory conversions to other religions are a terrible scar on the history, even the current history, of the world of our own day.

However, at a spiritual level, there is a 'holy compulsion' to turn and believe, which is clearly of God. The apostle Paul experienced that on the road to Damascus, and many of God's most eminent saints have known it through the running centuries, but it is absolutely not for man to 'compel'.

In genuine revival the Lord God uses mere preachers – sometimes men as 'ignorant and unlearned' as the rulers and elders considered the apostles Peter and John to be – and men and women find themselves compelled to cry out to God for mercy and are brought into the kingdom of heaven from the 'highways and hedges'. But such happenings are a work of the Holy Spirit of God – and not because of man's compulsion.

There is a noteworthy balance in the account Luke gives us in the Acts of the Apostles as he describes Paul 'arguing, debating, persuading, entreating' and even 'in Christ's name beseeching' and then, on his return to Antioch, reporting to the church 'all that God had done'. Paul had put in tremendous personal effort and suffered greatly in doing so, and yet the founding of the churches, in Philippi, Thessalonica and many other towns and cities, was a wonderful work of God.

Something beyond the parable, but a great privilege

The primary purpose of the parable was to challenge the Pharisees' assumption that by their careful law-keeping they would be certain to secure a place at the heavenly banquet.

However, we are also told that the master of the banquet was determined to have his house filled, even by those who would be judged by others, and perhaps by themselves, to be totally unworthy of such an honour. As we come to look at the parable in these days, this has implications for 'those from the highways and hedges' who have been 'invited to the banquet.'

In the parable, only one servant is mentioned, and it is his task to bring many people to the banquet. Applied to our modern world, the one Great Servant who can fulfil this role is the Holy Spirit, whose task it is to open eyes to see the kingdom of heaven and to convict the world of sin, righteousness and judgement. Should the parable stir us to be praying for a mighty outpouring of the Holy Spirit in our day and a dramatic gathering in of people for the great heavenly banquet?

Further, although it forms no part of the parable, from our Lord's teaching elsewhere and from the rest of the New Testament, it is clear that, before we take our seat at the great banquet, we have a task to fulfil. Like the first disciples, those who have come to believe through their witness, are called, indeed commissioned, to join the ranks of those who are his willing servants in inviting as many others as we can to the feast. It is a call to encourage our friends, colleagues and neighbours to accept this invitation and then do our very best to accompany them on the journey to the banqueting hall. Until on the last day, together, we take our place at that greatest of all banquets; 'the Marriage Supper of the Lamb'.

It is the task of those who believe, with gentleness, respect and courtesy, to be ready to give a reason for the hope that is in us. It is our task to share and invite, persuade and implore, as the Lord gives us opportunity, but never to use underhand methods let alone force.

In conclusion, three things for modern Christians to ponder and take away from this parable and its setting.

Firstly, the great danger of presuming, as the religious leaders at the feast did, that because we are associated with church or chapel we are destined for heaven. As George Whitfield was constantly reminding his hearers, for a place in the kingdom of God, 'You must be born again.' Our relationship with the living God and his Son must not be merely formal and resting on our membership of a church; it needs to be personal, humble and deeply grateful for his patience, kindness and mercy towards us.

Secondly, God's purposes are not frustrated. If we in the secular West turn our back on the Lord God – who has so blessed and prospered us in these last centuries as we shaped our laws and society according to his holy ways – we can only expect his good hand to be withdrawn, his protection taken away, and ultimate disaster. Is the kingdom being taken from us and given to the people of Africa and Asia and some parts of the Middle East who are flocking in and gratefully taking our place?

Thirdly, if we have truly been compelled by the Holy Spirit of God to come to his banquet, we are called to pray to the Lord of the banquet to send out his servant, the Holy Spirit, afresh in our day. We are also personally called to join in the task of that Mighty Servant as he enables us to share the gospel invitation and urge and encourage others to accept the place graciously offered to them at the Lord God's great banquet.

Lord God, we thank you for our Lord's parables which are so deep and so searching. By your Holy Spirit, give us ears and eyes to heed the warnings and challenges of this parable. Glorify your name among modern Jewish people and among Christian people gathered from the highways and hedges throughout the word.

Questions for discussion and personal reflection

1. Like the well-intended Pharisees, how easy is it for us to assume that our own good-living and good deeds, or our busyness in religious activities, will secure us a place in heaven?
2. How natural is it to become so immersed in this world's matters as to be unaware of God and his Son and his ways?
3. The Lord God, the Master of the Banquet, has graciously extended his invitation to non-Jewish people. How grateful should we be that God has included us?
4. What part can we humbly play to encourage God's ancient people, the successors of those to whom the invitation was originally given, to turn and to look again at God's gracious invitation in his Son?
5. Do you know anything of 'God's holy compelling' in your own spiritual journey?
6. What positive steps are suggested by the parable that we can take as individuals to live and speak faithfully in a very challenging world?

References

Provision for a newly married man – Deuteronomy 24:5
John the Baptist's witness to Jesus – John 1:29 and 34-35
He came to his own people – John 1:11-12
The stoning of Stephen – Acts 7:59

Simeon, 'Israel's glory' – Luke 2:25-32
Philip in Samaria and with the Ethiopian – Acts 8:4-5 and 26-29
Peter at Cornelius' house – Acts chapter 10
Paul and Barnabas – Acts 13:43-49
Jesus' warnings: – 'weep and gnash your teeth,' Luke 13:28&29, – 'the kingdom taken away,' Matthew 21:43
Ephesian Christians, 'adopted, redeemed. . .' – Ephesians 1:1-14
The marriage supper of the Lamb – Revelation 19:6-9
The kingdom taken from you – Matthew21:43
Well done good and faithful servant – Matthew 25:23
Saviour who is Christ the Lord – Luke 2:11
Seek first the kingdom of God – Matthew 6:33
Paul on the road to Damascus – Acts 9:1-9
Ignorant and unlearned – Acts 4:13
Paul on his return to Antioch, '. . . all that God had done' – Acts 14:27
Open eyes to see the kingdom – John 3:3-6
Convict the world – John 16:7-11
Reason for the hope that is in us – 1 Peter 3:15-16

The Tower, the King going to War and the Salt

Now great crowds accompanied him, and he turned and said to them, "If anyone comes to me and does not hate his own father and mother and wife and children and brothers and sisters, yes, and even his own life, he cannot be my disciple. Whoever does not bear his own cross and come after me cannot be my disciple.

"For which of you, desiring to build a tower, does not first sit down and count the cost, whether he has enough to complete it? Otherwise, when he has laid a foundation and is not able to finish, all who see it begin to mock him, saying, 'This man began to build and was not able to finish.'

"Or what king, going out to encounter another king in war, will not sit down first and deliberate whether he is able with ten thousand to meet him who comes against him with twenty thousand? And if not, while the other is yet a great way off, he sends a delegation and asks for terms of peace.

"So therefore, any one of you who does not renounce all that he has cannot be my disciple.

"Salt is good, but if salt has lost its taste, how shall its saltiness be restored? It is of no use either for the soil or for the manure pile. It is thrown away.

"He who has ears to hear, let him hear."

Luke 14:25-35, English Standard Version

The Parables of the Tower, the King going to War and the Salt

Strong and weighty words
'If anyone comes to me and does not hate his own father and mother and wife and children and brothers and sisters, yes, and even his own life, he cannot be my disciple. Whoever does not bear his own cross and come after me cannot be my disciple.'

These very serious, very weighty and indeed, very frightening words introduce the parables of the tower, the kings and the salt. They do not fit modern comfortable and respectable Christianity. They do not fit at all with 'gentle Jesus meek and mild'. And yet they are words recorded as coming from the lips of our Lord.

James Steward in his book *Heralds of God*, urges young preachers to, 'Preach Christ today in the total challenge of His high imperious claim. Some will be scared, and some offended: but some, and they the most worth winning, will kneel in homage at His feet.' 'His high imperious claim'? Here is the claim of one whose power and authority is absolute; one in total command. Such is the claim on our lives that we are compelled to face as we consider these verses.

The setting of these parables
Over several chapters Luke records the Lord's journey to Jerusalem and the cross of Calvary. The journey, on foot, is told in three sections. In Luke 9 verse 51, we read, 'He set his face to go to Jerusalem.' In chapter 13 verse 22, Luke records, 'He went on his way through towns and villages, teaching and journeying towards Jerusalem.' It is in this second section that we find the famous parables of the narrow door, the marriage feast and great banquet, the prodigal son, the dishonest manager, the rich man and Lazarus, together with these very challenging claims and the three short parables associated with them. The claims and their parables are so demanding that it is easy to see why,

unlike other parables, they are not found among a preacher's favourite texts! In fact, they are very rarely spoken about.

The immediate setting is given in Luke 14 verse 25: 'Now great crowds accompanied him and he turned and said to them . . .' and then follows this very challenging teaching on the essential conditions of discipleship, which our Lord illustrates with the parables of the tower, the king and the salt.

There was a great misunderstanding. The people had heard him speak with great authority, they had seen him heal the sick, restore sight to the blind and hearing to the deaf, and they had seen him set free those enslaved to demonic forces. Rightly, they had become convinced that here among them was the fulfilment of Isaiah's prophecy, the long-promised Anointed One, the Messiah. However, the Messiah they had in their minds and longed for was one who would rid them of their Roman overlords and restore Israel to the glory days not seen since the reigns of King David and his son Solomon. It seems that they imagined they were following Jesus to this kind of national glory.

In part, the crowd was right. He was indeed Emmanuel, God among them, come 'to visit and redeem his people'. He was, indeed, Israel's promised Saviour and Redeemer. But he was also 'the suffering servant of the Lord'. Ultimately, to him every knee will bow, for God has anointed him King of kings and Lord of lords. But first, it was necessary for him to suffer; to be despised and rejected, and put to death on a cross.

So, very dramatically, the Lord Jesus turned and said these very strong words to them, setting out the most severe demands on those who would be his disciples.

Our Lord spoke in dramatic terms of 'hating' family members and even life itself, but, of course, elsewhere in the Bible we are commanded to love our neighbour and to honour our parents. His point is that, where there is a clash of loyalty and obedience, he must take first place. Matthew makes this even plainer, 'He who loves father or mother . . . son or daughter more than me is not worthy of me; and he who does not take his cross and follow me is not worthy of me.'

Conquering kings promise houses, lands, grand titles and great honour to their faithful followers. The Lord Jesus, on his journey to Jerusalem and the cross, confronted them with loss, great suffering and death. The terms are hard, but he made it absolutely plain that he must take first place – over family, over possessions, even over life itself. The way to glory was the via dolorosa, the way of tears; the way of the cross.

If they, or we, would be a disciple, it is not enough to be carried along by the enthusiasm of the good folk around us – each of us must 'be prepared'. We must count the cost.

Such loyalty to the Lord Jesus may drive a wedge between us and those around us and make us, in their eyes, very odd. It may result in us being shamed, thrown out or persecuted – even by our own family. The picture the Lord gives us is that of carrying a cross through jeering crowds, as he was so soon to do.

The Man Building a Tower

'For which of you, desiring to build a tower, does not first sit down and count the cost, whether he has enough to complete it? Otherwise, when he has laid a foundation and is not able to finish, all who see it begin to mock him, saying, "This man began to build and was not able to finish."'

It is not hard to imagine onlookers joking with one another at the builder's expense, 'What a fundamental error!' 'A good foundation, a grand start – but he can't afford to complete it!' 'He's built a folly!' 'What a fool!'

'Which one of you . . .' these words tell us that the tower the Lord had in mind was not something exceptional, a great monument, but an ordinary tower and lodge. The kind any person in that age might have built to keep watch over sheep, or in his vineyard to keep watch over his precious crop at harvest time.

Matthew Henry suggests that, to help us understand, we could think of it as a house. In our own times this is even more sharp and painful. For example, 'He's put the deposit on a large house, but he can't afford to pay the mortgage!' 'He could have bought a smaller place, but the bailiffs come in tomorrow. Poor man – repossessed, with nothing left!' 'He didn't do his sums. He didn't count the cost. He didn't get his priorities sorted out.'

To the eager crowds flocking to follow him, Jesus turns and says, 'Do you really understand? Are you serious? Have you counted the cost?'

As in everything, the Lord Jesus is the pattern for disciples to follow. Jesus was not on a comfortable pathway as he journeyed toward Jerusalem, but on a very costly mission, given to him by his Father; to 'lay down his life a ransom for many'.

As he willingly submitted to his Father, so he challenges these would-be disciples to submit to him; to put him first in glad obedience, and in determined loyalty – even if that should cost everything; even life itself.

How does this apply to us in our generation?
Does this seem all a bit extreme? Well, maybe it is at present in the West, but for a moment just look back and reflect. What did faithful discipleship cost those first disciples and those who joined their number in the early days of the Christian church?

For that faithful witness Stephen, it meant martyrdom by stoning. For the apostle John's brother, James, again it cost him his life as Herod had him put him to death by the sword. John himself suffered imprisonment, and almost certainly slave labour, on the isle of Patmos; and Peter is believed to have been crucified.

For so many other early believers it meant leaving everything as they fled for their lives throughout the Roman Empire, carrying the gospel with them. Years later, the apostle Paul lists lashings, beatings, toil and hardship, hunger, thirst and shipwreck – and all that before his attempted assassination and final long imprisonment in Rome.

In England, and throughout the English speaking world, the Christian freedoms we enjoy were bought at a very high price. Godly Reformers like Latimer, Ridley and Cranmer, facing Queen Mary's determined hatred, were imprisoned and then burnt at the stake. John Bunyan, whose *Pilgrim's Progress* is still so loved and valued, wrote it from jail, imprisoned for the gospel's sake. The God-fearing Pilgrim Fathers sailed to America, facing great peril and leaving all for the sake of gospel freedom.

Even today, with our great Christian heritage, disciples are called to submit to the Lord Jesus; put him first – even if that costs the great displeasure, the scoffs and slurs of those we hold most dear. We might find ourselves on the uncomfortable side of conversations like these: 'What! Son, have I spent all this time and money training you up to follow me in the business and so be wealthy and successful – and you dare to tell me that you want to utterly waste your life? You want to become a preacher! You want to become a missionary!' Or, even if it means being denied the fulfilment of our dearest hopes and ambitions – 'This person is not appropriate for this post as it is clear that, in all conscience, he or she would not be able to . . .' Or even more costly to ourselves, if it means laying down life itself, as indeed it has for so many Christian disciples in other lands in our own days; violently beaten-up and chased from their homes, imprisoned, sent to labour camps, or even beheaded.

It is salutary to discover that there have been more Christian martyrs in the last hundred years than in all the centuries before.

Wise words from those who have run the race before us
John Calvin notes that we should not bring rejection or persecution upon ourselves. It is perfectly possible to gain the hatred of those around us and make ourselves quite unnecessarily 'martyrs' by our ill-judged or inflammatory words or deeds. Our Lord was full of grace as well as truth. As his followers, we are called to give a reason for the hope that is in us – but to do so with courtesy and respect.

J.C. Ryle urges no one to hold back from being a true disciple for fear of what it may cost. He who claims our complete loyalty is also the good shepherd who tends his lambs and feeds his sheep. As believers through the centuries have testified, his 'yoke is easy and his burden light' and, despite outward circumstances, he keeps his promise and gives inward rest and peace.

The crown of life
The Lord's words of warning to his over-eager followers were dramatic and arresting. They were meant to be so. But the Lord is no man's debtor. When we put in second place our loyalty to our own brothers and sisters and our own treasured hopes and plans, we find that we are given, as our Lord promised Peter, so many more brothers, sisters, houses and . . . life which not even death can snatch away.

Our Lord did not promise that it would be easy, but, again, for our encouragement, hear the words of that faithful disciple, Paul the apostle, 'But whatever gain I had, I counted it as loss for the sake of Christ. Indeed I count everything loss for the surpassing worth of knowing Christ Jesus my Lord.'

Here is one of the strange paradoxes of the kingdom of God. If we cling to everything for ourselves, we will ultimately lose it all. If we give up our pursuit of everything this world can offer for Jesus' sake we will be given so much more, together with the promise of eternal life.

Heavenly Father, these are stern and challenging words; give us grace to 'read, mark, learn and inwardly digest them' so that we may 'embrace and ever hold fast' the glorious gospel of your Son and 'the hope of everlasting life'.

(The quotations in this prayer are from the 1662 Book of Common Prayer; the collect for the second Sunday in Advent.)

Questions for group discussion or personal reflection

1. In your experience have these parables of the Lord Jesus often been seriously considered in Bible study groups or church services? Can you see reasons why they might not have been?
2. Do you think there could be times when family, social or even church loyalty might take priority over the reverence, loyalty and devotion that is due to the Lord Jesus?
3. If you have read John Bunyan's *Pilgrim's Progress*, can you perhaps relate to some of the scenes he describes? For example the personal cost of the initial scorn he experienced from his family and neighbours.
4. Have you ever found yourself in difficulty because you stood by godly principles?
5. Regarding John Calvin's warning, have you ever seen other people bring upon themselves rejection and some level of 'martyrdom'? How could we lay ourselves wide open to, or invite such hostility?
6. How can we learn to act with grace and compassion, while holding to God's truth?
7. How can we encourage one another to face an unbelieving world that can, at times, be very hostile?
8. In what ways can parables like these prepare and strengthen us for living as faithful disciples?
9. What certain and glorious hope does the true disciple have?

References

Sight to the blind, hearing to the deaf – Luke 7:21&22
Visit and redeem his people – Luke 1:68
Suffering servant of the Lord – Isaiah 52:13- 53:12
Not worthy of me – Matthew 10:37-39
Lay down his life a ransom for many – Mark 10:45
Stephen – Acts 7:54-60
James – Acts 12:1-3
Early disciples fleeing – Acts 8:1
Paul: Toil and hardship, hunger and thirst – 2 Corinthians 11:23-28
The attempt on Paul's life and his imprisonment – Acts 23 12-15 and the following chapters of Acts.
Full of grace and truth – John 1:14
Reason for the hope that is in us – 1 Peter 3:15
The good shepherd – John 10:11
His yoke is easy and his burden light – Matthew 11:28-30
As our Lord promised Peter – Luke 18:28-30
Surpassing worth of knowing Christ – Philippians 3:7&8 (RSV)
Life abundant and eternal – John 10:10 and Luke 18:28-30

The Parables of the Tower, the King going to War and the Salt – part 2

The King Facing Defeat

'What king, going out to encounter another king in war, will not sit down first and deliberate whether he is able with ten thousand to meet him who comes against him with twenty thousand? And if not, while the other is yet a great way off, he sends a delegation and asks for terms of peace.'

Of course, it is counting the cost again – but is it? A.M. Hunter pinpoints a very subtle but significant difference between the two parables. The builder could choose whether to build or not to build his tower. He could choose how large a tower to build and he could choose when it might be a good time to begin. But did this king have such freedom of choice? He has been informed that a conquering king with 20,000 armed men is advancing against him. What is he going to do? The situation is desperately serious. The king has no choice. He has got to make a decision, and to do so very speedily.

Our Lord shows us the gravity of the situation as he pictures the king sitting down to consider and, perhaps, take counsel with his army chiefs and best advisors. His choice is very limited.

Firstly, he could dismiss the report; regarding it as a very unlikely story. And yet if the report proves to be true, and he has taken no action, that would result in the total, overwhelming defeat of an unprepared people, captivity and slavery for his subjects and almost certain death for himself.

Secondly, he has only 10,000 men. Could he stand against a king coming to crush him with such overwhelming power and force? The advancing king would inflict terrible, devastating judgement on any resistance or refusal to submit that proved too feeble. He could expect no mercy.

Thirdly, if he believes the report to be true, and he knows he cannot stand against the advancing king, he has no choice at all, he must submit. While still at a safe distance, he must send and ask, 'What are the terms of peace? What must I forfeit? What will peace cost?'

No wonder the king 'sat down' to consider and take advice!

Certainly the parable of the king is about 'counting the cost', but this time it is about counting a different cost. Rather than addressing his over-eager hearers, is the Lord challenging those who had no intention of submitting to him and his 'imperious claim'?

The crowds of people following Jesus contained those who were, mistakenly or unthinkingly, too ready to count themselves his disciples. But the crowds also contained those who had no intention whatever of doing so. The Lord Jesus opened the eyes of the over-enthusiastic ones to the true cost of discipleship with the parable of the tower. Did he tell the parable of the king facing devastating defeat to open the eyes of those who were determined not to submit to him – such as the religious leaders, who were always present in the crowds? If so, to these he is putting the same challenge, 'count the cost'. But this time, it is not the cost of submitting to him but the cost of not submitting to him; of refusing to become his disciples. The cost will prove to be absolutely devastating – they will perish – as he had warned them and would continue to warn them as he approached Jerusalem.

How does this touch us?
Centuries earlier, Matthew Henry had also taken note of this subtle difference and applied the Lord's words very sharply. He notes that those who ignore the Lord God and his commands are in rebellion against him, and that, 'Even the proudest and most daring sinner is no equal match for God.' It is in our interest to make peace with him, and 'to do so long before the day of terrible reckoning'. We do not need to 'send', his terms are plainly set out both in John chapter 3 verse 16 and in these parables. If we will not believe, if we will not submit – we perish.

Matthew Henry sees our Lord provoking each one of us to ask, not this time, 'Can I afford to be a disciple of the Lord Jesus?' but, 'Can I afford not to be? Can I afford not to submit? Can I afford to live in God's world as if there were no God? Can I afford to ignore the claims of the Lord God and his Son the Lord Jesus – to whom he has given all authority and whom he has appointed both Lord and Judge? Can I afford to ignore him, recognising that he has made plain his promised return; this time, not in humility but in great glory and power?' We are plainly warned that on that day, to him every knee will bow.

In John Bunyan's *Pilgrim's Progress*, Christian must choose between staying in his home city, a city destined for destruction, or leaving all for the sake of following his new-found Lord and Master. The cost of leaving the City of Destruction and walking Christian's pilgrim path is very great. But, the cost of remaining in the City of Destruction is ultimately far greater.

There is a day of judgement coming. As the apostle James puts it, 'The judge stands at the door.' The King is on his way, his authority is irresistible and power totally overwhelming. Before him, on his final word, hangs our eternal destiny. At his word, we either live and by grace are heirs of glory, the Celestial City, the everlasting favour of God – or we perish. Can we afford not to let him rule our lives? Can we afford not to be a disciple?

Who, like the king in the parable, can 'consider' these things without quaking? Yet many church leaders have followed the king's first option. All the warnings in scripture of 'separating', of 'perishing', of 'judgement', and of 'the wrath of God and of the Lamb' are dismissed as the products of the over-active imagination of a 'less enlightened' generation. And the result? The watchmen do not sound the alarm, God's people are not warned, and, on the great and terrible day of our Lord's return, both will be found totally unprepared.

From this short parable, it is painfully clear that none can stand against the wrath of God or of his Son. It is only those willing to accept the apostolic witness to the necessity of following the king's third option – of submitting and accepting the coming king's terms – who will escape.

This sounds extreme to our modern ears, accustomed as we are to a greatly watered-down, comfortable and self-centred version of Christianity. And yet such warnings of the judgement to come lie at the very heart of the authentic gospel as taught by the Lord Jesus, by the apostle Peter and by Paul. For example, Luke records our Lord's direct warning of the suddenness of his coming on an unprepared people, 'As it was in the days of Noah . . .' and, 'As it was in the days of Lot . . . so it will be when the Son of man comes.' People, going about their lives in their ordinary God-ignoring way, will suddenly be overwhelmed by judgement and destruction.

The apostle Peter, speaking to the Gentiles gathered in the house of Cornelius, said, 'And he (the Lord Jesus) commanded us to preach to the people and to testify that he is the one appointed by God to be judge of the living and the dead. To him the prophets bear witness that everyone who believes on him receives forgiveness of sins through his name.'

Brought for examination before the leading men of Athens, the apostle Paul proclaims, 'The times of ignorance God overlooked, but now he commands all people everywhere to repent, because he has fixed a day on which he will judge the world by a man whom he has appointed, and of this he has given assurance to all by raising him from the dead.'

Truly, God has so loved this world as to give his only Son. But, it is in order that those who believe in him, accept him as Lord of their lives, might not perish. Only those who yield their lives to him are promised life that not even death can snatch away; life that is eternal.

Lest we modern 'heralds of God' become too harsh, and for the strong encouragement of all who have ears to hear, notice the reassuring words found in the second letter of Peter, 'The Lord is not slow to fulfil his promise as some count slowness, but is patient towards you, not wishing that any should perish but that all should reach repentance'.

Like the king, when we 'sit down and consider', and our eyes are opened to see our true and desperate situation and to recognise that we must yield to the Lord Jesus, what are his terms? What are his conditions? What must we do? Firstly, unlike the religious leaders of Jesus' day, it is essential that we recognise him for who he truly is, the promised Messiah, the Son of God; the Lord God's anointed judge, King of kings and Lord of all lords. Secondly, we are called to accept the amnesty, the free forgiveness of God, that he was on his way to Jerusalem to purchase for us by his precious death. Thirdly, as the Lord Jesus had just described to the great crowd following him, we are called to put him first; laying our lives, our time, our money, our very selves at his feet; putting ourselves entirely and absolutely at his disposal.

The Lord Jesus does not relax his terms. His imperious claim on our lives is absolute. Immediately after the parable he says 'So therefore, any one of you who does not renounce all that he has cannot be my disciple.' Peter, James and John understood these things and left their nets, Matthew left his accounting table, and Paul counted all his privileges and achievements as 'dung' in comparison with the surpassing worth of knowing Christ Jesus his Lord.

In conclusion

The parable of the tower challenged the over-enthusiastic crowd and, it would seem, this parable of the king facing certain defeat was directed to the less-than-enthusiastic religious leaders.

How encouraging it is to read in Luke's account of the early church that, after Pentecost, '. . . the number of the disciples multiplied greatly in Jerusalem, and a great number of the priests became obedient to the faith.'

Pray earnestly that the Lord God, by his Holy Spirit, would do a work like that in our day. Pray for ourselves, that our discipleship might be real and not just in name only. Pray that at his coming, the Son of man may find a people prepared.

Questions for group discussion or personal reflection

1. Matthew Henry warns that those who ignore the Lord God and his commandments are in rebellion against him, yet, 'Even the proudest and most daring sinner is no match for God.' Where does that leave us and those we know?
2. Has all thought of 'judgement', of 'perishing', of 'the wrath of God' been air-brushed out of the thinking and preaching of almost all of our churches today? If so why?
3. On his return, will the Lord Jesus find a people ready, about his business and prepared? What would that look like in practice? Will many of us find ourselves totally unprepared?
4. What are his terms of peace, and how do we react and respond to them?

References

Lord and Judge; the judgement seat of Christ – 2 Corinthians 5:10
Every knee – Philippians 2:9&10
The judge stands at the door – James 5:9
Separating – Matthew 13:36-43
Perishing – John 3:16
Judgement – Luke 11:31-32
The wrath of God and of the Lamb – Revelation 6:15-17
As it was in the days of Noah – Luke 17:26-30
Peter in the house of Cornelius – Acts 10:42&43
Paul in Athens – Acts 17:30&31
God so loved – John 3:16
Not the will of God that any should perish – 2 Peter 3:9
The surpassing worth of knowing Christ Jesus – Philippians 3:3-8
Priests obedient to the faith – Acts 6:7

The Parables of the Tower, the King going to War and the Salt – part 3

The Tasteless Salt

'Salt is good, but if salt has lost its taste, how shall its saltiness be restored? It is of no use either for the soil or for the manure pile. It is thrown away. He who has ears to hear, let him hear.'

Luke records Jesus concluding this section on the cost of discipleship with this tiny parable of useless salt, salt that had lost its 'tang' or its savour. Our modern minds may question how this could happen, but salt in ancient Israel would almost certainly have been very impure. The ordinary people harvested sun-dried salt by hand from sea shores. To use it you would simply add water, stir or shake the mixture and when it had settled, use the salty water for cooking and throw away the sandy grit that was left. You can see that it would be possible for the actual salt to have been washed out before it came to be used, with just the grit left. It would look much the same, but for use in cooking or for preserving it would be totally useless. It could not even be used as a fertilizer to enrich the soil as a whole range of soluble mineral salts would have been lost.

The Lord used this brief saying or parable several times in different settings during his ministry, but always with the same thrust: as a picture of those who begin well but, for one reason or another, fall short.

Following Luke's account, C.H. Dodd suggests that one clear application of the parable of the salt would have been to the religious leaders of Israel, some of whom would have been among the crowd listening to Jesus. The Pharisees in particular prided themselves in being the descendents of Abraham and believed both their teaching and lives to be pleasing before God. But unlike Abraham, they were not men of vital faith and humble obedience who were open to the Lord

God's leading. How could they, or the nation they led, be the blessing to the world that Abraham's descendents were called to be? They were like the salt that had lost its saltiness, the very property that gives it its value.

Matthew records Jesus teaching the disciples, "You are the salt of the earth, but if salt has lost its taste, how shall its saltiness be restored? It is no longer good for anything, except to be thrown out and trampled under people's feet." Later in his ministry, as Jesus was teaching his disciples, Mark records our Lord saying, "Salt is good, but if the salt has lost its saltiness, how will you make it salty again? Have salt in yourselves, and be at peace with one another."

Many commentators separate Luke's record of the tiny parable of the salt from the parables of the tower and the king, but as G. Campbell Morgan points out, in the Greek it begins with a 'therefore'. 'Salt, therefore, is good, but if salt has lost its taste . . .' The parable is continuous with our Lord's challenges to 'count the cost,' and here, those challenges are re-enforced with the challenge to 'hold fast.'

Although the Lord Jesus was still addressing the great crowds who were following him, was this first a warning to his immediate disciples? They had been with him for nearly three years, heard so much of his teaching, witnessed the clear evidences of his being the Son of God, the long-promised Messiah, Emmanuel, God amongst us. Would they hold steadfastly to all they had seen and heard, or would they turn their backs on it all and prove useless before Almighty God?

Peter knew and publicly professed that the Lord Jesus was the Christ, the Son of God – and yet, on that terrible night when he denied his Lord, the cost was too great. His own life was on the line. To admit that he was a disciple could well have meant imprisonment or even death. That is why our Lord charged disciples to 'count the cost', to be prepared. Forgiven and restored Peter went on to be very far from useless.

A spiritual fall or stumble can happen very suddenly, as it did for the apostle Peter. Or, it can happen gradually as it did for John the Baptist during the time he was imprisoned by Herod. Thomas Bilney and Thomas Cranmer were leading figures in the Reformation in England; each temporarily 'crumpled' under the prolonged and intolerable pressures put on them to renounce their biblical faith.

Demas was at one time a fellow partner in the gospel with the apostle Paul, but the pull of this world proved too great and so, it seems, Demas gave up – salt that had lost its saltiness.

Would we do better? I very much doubt it. However, like each of these men, what cause we have to thank our gracious Lord that he was, and still is, 'the God of the second chance.'

How should we apply this solemn warning to today's disciples and today's churches?
Down the centuries, the parable has remained a warning lest a spiritual tumble should befall us personally . . . or befall our churches.

Sir Francis Drake wrote, 'There must be a beginning of any great matter, but the continuing unto the end, until it be thoroughly finished, yields the true glory.' Like the undertaking of some great task, true discipleship is much more than a single profession of faith. It is a lifetime of growing in faith, and of glad and willing submission to the Lord Jesus; a constant seeking first of the kingdom of heaven and of his guiding in our lives.

Some examples from three stages of life may help. Perhaps as a younger person, you set out as a disciple on the pilgrim way. Ten or fifteen years pass and you have done well in your job and gained more and more responsibility. But this has come at the cost of long hours, travelling and the job becoming far more demanding and stressful. On top of this, family commitments are crowding in; your wife and youngsters need your attention, your parents are getting older and needing more help. There just doesn't seem to be time in the day or energy left for spiritual things.

Or, life goes on but you have gradually drifted far from the joyful faith of earlier years. You've lost contact with the enthusiastic Christians with whom you used to meet and pray, and the Bible no longer thrills or speaks to you. Where you now live, the local church is very welcoming and yet not able to help you spiritually. Its chosen priority is to be a social hub and gathering for local people with the common aim of fund-raising for the church and the arranging of social activities in the community – rather than these things, good and necessary as they are, being a small part of the greater priority of the making, strengthening and building up of disciples.

Later in life, perhaps now isolated from Christian fellowship, that first public profession of faith and promise of lifelong loyalty has never been forgotten. But, having held fast to godly ways for fifty or sixty years, things are now becoming more difficult with loss of independence, failing eyesight, failing hearing and constant aches and pains. In some seeming 'prison cell' situation like this, will our faith falter, like the imprisoned John the Baptist? – Or will we be like the equally imprisoned apostle Paul, 'rejoicing in the Lord', looking forward to being 'with the Lord' and seeking to encourage all around us to rejoice and to hold fast?

If such things can befall individuals, can they befall churches too?
The commentaries unite in applying these warnings to today's individual disciples and to today's churches and their leaders. But, before looking at that in detail, it is very challenging to look at the risen Lord's words to the seven ministers and churches as recorded in the first chapters of the book of the Revelation. These were churches where true, single-minded discipleship was proving to be very costly, and where for one reason or another they were in great danger of losing their saltiness. Ephesus, 'abandoned the love you had at first'; Smyrna, shaken by tribulation and poverty, subjected to slander and facing suffering; Pergamum, embracing false teaching: Thyatira,

squeezed by society around them into creeping idolatry and immorality; Sardis, both minister and church 'have the name of being alive, and you are dead,' their works far from perfect in the sight of God; Philadelphia, with its challenge to hold fast; and 'lukewarm' Laodicea, claiming to be rich, prosperous and in need of nothing, and yet, before the Lord, found to be 'wretched, poor, blind and naked.'

Although we can visit the ruins of these cities today, there is not a hint of the churches left. Although there are wonderful exceptions, could that be the fate of so many of our traditional Western churches today as we see true Christian discipleship, of the kind the apostles would recognise, all but evaporating around us? Or what of our Lord's terrible question, 'When the Son of man comes, will he find faith on earth?'

Sadly, it is possible for both disciples and churches to cease to hold fast and to hold out the apostolic gospel, and be salt and light in this world, and so before God become useless. It was not for nothing that the old Reformers taught both minister and people to take pains to take good care of the heart. Not just the important physical one, but our inner, secret walk and fellowship with the Lord God and his Son, the Lord Jesus.

Overall conclusion

These are our Lord's very serious words to his would-be followers.

To those too eager and unprepared – count the cost of submitting; the parable of the tower.

To those too reluctant or stubborn – count the cost of not submitting; the parable of the kings.

To those who begin but fall short – take care, watch and pray; the parable of the salt.

James Steward wrote, 'Preach Christ today in the total challenge of His high imperious claim.' Here, in these parables, that claim is plainly and painfully set before us. Is it surprising that they do not rate highly on the preacher's list of favourite texts?

These three very demanding parables stand as a challenge to the modern church and its leaders. Have we failed our people by calling them to a 'self-comforting level of belief' – without ever telling them of, let alone challenging them with, the unsparing call to single-minded discipleship that Jesus demands in these parables?

Although many will have no time for such things, as our Lord said, 'He, who has ears to hear, let him hear.'

Heavenly Father, we acknowledge our weakness and vulnerability before you. In our own strength, we are bound to fall or be gently drawn away by the world, the flesh or the devil. As it is only by your grace that we can enter the kingdom of heaven, so it is only by your grace that we are able to stand. Keep us faithful, keep us watchful, keep us walking closely with yourself and, in your mercy, restore and revive your wonderful but faltering church.

Questions for group discussion or personal reflection

1. Can you identify with any of the scenes described, where, faith has become a struggle?
2. When compared with the message delivered by the apostles, is today's church too often giving us short measure?
3. Why do you think these parables are not every preacher's favourite subject?
4. How can the warnings of parables like these prepare us and help us stand firm?
5. In what ways can we help one another to 'hold fast'?

Footnote

For those with a strong stomach! In the light of parables such as these, should comfortable Christians in the West perhaps take more notice of the reality underlying the risen Lord's words to the church in Smyrna? Some of the people of this church were about to be thrown into prison and tested terribly. To the whole church, the risen Lord is recorded as saying, 'Be faithful unto death, and I will give you the crown of life.'

Only a couple of generations ago, in some churches, these stirring and challenging words of the risen and ascended Lord would have been sung by the choir and congregation as each candidate came up out of the water of baptism. The note is also clearly sounded in the Methodist Covenant Service, and within the Anglican church a similar challenge can be found in the commitment at baptism, '. . . not to be ashamed to confess the faith of Christ crucified, and manfully to fight under his banner against sin, the world, and the devil, and to continue Christ's faithful soldier and servant unto your life's end.'

References

You are the salt of the earth – Matthew 5:13
If the salt has lost its saltiness – Mark 9:50
Abraham's call to be a blessing to the world – Genesis 12:1-3
Peter's denial – Luke 22:54-62
John the Baptist imprisoned by Herod – Luke 3 18-19 and 7:18-19
Demas – Philemon 23 & 24 and 2 Timothy 4:10
Rejoicing in the Lord – Philippians 1:12-14, 4:4-13 and Acts 16:24-25
The churches of Revelation – Revelation chapters 1-3
Will the Son of man find faith on the earth? – Luke 18:8
Be faithful unto death – Revelation 2:10

The Lost Sheep, Lost Coin, Prodigal Son and his Elder Brother

Now the tax collectors and sinners were all drawing near to hear him. And the Pharisees and the scribes grumbled, saying, "This man receives sinners and eats with them." So he told them this parable: "What man of you, having a hundred sheep, if he has lost one of them, does not leave the ninety-nine in the open country, and go after the one that is lost, until he finds it? And when he has found it, he lays it on his shoulders, rejoicing. And when he comes home, he calls together his friends and his neighbours, saying to them, 'Rejoice with me, for I have found my sheep that was lost.' Just so, I tell you, there will be more joy in heaven over one sinner who repents than over ninety-nine righteous persons who need no repentance.

"Or what woman, having ten silver coins, if she loses one coin, does not light a lamp and sweep the house and seek diligently until she finds it? And when she has found it, she calls together her friends and neighbours, saying, 'Rejoice with me, for I have found the coin that I had lost.' Just so, I tell you, there is joy before the angels of God over one sinner who repents."

And he said, "There was a man who had two sons. And the younger of them said to his father, 'Father, give me the share of property that is coming to me.' And he divided his property between them . . ."

Luke 15:1-12 English Standard Version

The reason why this series of parables was told and the first two parables explored

The key to understanding the whole 'parable'

Although Matthew records the parable of the lost sheep, no other gospel writer records the series of parables found in the fifteenth chapter of Luke's gospel. The Reformers taught that the key to understanding the whole chapter is the murmuring of the scribes and Pharisees recorded in the opening verses.

'Now the tax collectors and sinners were all drawing near to hear him. And the Pharisees and the scribes grumbled, saying, "This man receives sinners and eats with them." So he told them this parable . . . '

The vivid word pictures of the shepherd searching for his lost sheep, the woman searching for her coin, the father welcoming his lost son and the angry displeasure of the elder brother, are all of a piece; a single parable in answer to the murmuring of the scribes and Pharisees. By this series of pictures, the Lord was showing the scribes and Pharisees who he was and why he was mixing with 'sinners'. He was also showing them, as in a mirror, their own religious but hardened hearts, and their greatly mistaken reaction to himself and to what he was doing.

Once we have grasped this, we will be saddened when we find this series of parables divided up and regarded simply as a collection of useful gospel pictures to be used without reference to the murmuring which opens the chapter, or to the elder brother at its conclusion. Like me, you may well have heard many talks on each of the first three parables and very few on the elder brother.

Why did Luke think it so important to record the presence of the scribes and Pharisees?

Throughout his ministry, the gospel writers record that the scribes and Pharisees were keeping an increasingly hostile watch on the Lord

Jesus. Many of his later recorded conversations and parables were specifically for their hearing, to show them who he truly was, how they were behaving, and the consequences of their rejection of him.

From the start, the religious leaders in Jerusalem had their attention drawn to the son of Mary. Zechariah, the priest who was to become the father of John the Baptist, was on duty in the temple. As he burned incense, the angel Gabriel, sent from the Lord God, assured him that his barren wife would have a son. He was full of doubt and, as a sign, was spectacularly struck dumb. Such an incident would have been drawn to the attention of those in authority. As would his equally spectacular release from that dumbness as, in obedient faith, he named his new-born son 'John'; a name quite unknown in his family. Filled with the Holy Spirit of God, Zechariah prophesied that the Lord God was about to visit and redeem his people Israel, and that this child, John, would be the Lord's herald; going ahead to prepare his way.

The godly Simeon had been assured by the Holy Spirit that he would not die before seeing the Lord's Christ. As Jesus' parents brought the infant Jesus to the temple for Mary's purification, Simeon publicly proclaimed him to be God's salvation, 'A light to lighten the Gentiles and the glory of his people Israel.' The widow Anna, who spent her life praying and worshipping in the temple, came into the temple at that time and gave thanks to God and publicly spoke of Jesus 'to all who were waiting for the redemption of Jerusalem.'

When Jesus was about twelve years old Mary and Joseph brought him to Jerusalem. Attention was again focused on him as he amazed the teachers in the temple by his questions, his wisdom and his understanding.

Years later, the religious leaders sent a delegation from Jerusalem to ask John the Baptist why he was baptising, and specifically about John's own role. John drew their attention to Jesus, who was now about thirty years old. He declared Jesus to be the one whose way he was preparing. He also declared him to be '. . . the Lamb of God who takes away the sin of the world,' and, '. . . the Son of God.' In the light of the prophetic words of Zechariah, as he named his infant son 'John', these were statements that could not be ignored.

So the Lord Jesus was a marked man from his earliest days and the scribes and Pharisees made sure that they always had representatives present. You can see this official presence in the crowds carefully recorded by the gospel writers throughout his public ministry.

Could he be the true Messiah?

There was an air of expectancy about the promised appearance of the Messiah, and yet there had been many false claimants. Was he, Jesus, the true Messiah? The scribes and Pharisees were trying to discern the truth. They had seen him heal the sick, give sight to the blind and hearing to the deaf. They had seen him set free captives of demonic spirits, and had witnessed the common people flocking to hear his gospel – all of these were signs of the promised Messiah as foretold by Isaiah.

So many of the promised signs had been fulfilled, and yet his ministry was, in the religious leaders' view, 'irregular'; he was not one of them. Further, he was clearly not the man to fulfil their nationalistic hope of a restored Israel, free from the yoke of Rome. And, perhaps most significant of all, he was constantly suggesting that their own religious leadership fell far short of being faithful shepherds of God's people. He was, in fact, posing an increasing threat to their dearly held position of privilege and of power.

Here in chapter 15, Luke records the Lord Jesus surrounded by the very lowest of society – tax-gatherers and sinners. He was mixing with them and even honouring them by eating with them. How, reasoned the scribes and Pharisees, could a truly 'religious' man associate with such people? How could a 'righteous' man so contaminate himself? How could the true Messiah of God eat with traitors, fallen women and the like? Their murmuring was not so much a grumble or complaint that he was doing so, but rather they murmured as they confirmed one another in their resolve to reject him as the promised Messiah. Their hearts and minds were hardened against him and they justified their rejection of him as they saw the people with whom he mixed.

'This man receives sinners and eats with them.' The scribes and Pharisees intended this as a slur so that they could discount him, but, actually, they honoured him by drawing attention to yet another of the hallmarks of the true Messiah. The prophet Ezekiel foretold the day when the Lord God himself with his Messiah, pictured as David the shepherd king, would tend and shepherd his flock – a flock so neglected and abused by his appointed under-shepherds as they grew fat and pampered themselves.

With the commendable aim, as they saw it, of wanting to please God, the religious leaders kept themselves ritually clean. The Pharisees were the 'separated ones' and had the ultimate aim of presenting themselves to the Lord God, 'perfectly righteous'. So, by their own logic they could never mix or associate with fallen men and women, let alone eat with them, for they would become ritually unclean; they would contaminate themselves. However, here before them was the Lord Jesus among the most despised and soiled of society, tax-gatherers for the Roman overlords and fallen sinners, mixing with them and eating with them. The Pharisees would never do such a thing; it would ruin their righteousness! They could accept a penitent sinner crawling to them for forgiveness, but to go amongst fallen people seeking their restoration, as the Lord was doing, was offensive to them. It was quite beyond anything they would consider acceptable, let alone doing themselves.

But the Lord Jesus cared about such people; bothered with them (and I for one am grateful that he did, and still does!) The religious leaders had no heart or sympathy for that. Theirs was an exclusive religious club or order – the great danger of the church in any age.

'This man receives sinners . . .' Here was the truth of God on the lips of the scribes and Pharisees. The Lord Jesus was mixing with tax-gatherers and sinners precisely because he, the true Messiah, 'came to call sinners to repentance', and 'came to seek and to save those who were lost'.

It is into this situation the Lord spoke the three parables of the lost, rescued and reinstated, and the one parable of the elder brother – to show, as in a mirror, the slavish self-righteous attitude of the murmuring scribes and Pharisees.

The Shepherd and the Lost Sheep

The scene

The picture of the shepherd looking after his flock of sheep was a very familiar one to Jesus' hearers. The local terrain was open, rugged, and at certain times of the year, very dry, so the shepherd must constantly lead his flock from one place to the next, searching for the best possible feeding area. Israel's most famous king, David, spent much of his early youth looking after his father's sheep, continually leading them to fresh pasture; and with rod and staff, sling and stone rescuing them and protecting them from wild animals. Although in the West, our pictures frequently show a single shepherd with his sheep, Eastern shepherds rarely worked alone. There would be a group of them – as Luke records there was on the night of the angel's announcement of the birth of the 'Saviour who is Christ the Lord.'

When Luke records Jesus as saying, '. . . leaving the ninety-nine in the open country'; almost certainly the main flock of sheep could be safely left in the care of fellow shepherds or the hired men who were there to help the family member, such as the youthful David. As the owner's representative, he would be the chief and responsible shepherd and so it would fall to him to give account of the sheep and to lead any search or rescue. On safely recovering a lost sheep, his return, full of joy, may well have been to the men looking after the main flock or, if he was long delayed by the rescue, could have been to the family at home.

What, then, is the relevance of the picture to the grumbling scribes and Pharisees?
The tax-gatherers with whom Jesus was mixing were not honourable men, but men who made themselves very rich by exacting the tax due to the Romans from their own countrymen – plus as large a 'handling charge' as they could . . . for themselves. They were fleecing their own kith and kin to pay the hated, occupying Romans and to line their own ample pockets. Hated, fallen men – regarded as thieves and traitors. And yet Almighty God cared about them and sent his Son, the Good Shepherd, to seek and rescue men like that.

The Lord mixed not only with tax-gatherers but with socially-outcast sinners of every kind; men and women whose appetite for money or sex – or whose desperate search for relief from the endless, grinding poverty – had caused them to fall. I do not suppose they meant it to end up this way, but, just like the nibbling sheep going from one green tuft to the next, 'one thing led to another' until here they were in the gutter of society, lost and despised.

'Which one of you . . . ?' Here is an appeal to conscience, the scribes and Pharisees first, but ourselves too, as Luke's readers. It is as if the Lord were saying, 'Which one of you – maybe, like King David in his youth, out on the hillsides with a few hired men and personally responsible for the family's sheep, a hundred of them – which one of you would fail to bother with the one that strayed, and fail to seek and search until you could bring it safely back? Of course you would search – and that is what I am doing. All heaven rejoices over each precious, rescued, restored, repentant person. And will you, murmuring, self-satisfied, self-righteous religious leaders fail to rejoice?'

Would such a picture reach the closed and hardened hearts of these men who so prided themselves in being 'not as other men'? If the scribes and Pharisees had truly listened to Moses and the Prophets, on whose writings they were regarded as experts and interpreters, God's prophet and spokesman Isaiah would have taught them that, before the One with whom we have to deal, all our righteous deeds and efforts are as 'filthy rags'. Noble and godly Isaiah, confronted with the majesty and glory of the Lord, found himself ruined, lost and undone. He would have taught them that we have all gone astray as lost sheep; that we are all in need of repentance and of the mercy and forgiveness of God.

Before Almighty God, the hard and compassionless, proud and self-righteous religious leaders did need to repent – just as much as the tax-gatherers and sinners they so despised. However, their own preferred but mistaken teaching was that by meticulous law-keeping they could make themselves so good, so religious, so perfectly acceptable before God as to need no repentance – hence the irony of the Lord Jesus' reference to the 'ninety nine' who considered that they did not need to repent.

What is the relevance of Jesus' picture to us as Luke's readers today?
How many of us have known good folk, friends, colleagues or family members, who have strayed from godly ways. Like grazing sheep, they have been drawn away in the pursuit of wealth, a career pleasure, a marriage partner or, perhaps, power and influence, until they are so immersed in these things, that God, and walking in his holy ways, are long forgotten.

Here is a constant risk. As the years move on, any of us can so easily be drawn away from walking closely with the Lord God. We just follow our desires – maybe like the scribes and Pharisees under a respectable cover of religion, – until like sheep nibbling from one good patch of grazing to the next, we end up far away and in great spiritual danger.

The Son of God searched, made himself known and rescued then, and he does so now. He welcomes, forgives and restores straying, lost sheep – could that be one of us? Just as a shepherd is listening for the feeble bleat of a lost sheep, so the Lord Jesus' ear is open to our cry for mercy and for rescue. Taste and see the joy of heaven over one sinner who repents – far greater than over ninety nine persons who, like the scribes and Pharisees, proudly imagined they needed no repentance.

On one occasion a Pharisee invited the Lord for a meal, but failed to give Jesus the customary Eastern courtesies of a kiss, an anointing with oil and foot washing. To the Pharisee's disgust, a 'sinner', a fallen woman, let her tears fall on the Lord's feet, wiped them with her hair and anointed them. The Pharisee concluded that Jesus was no prophet or he would have known the kind of woman she was. But actually, she was showing her love and faith in the one who alone could rescue and forgive her, a love so conspicuously absent from the Pharisee's attitude toward Jesus. To the fallen woman Jesus said, 'Your sins are forgiven.' . . . 'Your faith has saved you; go in peace.' The Pharisees at the table with him were left to ponder the question, 'Who is this, who even forgives sins?'

The scribes and Pharisees murmured. But the angels of God, all heaven, rejoice over each sinner who repents; each person who, in Henry Lyte's words, is 'Ransomed, healed, restored, forgiven . . .'

The Woman Diligently Searching for her Lost Coin

"Or what woman, having ten silver coins, if she loses one coin, does not light a lamp and sweep the house and seek diligently until she finds it? And when she has found it, she calls together her friends and neighbours, saying, 'Rejoice with me, for I have found the coin that I had lost.' Just so, I tell you, there is joy before the angels of God over one sinner who repents."

Was the coin part of her dowry, or a coin she wore as jewellery, or just of great value in a society where bartering was the common practice and money very scarce and rarely used? We do not know. But the woman regarded that coin as exceedingly precious and so she spared no pains in her search until she found it – just as the Lord Jesus was doing with these fallen, lost, but in his sight exceedingly precious people.

Once the woman had found her treasured coin, she called together the neighbouring women to rejoice with her over the recovery of the coin. The coin was that valuable and significant to her. Before God, this is the kind of great value and significance the Lord Jesus was placing on each fallen person who is rescued.

How did this picture speak to the murmuring scribes and Pharisees?
Zacchaeus, the little man who climbed the sycamore tree to see Jesus, was a very rich, chief tax-collector; the sort of person the Pharisees totally despised. When the Lord showed compassion toward him and went to his house, the crowd murmured, 'He has gone to be the guest of a sinner.' But after Zacchaeus had clearly turned from his ungodly ways, Jesus said of him, 'Today, salvation has come to this house, since he also is a son of Abraham. For the Son of Man came to seek and to save the lost.'

Matthew, the gospel writer, was also a tax collector. After Jesus had called him to be a disciple, he invited Jesus and the other disciples for a meal and they were joined by many other tax-collectors and sinners. The self-righteous Pharisees were not slow to question Jesus' willingness to eat with such people. But Jesus replied, "Those who are well have no need of a physician, but those who are sick. I have not come to call the righteous but sinners to repentance."

In the eyes of the self-righteous Pharisees, such people were soiled and of no value. But before God, each one was very precious. Here was the Son of God reaching out in mercy to rescue those who had fallen.

Can this picture speak to us in our day as Luke's readers?
Unless it is carefully looked after, a typical coin will, by its nature, just fall and roll under or behind something that will hide it from view. It does so because of its weight and shape. In the same way, we love to excuse ourselves by claiming, 'It is just the way I'm made,' or, 'It is just the way I am.' We may blame our genes, our upbringing or our environment; anything, just as long as we can convince ourselves that our straying from the ways of God is not our fault. It is true that we do have differing inherited challenges or genetic predispositions – to lie, to cheat, to steal or to have to face strong, difficult and ungodly passions and desires; for example uncontrolled anger.

The apostle Paul recognised such things as he spoke of 'keeping under his body in case after preaching to others he himself was a castaway'. Many of us have character flaws; 'secret corruptions' and inclinations that, unrecognised and allowed to run out of control, would bring us down. We also 'suffer' from the universal human inclination to ignore the God in whose hand is our breath; to cut free and do as we want to do. Together these would sweep us down the great, broad way that, before the judgement throne of God, would lead us to loss and ruin.

Just like the woman diligently searching for her precious coin, the Son of God was mixing and 'even eating' with tax gatherers and sinners because he came to seek and to save those who had fallen and were lost. Each one who turned from ungodly ways was forgiven, and all heaven rejoiced.

Down the centuries, this same great work is the task the Lord commissioned his believing people to fulfil – to seek the lost, the broken and the neglected and tell them of the free, gracious forgiveness God offers to those who truly turn from ungodly ways and put their trust in the One who told these parables.

"And when she has found it, she calls together her friends and neighbours, saying, 'Rejoice with me, for I have found the coin that I had lost.' Just so, I tell you, there is joy before the angels of God over one sinner who repents."

Lord God, thank you for these penetrating parables that fell from the lips of your Son the Lord Jesus Christ. Show us, in our day, how far we have strayed and bring us home. Disturb our self-righteousness and awaken us to our true plight before you. By your grace enable us to truly repent, and then, as members of your forgiven people reach out to others.

Questions for discussion or personal reflection

1. The scribes and Pharisees were murmuring because Jesus mixed with outcasts and sinners. How does noticing this help us to understand this whole series of parables?
2. Have we ever found ourselves looking down on and perhaps despising those who have strayed far, got caught up in some way or just tripped themselves up, and so landed in dire straits before Almighty God and their fellow human beings?
3. How can we prayerfully be playing our part in bringing others to know the mercy and forgiveness of God?
4. Why did the scribes and Pharisees discount Jesus as the true Messiah? Did he fit the pattern they expected?
5. Have you had opportunity to seriously consider who Jesus really is?
6. Have we known anything of straying from godly ways? But for the mercy and loving care of our wonderful Shepherd, would we have been lost?
7. Do we see in ourselves traits and inclinations that would lead us to be eternally lost but for the grace of God and his patience, kindness and the clear instructions of his word?

References

Lost sheep – Matthew 18:12-14
Zechariah – Luke 1:1-25 & 57-80
To seek and to save the lost – Luke 19:10
Simeon – Luke 2:22-35
Anna – Luke 2:36-40
The boy Jesus in the temple – Luke 2:41-52
John the Baptist questioned – John1:19-34
Official presence – Luke 6:7, 14:1, 20:20, Matthew 27:41-43
Signs of the Messiah – Isaiah 35:3-6 & 61:1&2
Ezekiel – God the shepherd, Ezekiel 34
Came to call sinners to repentance – Luke 5:32
Came to seek and to save the lost – Luke 19:10
'A Saviour who is Christ the Lord' – Luke 2:11
Not as other men – Luke 18:11
Filthy rags – Isaiah, 64:6
Isaiah ruined and undone before Almighty God – Isaiah 6:1-7
Straying sheep; '. . . all we like sheep have gone astray' – Isaiah 53:6
Woman anointing Jesus – Luke 7:36-50
Zachaeus – Luke 19:1-10
Came not to call the righteous, but sinners – Luke 5:27-32
To be as gods; 'be like God' – Genesis 3:5
Broad way; the wide and easy way – Matthew 7:13
Paul, a castaway – 1Corinthians 9:25-27
God, in whose hand is our breath – Daniel 5:23

The Lost Sheep, the Lost Coin, the Prodigal Son and his Elder Brother – continued

The Prodigal Son

Now the tax collectors and sinners were all drawing near to hear him. And the Pharisees and the scribes grumbled, saying, "This man receives sinners and eats with them." So he told them this parable . . .

. . . And he said, "There was a man who had two sons. And the younger of them said to his father, 'Father, give me the share of property that is coming to me.' And he divided his property between them. Not many days later, the younger son gathered all he had and took a journey into a far country, and there he squandered his property in reckless living. And when he had spent everything, a severe famine arose in that country, and he began to be in need. So he went and hired himself out to one of the citizens of that country, who sent him into his fields to feed pigs. And he was longing to be fed with the pods that the pigs ate, and no one gave him anything. But when he came to himself, he said, 'How many of my father's hired servants have more than enough bread, but I perish here with hunger! I will arise and go to my father, and I will say to him, "Father, I have sinned against heaven and before you. I am no longer worthy to be called your son. Treat me as one of your hired servants."' And he arose and came to his father. But while he was still a long way off, his father saw him and felt compassion, and ran and embraced him and kissed him. And the son said to him, 'Father, I have sinned against heaven and before you. I am no longer worthy to be called your son.' But the father said to his servants, 'Bring quickly the best robe, and put it on him, and put a ring on his hand, and shoes on his feet. And bring the fattened calf and kill it, and let us eat and celebrate. For this my son was dead, and is alive again; he was lost, and is found.' And they began to celebrate."

Luke 15:1-2 and 11-24 English Standard Version

The Prodigal Son

The temptation to live in God's world as if there were no God is always with us. It is the constant inclination to ignore the Lord God, his commandments and his holy ways and so be free to do as we will and be the master of our own destiny. The Lord Jesus portrays this so vividly with the parable of the younger son saying, 'Father, give me the share of the property that will fall to me.' What was he asking for? Like so many of us when young, he longed for independence; the 'freedom' and the 'happiness' that he believed was being denied him. All this would be his – if he could escape home, do what he wanted, and have what he wanted when he wanted it, and had the money to pay for it.

By far the greater share of the inheritance would fall to the elder brother, and the younger son would be expected to stay and, with his elder brother, build up the whole estate. Clearly, it is most honouring to the Lord God when family members can live and work in harmony. But was the younger son unwilling to do this? Or, could he see that once his father had died, he would become subject to his elder brother? Why wait? He might as well ask his father to settle the inheritance now, escape home and so avoid the risk of being trapped as the servant of his elder brother. With the inheritance settled, he would be free and have wealth to do whatever he wished – and to do so now.

John Calvin comments that young men, once they are determined to follow their desires and passions, are extremely head-strong. No matter how clearly destructive of themselves or of others, neither reason nor threats, neither fear nor shame will restrain them. Yet, what an affront; how offensive! 'Father, could you break up your estate and regard yourself as dead – so that I can turn my back on you, leave home and please myself . . .' But isn't this exactly how we treat Almighty God, our heavenly Father – in whose hand is our breath and all our circumstances?

Mirroring the Lord God's treatment of us, with great patience and wisdom, the father did not refuse, confine or punish his son. Perhaps with great sorrow, he raised his share and let him go.

The younger son took the share and moved far away where he spent freely, not necessarily immorally, as many commentators assume, but just carelessly; following the desires of the moment. He was a spend-thrift, a waster – a prodigal. However, the younger son's share was a definite amount, not an income stream, and so, of course, after a while it ran out.

It takes effort, discipline and restraint to build up or maintain wealth, and no effort whatsoever to waste it. The turn of a card, a throw of dice and another round of drinks will do it. Anyone can waste money – and you can give such a person as much as you like (from your own wallet or from the public purse) and they will still run out. Unfortunately for the younger son, his wealth completely gave out just at the beginning of a severe famine.

The young man found himself in a desperate situation. Without money, no one cared about him. The new companions and admirers that his wealth had bought him had all melted away. He was friendless and penniless in a foreign country; no cousins, aunts or other relatives who might take pity on him; just on his own and in dire need of both food and shelter. He took what action he could to enable him to stay in the far country and avoid the shame of having to return home. He took a job, but found himself exploited by a man who sent him to feed pigs.

As the murmuring scribes and Pharisees would well understand, for a Hebrew person to fall so low as to be feeding pigs was a terrible fate. But worse still was the gnawing hunger that made even the husks, probably wild carob pods, that the pigs were eating look desirable. And perhaps worst of all, the phrase 'nobody gave him anything'. He was quite dispensable. If he died it would matter to no-one; just one less hungry mouth in a time of severe famine.

The younger son had grasped at freedom, and found himself in slavery. He had grasped at wealth, and found himself in poverty. Far from discovering happiness, he was in a desperate plight – as, ultimately, we will find ourselves in, if we try to live in God's world without reference to him.

A shaft of light; a glimmer of hope
John Calvin comments that we will not change our way of life until we come to see that we absolutely have to do so. Under the hand of God, as the younger son compared life at home with his present situation, his desperate hunger drove him to that point.

"But when he came to himself, he said, 'How many of my father's hired servants have more than enough bread, but I perish here with hunger! I will arise and go to my father, and I will say to him, "Father, I have sinned against heaven and before you. I am no longer worthy to be called your son. Treat me as one of your hired servants."' And he arose and came to his father."

Facing inevitable death, he 'came to himself' – or, as we might say, he came to his senses. It was the moment truth dawned. He had escaped home and pursued his own desires but now it had all gone terribly wrong. He had tried to rescue himself by taking a job – and failed; he was just being exploited. There was no possible future for him in the far country. Painfully clearly, he saw that he must turn his back on all that he had tried to gain by leaving home. Far from being the road to freedom, success and happiness, it had proved to be the road to his total ruin. There was only one option left to him; he must 'lose face', 'eat humble pie' and creep home. He had no other option but to throw himself on the totally underserved kindness and pity of his father.

I would have loved to have read, "But when he came to himself, he said, 'I have wronged my father terribly, I will arise and go to him, and I will say to him, "Father, I have sinned against heaven and before you. I am no longer worthy . . ." ' That would have been a clear and noble statement of his genuine repentance. However, at this point, his priority does not seem to be, to humbly do all he could to put things right with his father – that will come later – but to escape starvation and fill his belly with bread. And so we read, 'But when he came to himself, he said, "How many of my father's hired servants have more than enough bread, but I perish here with hunger! I will arise and go to him, and will say to him . . ."' How clearly our Lord sees and understands our self-centred ways!

The younger son's resolve to return home with carefully chosen words of confession may have been his plan of action to escape death. Do note, however, that our Lord is portraying repentance from a human point of view. No matter how mixed our motives, once we have been given clear insight into our true and frightening situation before Almighty God, to take action – by throwing ourselves on his mercy – is our responsibility and the essential first step in true, biblical repentance.

The place of desperate times in the purposes of God
Surrounded by pigs and husks, the younger son's eyes were opened and he resolved to change. It took his desperate hunger to bring him to this point, but now he plainly saw that he must go home and plead for mercy. Can it be like that for us? On occasion, the Lord God does graciously use terrible times to open our eyes to see our mistakes and to open our ears to hear his voice. He uses disappointment, tragedy, even prison, to soften our hardened hearts to see the emptiness of our godless pursuit of the pleasures or the possessions of this world – despite all their enticing promises. Pain itself can be, as C.S. Lewis pointed out, 'God's megaphone' to call us to turn to him. How many of us have cause to thank God for such times. Perhaps we had an awareness of the Lord God in the background but, like the prodigal son, turned our back on him and on godly ways to 'plough our own furrow', to 'do our own thing'. It is not until we have some desperate wake-up call or

find ourselves 'floundering about', utterly lost that we are enabled to see our need to get right with our heavenly Father; that with him, and with him alone, is life and without him we perish.

Sadly, we often want to be right with God – without being willing to leave the 'far country'; without being willing to turn our back on godless ways. But the younger son was willing; he acted on his moment of solemn insight. He did not delay or linger any longer. Ragged and penniless, starved and stinking of pigs, he began to make his way home.

In our day, this is the testimony of many, including, one young drug addict who was granted just such a God-given, life-changing moment. In an equally clear moment of insight, he saw his life, what he was doing, where it must lead and what he must do – and he did it. By God's grace he totally turned his back on that lifestyle, cast himself on the mercy of God in the name of the One who told this parable, and is now a radiant Christian, gladly working as a servant in his heavenly Father's household.

Christians in the days of great preachers like Whitfield and Wesley had a word for this. They called it 'awakening'. It is when, by the sovereign work of the Holy Spirit of God, we 'wake up' – or are 'awakened' – to our desperate situation before Almighty God, our need to be right with him, and are moved to take action; to flee to him for mercy.

The home-coming; a repentance that became deep and real

Initially, the younger son's resolve to return home may have been due to his desperate need to secure bread, but there are clear signs that his repentance grew to be far deeper than that. In the far country, the younger son was pursuing his vision of a new life, free from any restraint whatsoever. All was going according to his wildest dreams . . . until the money ran out and the famine struck. Everything had changed.

Faced with a famine and with no one to help him, did he come to see that the apparent freedom of the far country was an illusion, an empty mirage? That everything he had so taken for granted and turned his back on for his longed-for 'freedom' was actually of great value? At home, the family and the hired servants worked together as a team and there was bread enough and to spare, even in a famine. Here, in his chosen far country, there was absolutely nothing. As a total outsider in a country faced with famine, no one gave him anything. He had made a great mistake and his only chance was to return home and to cling to the one remaining thread of hope. Destitute and totally unworthy as he now was, he was still his father's son. Maybe his father would let him return, perhaps as a servant.

The justice he deserved? . . . . or amazing grace, which he most certainly did not?
For the prodigal son of the parable there was still an insuperable barrier about which he could do nothing. There was only the slimmest of chances that his father would accept him, even as a hired servant. He had brought such public dishonour on his father as he damaged the family's prosperity and totally wasted the family wealth. Would his father, let alone his elder brother and the men about him, ever let him return? Justice demanded that with rocks and stones, dogs and sticks, they would be determined to drive him away and make sure that he would never darken their doors again.

With the same thinking, the murmuring scribes and Pharisees would have kept these tax-gatherers and sinners from the kingdom of God. The people with whom the Lord Jesus was mixing and even eating had brought shame on the nation. Some had greedily devoured their fellow countrymen's wealth; fattening themselves as they collected taxes for the Romans. Some of them, the 'sinners', had soiled everything the Pharisees professed to stand for. Far from welcoming their rescue and forgiveness, the self-righteous scribes and Pharisees would have loved to have been able to drive these tax-gatherers and sinners far from God's Israel.

For this reason, the scribes and Pharisees listening to the parable would naturally expect the father to make a 'principled' and 'righteous' response to the younger son's attempt to return home. Although he was a son, they would be eager to see textbook justice applied impartially, and such a wayward son banished forever. But, to their horror, the parable takes a shocking twist. The father's intention is very different from the strict course of justice that they were expecting. It mirrors the wonderful patience and mercy of the Lord God. Maybe the father had been waiting and watching for this moment, for he saw his ragged, returning son while he was still a great way off. Eastern fathers rarely run, it is a matter of dignity and position. However, deeply moved with love and compassion, and a determination to get there before anyone else, he ran to rescue, restore and forgive his precious, starving son.

Here is the vital heart of the parable; the meeting, tempering, even replacement, of the demands of strict legal justice with mercy and compassion. The scribes and Pharisees knew nothing of such mercy, such totally undeserved forgiveness, or of such compassion; of being moved to the depths of their being, 'to their bowels', as the original Greek has it.

Compassion is a key word, often used by the Lord as he explained what he was doing and by the gospel writers as they record how the Lord Jesus was deeply moved by the lostness, pain and suffering of those before him. It was out of compassion that he taught the great crowds, healed the sick, gave sight to the blind, hearing to the deaf and set captives to evil spirits free. It was out of compassion that he was taking the trouble to help and rescue these tax collectors and sinners.

Such mercy and compassion had no place in the thinking of the scribes and Pharisees. How could you 'perfectly keep the Law' if, out of compassion, you were constantly breaking it? By healing on the

Sabbath and, as now, eating with sinners, this is exactly what the Lord Jesus was doing – and it caused the scribes and Pharisees great offence. However, mercy and compassion were the hallmarks of our Lord's ministry and have been the hallmarks of his true followers ever since.

A repentance that became deep and true

In love and pity for his son, the father's greeting was not a well-deserved, 'Get out and never come back,' nor even, 'Go and wash and I'll see you later.' But there and then, publicly, he restored and honoured his son. Filthy and stinking as he was, his father fell on his neck, embraced and welcomed him.

Matthew Henry notes that as the younger son actually comes to confess his failure and unworthiness to be regarded as a son, he did so not before – in order to win his father's favour – but after his father had embraced and welcomed him. So, clearly, by this time his sorrow for his blindness and error had become both real and deep. This was a genuine repentance, with a longing to be right with his father.

Receiving such totally undeserved and overwhelming forgiveness, the younger son poured out his confession. It was 'against heaven', against the Lord God, that he had sinned as well as before his father. He had turned his back on his father and on his duties as a son. He had pampered himself and fulfilled his desires at his father's expense and ultimately had wasted everything. He freely acknowledged that he had sinned against heaven; failed to 'honour his father', and had justly forfeited the privileges of being a son.

The younger son offered no explanations, excuses or defences. He just said, 'Father, I have sinned against heaven and before you. I am no longer worthy to be called your son.' Not, says Joseph Parker, until we both feel and own our utter unworthiness, our nothingness, will he, our heavenly Father, put all heaven into our hearts. For us to come to that point can be as long a spiritual journey, as it was a physical one for the younger son. A real and deep outpouring of the heart, in tear-stained repentance, faith and gratitude, may well be brought about, as it seems to have been in this parable, by an overwhelming awareness of the greatness of our heavenly Father's mercy and love toward us.

Richard Trench comments, '. . . and thus the truest and best repentance follows, and does not precede, the sense of forgiveness; and thus too will repentance be a thing of the whole life long, for every new insight into that forgiving love is as a new reason why the sinner should mourn that he ever sinned against it.'

The joy of heaven over one sinner who repents
With fine clothes, the father restored his son, not to slavery but to sonship. With sandals and a ring, he gave him not a position of servanthood but of authority in the household. Finally, to publicly seal the welcome and forgiveness of his son and leave no room for doubt, he ordered a lavish celebration.

Just as in the parables of the rescued sheep and recovered coin, there was great joy over the young man who 'was dead' and is alive – family, friends and neighbours rejoicing together over the son who was lost and is found. The music and feasting Jesus described in the parable, is a picture of the joy in heaven over one sinner who repents.

What a beautiful illustration of true repentance. It begins with the Holy Spirit opening our eyes to see our true and desperate situation before God and where it must lead. Such an awakening stirs us to turn our back on God-ignoring ways, and, with feeble trust, put our hopeless case before him and plead for his forgiveness. As with the younger son, such a genuine turning and seeking his forgiveness is met by the overwhelming mercy and generosity of our heavenly Father. Totally unworthy as we are, he clothes us with the robe of his righteousness, restores, forgives and adopts us as the sons and daughters of his household and calls all heaven to rejoice.

However, until we are 'awakened', we will comfortably go on in our blindness, living in this world as if we were not accountable to

God and, like the younger son, doing as we please. Or else, like the religious leaders to whom Jesus was speaking, presuming that we are fine before the Lord God and again doing as we please, but this time doing it wearing a cloak of respectability and religion.

As 'sinners' or as 'Pharisees', we desperately need to be enabled to see our true plight before Almighty God, the judge of all the earth, and our need to be right with him. Not until we see these things, will we turn to him in genuine repentance and plead for forgiveness. Not until we admit our failure to honour and obey him, will we be given, freely given, that which is of greater value than anything this world can offer – the precious 'jewel' of mercy, forgiveness and adoption as a child of God in and through his Son who told these searching parables.

The kingdom of God is filled with totally undeserving sinners who have come home to the Lord God; who have cried to him for mercy and have been given far more than any of us could ever hope for, let alone deserve. The true sons and daughters of God are made so by the totally unmerited favour of God; rescued, restored, forgiven and brought into the family by grace alone – just like the prodigal son.

Can you sing with John Newton?

> 'Amazing grace! How sweet the sound
> That saved a wretch like me.
> I once was lost, but now am found;
> Was blind, but now I see.'

Heavenly Father, have mercy upon us, show us with great clarity where we really stand before you. By your grace enable us to turn our back on our deeply-ingrained, self-seeking ways and run to you knowing that our only hope lies in your unmerited, undeserved mercy and favour offered to us in and through your Son.

Questions for reflection or discussion

1. How natural is it for us to want to break free from the 'restrictions' of godly ways and follow our own desires? Where does it ultimately lead?
2. How dangerous was it for the younger son, and can it be for us, to run out of money far from friends and family?
3. Although terrible at the time, why might the younger son come to bless God for the famine and for his desperate hunger?
4. Has the Lord God used particularly difficult times to open your eyes, draw you to himself or to speak to you?
5. How easy is it for us to presume on the forgiveness of the Lord without turning from our ungodly ways?
6. How hard is it for us to humble ourselves before our heavenly Father and acknowledge our total unworthiness of his mercy and favour?
7. How much does the love and mercy of God, found in the One 'who came to seek and to save the lost' feature in your life?

Footnote

From our Lord's vivid description, it was the need to escape death and find food to eat, that drove the younger son to return home – rather than a longing to be reconciled with his father. It was his desperate situation that drove him to pursue the only option left to him; to return to his father and to beg for mercy.

Nevertheless, if repentance can be seen as a 'journey' rather than a 'single event', the great and outward stepping stones that can lead to a true, deep and life-changing repentance are to be seen here. The Lord God has given us the pattern, 'If my people, who are called by my name, will humble themselves and pray, and seek my face and turn from their ungodly ways; then I will hear from heaven, and will forgive their sin and heal their land.' As our Lord describes the younger son resolving to return home, this pattern is followed.

His eyes opened by his desperate plight, the younger son was willing to humble himself; to admit that, without his father's mercy and help, he must inevitably perish. He was willing to plead for forgiveness without offering any excuses or claiming any merit. To do so, he was willing to seek his father's face; to make his way home and come before the father he had so dishonoured and wronged. Finally, he was willing to turn his back on the independence and freedom of the far country and on its ways, and to submit to the discipline of being a servant of his father at home.

References

Failed to honour his father, Exodus – 20:12
Robe of righteousness – Isaiah 61:10
Came to seek and to save the lost – Luke 19:10
'If my people . . .' – 2 Chronicles 7:14

The Lost Sheep, the Lost Coin, the Prodigal Son and his Elder Brother – concluded

The Return of the Elder Brother

". . . And the son said to him, 'Father, I have sinned against heaven and before you. I am no longer worthy to be called your son.' But the father said to his servants, 'Bring quickly the best robe, and put it on him, and put a ring on his hand, and shoes on his feet. And bring the fattened calf and kill it, and let us eat and celebrate. For this my son was dead, and is alive again; he was lost, and is found.' And they began to celebrate. Now his older son was in the field, and as he came and drew near to the house, he heard music and dancing. And he called one of the servants and asked what these things meant. And he said to him, 'Your brother has come, and your father has killed the fattened calf, because he has received him back safe and sound.' But he was angry and refused to go in. His father came out and entreated him, but he answered his father, 'Look, these many years I have served you, and I never disobeyed your command, yet you never gave me a young goat that I might celebrate with my friends. But when this son of yours came, who has devoured your property with prostitutes, you killed the fattened calf for him!' And he said to him, 'Son, you are always with me, and all that is mine is yours. It was fitting to celebrate and be glad, for this your brother was dead, and is alive; he was lost, and is found.'"

Luke 15:21-32 English Standard Version

The Elder Brother

I freely confess that I do not easily find 'ears to hear' this final part of the parable series. It is not comfortable, but that is almost certainly because it often, and painfully accurately, mirrors the secret inclinations of my own heart. Maybe I am not alone, and this is the reason why the elder brother is far less frequently spoken or written about.

Keeping in mind the key verse: 'Now the tax collectors and sinners were all drawing near to hear him. And the Pharisees and the scribes grumbled, saying, "This man receives sinners and eats with them."'

Was the elder brother's anger the passing anger of surprise and horror?
Full of the joy of his son restored, the father said, '. . . let us eat and celebrate, for this my son was dead, and is alive again; he was lost, and is found.' Everyone joined the celebration, sharing the father's joy – everyone, that is, except the elder brother. Will he come in? Will he join such a celebration? Will he stand alongside his father to rejoice and welcome the son who 'was lost and is found'? He most certainly will not! His anger is red hot. Coming in from the field, he discovers that, without a word to him, his father has very publicly forgiven and reinstated his dreadful brother. Even now as he approaches home, the celebration is in full swing with friends, neighbours and the wider family all there. He is absolutely furious and has no intention of celebrating such a homecoming.

Was the elder brother's anger just an instant, and understandable, flaring up of horror that a brother, who had brought such dishonour and damage to the family, could be so easily reinstated? Suddenly and unexpectedly he had a lot to come to terms with. His anger may just have been an expression of his instant inner turmoil; a blend of frustration, envy, resentment and a total inability to accept his brother's return and forgiveness, let alone this great celebration.

It is not hard for us to identify with the elder brother's heated anger and indignation. He has good reason: *He* has remained steadfast, working on the family estate. *He* has not strayed. *He* has not wasted the family wealth. *He* has not brought shame and dishonour on his father and on the family. In fact, in his view, he has been a thoroughly good and devoted son – exactly as the scribes and Pharisees saw themselves before God, as they refused to rejoice over the rescue of these dreadful and dishonourable tax-gatherers and sinners.

Or was his anger the settled anger of perceived injustice?
The father and his elder son viewed the younger son with very different eyes. Even at great cost, the father longs for the well-being of each of his sons in a way that the elder brother simply cannot imagine. The elder brother sees his younger brother's plight as his just reward; he was reaping what he had sown, so let him stay in his far country, 'stew in his own juice'. The father's longing was for the best for his son, and so strict justice was laid aside and the wayward son treated with totally undeserved mercy and kindness.

The thinking of the father and that of the elder brother were very far apart. In no sense did the elder brother share the father's joy over the safe return of his younger brother. In anger and frustration, he recognises that his father's actions have over-ridden the exclusion from the family which iron-fisted justice demanded.

Helped by his men, he could no longer justly drive away and permanently exclude his rotten, wretched, returning brother. Grace had triumphed over justice! But it was so hard to accept, as, in the elder brother's eyes, the younger son was rotten because of the great damage he had done to the prosperity of the family. He was wretched because he returned as a beggar to live the rest of his life at the family's, and what would ultimately be the elder brother's, expense.

Or was his anger the ugly anger of self-righteousness?
As Kenneth Bailey explains, in refusing to join the celebration, stand by his father and welcome home his younger brother, the elder brother, in his turn, publicly dishonoured his father and brought shame on him before the wider family and their friends and neighbours.

His father left the feast to come and speak with him, not to compel, but to entreat him to come in. But his kindness is met by an outpouring of the elder brother's anger and resentment together with an unjust accusation. 'This son of yours,' words suggesting that, at the very least, his brother should, justly, have been banished, and that to forgive and restore him to the full status of a son was showing blatant favouritism toward him. The elder brother continues this theme as he compares the killing of the fattened calf with his own lack of any reward; not even a young goat. The younger brother had undoubtedly squandered the family wealth, but nobody had accused him of wasting it on prostitutes until the elder brother did; dredging the accusation, as we can so easily do, from the darker caverns of his own imagination. And as for the calf, kept and fattened for a quite exceptional occasion, in the elder son's opinion, to kill that to celebrate the sneaking return of such a dishonourable wretch was absolutely outrageous.

As the elder brother pours out his heart and mind, it becomes painfully clear that he was not in close communion with his father and one at heart with him. Had they spoken together of the possibility of the younger son's return? Had there been a very long-standing difference of opinion, with the elder brother determined 'to see justice done'? Even the father's running to meet his younger son, in joy but also to receive him first and so stop anyone else intervening, suggests that there was not a common mind concerning his possible return and that the elder brother had a settled rejection of him – just as the scribes and Pharisees had for these tax gatherers and sinners, their fallen but fellow sons and daughters of God's Israel.

Has the father one or two estranged sons?

Notice the elder brother's vainly imagined superiority, 'he would never do such a thing'. His assumption, that he deserved better treatment than he was being given; at the very least 'a young goat to celebrate with his friends.' His technical correctness, years of service and obedience, and yet his total lack of family affection, grace or humanity toward his fallen, but now rescued, brother. The younger son may have displayed obvious, self-indulgent failures; the elder brother's sin was hidden. It was spiritual and mental and yet here it begins to show itself in attitudes of pride and arrogance, and of disdain – attitudes that so closely mirrored those of the scribes and Pharisees.

It appears that, although the elder son was dutiful, his relationship with his father was now completely broken over this issue of the younger son's welcomed return. He was aware that anything spent on the younger son, now or in the future, was at his expense. So, even the cost of this feast, and in particular the killing of the fattened calf, left him just that much less to inherit. Although unspoken, might we reasonably conclude that, just as much as the younger brother, he longed for the day when he could inherit the estate, do as he will and celebrate with his friends as and when he pleased?

Although the father clearly shows his appreciation for his elder son's steadiness and support, 'You are always with me,' and assures him that he already has great freedom and that the total remaining estate would fall to him, 'All that is mine is yours,' it seems that the father has not one, but two lost sons. The younger one 'cut free' and went far from him. The elder one remained physically close, but in heart and mind was at least as distant from him.

The scribes and Pharisees were experts in the laws and practice of religion, but were strangers to the heart and compassion of the One they professed to serve. Our Lord's picture of the elder brother strikingly illustrates his quotation from Isaiah on an earlier occasion. Describing the religion of the scribes and Pharisees, he said, '. . . this people honours me with their lips, but their hearts are far from me . . .'

A challenge to the scribes and Pharisees then – and to ourselves today
Did the elder brother come in and join the feast? Would he stand alongside his father and rejoice with him in the restoration of his brother? We are not told. The question and the invitation are left with the scribes and Pharisees – and with those of us in every generation who feel that we are more respectable, more religious, more dutiful

and more devoted than others, and are, therefore, more worthy of the Lord God's favour.

Like the elder brother, how easy it is to despise those who have fallen, and how natural to find it hard to accept the mercy, generosity and grace the Lord God shows toward such people. We have not sunk to such depths, and so, like the scribes and Pharisees before us, count ourselves above them; without need of such forgiveness – and so without need of repentance.

As the scribes and Pharisees compared themselves with the fallen tax-gatherers and sinners, they were essentially proud that they had not fallen, as was the elder brother of our Lord's parable. However, pride and self-righteousness before the Almighty and All-Holy God are the most deep-rooted of offences and the greatest of barriers to entering the kingdom of heaven.

The old proverb has it that we should not judge a man until we have walked a few miles in his shoes; actively recognising and reminding ourselves that '. . . there, but for the grace of God, go I.' Why? – because, sadly, as the Bible teaches, in the thinking of those at ease there can so easily be contempt for those who have stumbled; 'whose feet have slipped,' or who have been overtaken by misfortune.

Matthew Henry so helpfully points out that, confronted with other people's tumbles, rather than allowing ourselves to feel a touch of pride, we should be humbly grateful before the Lord God for his hand on our lives: – Grateful that we have been spared the genetic inclination or overwhelming desire that has caused a fellow sinner to fall. – Grateful for the more helpful or more godly environment in which we have grown up. – Grateful that the worldly or 'fleshly' people, with whom we have mixed, have not dragged or enticed us into their ways. – Grateful that desperate shortage of money or other dire circumstances have not driven us to such depths.

The scribes and Pharisees had just such a helpful environment around them. They were a well-bred, religious 'middle class,' set aside to study godly ways. They were surrounded by men with the same aim, and so they were greatly helped not to stray or fall by both the company they kept and by their studies of the Scriptures. They were also spared from the poverty to which the common people were subjected, and had both social status and honour heaped on them. They really had no excuse for pride and arrogance; only for humble and on-going gratitude. However, that is not the way fallen human nature takes us!

An ever-present danger

The parable was addressed to the scribes and Pharisees. But there are those who assume they are worthy of the favour of God found in every generation of the church. In fact, it is a great danger for those who have grown up in the church.

Surrounded by the people of God and the things of God we naturally assume that we are truly part of God's favoured people. After all, we share the same rituals, talk the same language and adopt the same habits and customs. And yet some of the most solemn words fell from the Lord's lips as he warned that on the last day many will say to him, 'Lord, Lord, have we not preached in your name . . . and done many mighty things in your name' and he responds with frightening finality, 'I never knew you, depart from me . . .' To how many busy and esteemed church leaders and members will our Lord have to say those words – some of the most terrifying words in the New Testament – 'I never knew you . . .'?

Even as a ransomed and forgiven child of God, after some years in the church, how easy it is to step into the elder brother's shoes and find ourselves secretly or openly satisfied when natural justice takes its course and ungodly ways lead to a fall. Like the elder brother, we can easily find ourselves all but resenting the free forgiveness of 'totally unworthy' people. Or, like him, feel that, taking into account all our years of devoted service, the Lord in some way owes us his favour – surely we deserve the equivalent of 'a young goat to celebrate with our friends;' and so be spared from some hardship or illness, or caused to flourish in some way.

If we grasp the Lord's great lesson taught in this parable, we will come before Almighty God as empty-handed as the returning prodigal son. Like him, none of us actually has anything to offer, indeed, justice demands our banishment. When we see this we will come to him pleading for mercy and forgiveness and subsequently asking, each day, for fresh forgiveness. Only then will we live a life of deep and on-going gratitude, and share the joy of heaven over each fellow sinner who repents; each person rescued and brought home to our heavenly Father.

One 'Elder Brother' Pharisee whose heart was totally changed
This series of parables clearly reflects how much God our heavenly Father and his Son, the Lord Jesus Christ, care about wayward and stumbling humanity. But the final section of the series displays how our heavenly Father also cares deeply about religiously-inclined people who are mistakenly convinced of their own self-made righteousness – like the scribes and Pharisees to whom Jesus was speaking. The picture of the return of the elder brother shows how our heavenly Father seeks to entreat people who share his kind of thinking, to put aside our pride and come in. In these parables we have set before us 'the joy of heaven over one sinner who repents' – be they wayward and fallen, or outwardly respectable and religious.

'. . . circumcised on the eighth day, of the people of Israel, of the tribe of Benjamin . . . as to righteousness, under the law blameless' writes that former Pharisee, the apostle Paul. But with deep gratitude he also writes, 'This is a true saying and worthy of acceptance by everyone, that Christ Jesus came into the world to save sinners, of whom I am the chief.'

Inscribed over the arch of the doorway of a little church – through which minister, church officers and people must pass – are the words of the murmuring scribes and Pharisees, 'This man receiveth sinners.' I, for one, have cause to praise God that he did and still does.

By the pulpit in another ancient church is a memorial tablet of the local, nineteenth-century Squire. It has his name, dates and then three short texts, clearly of his own choosing, '. . . God, be merciful to me, a sinner.' 'Jesus said, "I am the way, and the truth and the life; no man comes to the Father but by me". ' 'I know whom I have believed.' Could such words be put on our memorial stone? For Squire, Parson and people there was, and still is, only one way – just as there was for tax-collectors and sinners, and for scribes and Pharisees.

'Not by deeds of righteousness which we have done,' writes the apostle Paul, 'but according to his mercy he saved us . . .'

True repentance begins when we see, with horror, where we truly stand before Almighty God, turn from own ways and plead with him for mercy. With overwhelming grace and forgiveness, he comes to meet us where we are, either 'to bring us home', as with the younger son; or 'to bring us in', as with the elder son.

Heavenly Father, have mercy upon us, show us with great clarity where we really stand before you. Enable us to turn our back on our determination to be the master of our own destiny and on our dutiful attempts to earn your favour, and bow our knee to you, recognising that our only hope lies in your unmerited and undeserved mercy.

Questions for reflection or discussion

1. Who might correspond in our society to the tax-gatherers and sinners?
2. Could you rejoice over their rescue and restoration; first to the Lord God and then to mainstream society?

3. How easily do we 'step into the elder brother's shoes' as we look in judgement on others and make assumptions concerning ourselves?

4. To what extent do we wrestle with the teaching of this parable, that all we ever hope for from the Lord God is always by his goodness and grace and never because we have earned his favour?

5. How easy is it for church and chapel folk to be correct and dutiful yet loveless and joyless in the things of God? What might underlie this?

6. Had the apostle Paul discovered something wonderful? What was it?

References

This people honour me with their lips, but their hearts . . .' – Isaiah 29:13, Matthew 15:8, Mark 7:6

Contempt for those who have stumbled – Job 12:5

I never knew you – Matthew 7:21-23

Circumcised on the eighth day – Philippians 3:5&6

Of whom I am the chief – 1 Timothy 1:15

God, be merciful to me, a sinner – Luke 18:13

I am the way, the truth and the life – John 14:6

I know whom I have believed – 2 Timothy 1:12

Not by deeds of righteousness – Titus 3:5

The Dishonest Manager

He also said to the disciples, "There was a rich man who had a manager, and charges were brought to him that this man was wasting his possessions. And he called him and said to him, 'What is this that I hear about you? Turn in the account of your management, for you can no longer be manager.' And the manager said to himself, 'What shall I do, since my master is taking the management away from me? I am not strong enough to dig, and I am ashamed to beg. I have decided what to do, so that when I am removed from management, people may receive me into their houses.' So, summoning his master's debtors one by one, he said to the first, 'How much do you owe my master?' He said, 'A hundred measures of oil.' He said to him, 'Take your bill, and sit down quickly and write fifty.' Then he said to another, 'And how much do you owe?' He said, 'A hundred measures of wheat.' He said to him, 'Take your bill, and write eighty.' The master commended the dishonest manager for his shrewdness. For the sons of this world are more shrewd in dealing with their own generation than the sons of light. And I tell you, make friends for yourselves by means of unrighteous wealth, so that when it fails they may receive you into the eternal dwellings.

"One who is faithful in a very little is also faithful in much, and one who is dishonest in a very little is also dishonest in much. If then you have not been faithful in the unrighteous wealth, who will entrust to you the true riches? . . . No servant can serve two masters, for either he will hate the one and love the other, or he will be devoted to the one and despise the other. You cannot serve God and money." The Pharisees, who were lovers of money, heard all these things, and they ridiculed him.

Luke 16:1-15, English Standard Version

The Dishonest Manager

Here is Jesus' teaching on the godly use of this world's opportunities and of wealth. The Pharisees despised his teaching, but disciples can learn much from it. Yet, what is this? The Lord Jesus would appear to be holding up, as an example for disciples to follow, a thoroughly dishonest man; a man who provided for his own future by taking advantage of the one who trusted him and making friends by giving away his master's income!

It is a parable that has puzzled and greatly embarrassed the church for centuries. Way back in AD 355, Julian became the Roman Emperor. He was the last of Constantine's Christian dynasty and he rejected Christianity in favour of paganism arguing, from this parable, the inferiority of the Christian faith and of the Lord Jesus Christ. It clearly is a parable that causes many to stumble.

Yet, to teach true godliness, the Lord Jesus did sometimes use bad men in his parables. For example, the unjust judge – not to teach the idle neglect of an injustice, as was shown by that judge, but to teach persistence in faith and prayer, the kind of steadfast persistence shown by the widow. Or, the man who would not help his neighbour with bread late at night, until that neighbour continued shamelessly to knock on his door – not to teach us to tell those in need to go away, but to teach us to really mean business with the Lord God in prayer, like the neighbour who persisted with his request for bread.

In looking at the parable of the dishonest manager, we need to be careful to hear what the Lord Jesus Christ is teaching and not be tripped up by what he is not teaching. The key seems to be in avoiding hastily assuming that the Lord is commending dishonesty.

The rich man and his manager
A rich man had appointed a manager who had his master's authority to administer his affairs. As many wealthy people have found, there is always a risk of being cheated by doing that, and after a time the man-

ager was charged with wasting his master's wealth. (The same word is used of the prodigal son's wasteful and extravagant spending in the far country.) The manager faced being called to account and dismissed. He offers no defence or excuse; he is silent, aware that the facts and figures will make only too plain the truth of the accusation.

'Turn in the account of your management, for you can no longer be manager.' Those words meant he was about to lose both his job and his home. Clearly, he needed to make preparation for what lay ahead, and to do so without delay.

What was he going to do? He was unwilling or unable to do heavy physical work – to dig – and was too proud to beg, but he uses his brains, 'I know!' 'I have decided what to do, so that when I am removed from management, people may receive me into their houses.' And he took the opportunity the remaining hours that his position as manager gave him to secure his own future. In doing so, he was forward-looking, clear-thinking and shrewd.

(Understandably, to avoid the possibility of such advantage being taken, modern employees about to be made redundant are often escorted straight from their place of work to the manager's office and then to the door.)

The debts the manager adjusted

There have been many suggestions regarding the nature of the debts, but clearly, without consulting his master, the manager greatly reduced the amount each debtor owed.

The manager could have removed the interest that had been agreed at the outset, but which over time had grown substantially on each debt. As interest charged to fellow Hebrews was forbidden, it would be extremely clever. It would win the manager great favour with the debtors, and his master could not possibly go to court to retrieve it, as the original unlawful agreement would be exposed.

Alternatively, as Kenneth Bailey suggests, the instruction, 'Take your bill, sit down quickly and write . . .' would very comfortably fit with an adjustment to a land rental agreement. A tenant farmer has the use of the land and agrees to settle by a set amount of the produce after harvest. The Lord Jesus refers to this kind of agreement in the parable of the vineyard tenants, the servants being sent to collect their master's portion of the vineyard harvest.

In the parable of the unjust manager, the manager's discreet conversations with the debtors could have been something like this, 'You agreed to a hundred measures, quickly sit down and replace that agreement for fifty, and I'll sign it.' 'You agreed to a hundred measures; sit down and rewrite the agreement for eighty, and I'll sign it.' And, of course, he made friends of the debtors, who would welcome him to their homes. It was wise because it provided for his future. It was clever because it made both his master and himself greatly appreciated for being generous, and in a close-knit, country community that is of great value. No one is going to be hasty to undo that. If that was the manager's plan, it was clever and it was shrewd.

We do not know for certain what kind of cunning wisdom the manager used, but his master commended him for it. His master did not commend him for his dishonesty; he is named as being 'dishonest'. The master commended him for his forethought and his clear-thinking, his shrewdness and his decisive action in the challenging situation in which he found himself.

Matthew Henry writes, the master 'of that servant, who, though he could not but be angry at his knavery, yet was pleased with his ingenuity and policy for himself . . .' 'He does not commend him because he had done falsely to his master, but because he had done wisely for himself.'

By this parable, the Lord challenged his hearers to learn from the manager – not sharp practice and dishonesty – but to learn clear-thinking and forward-looking use of the limited time and opportunities we have. The Lord's challenge is to be as clear and active with regard to our eternal future, as the manager was in preparing for his earthly future.

Yet again, this is very far from a comfortable parable. It is a clarion call for those who have ears to hear, believers and unbelievers alike, to a searching re-alignment of our life, lifestyle and priorities in the light of eternity. It is a warning to be noted, for, as the Lord said, 'The sons of this generation are wiser, are shrewder, in their affairs than the sons of light.'

How did the parable apply to Jesus' hearers, and how does it apply to us today?
Firstly, it is a word of warning to those who, like the Pharisees, would scoff and ridicule, and a call to those, who, like many in the listening crowd of Jesus' day, have yet to believe; have yet to realise who the Lord Jesus truly is and what he came to do.

Even if, like the Pharisees, we choose not to acknowledge it, or, like the ordinary people, we are as yet unaware of it, life itself, our very breath and all our circumstances, are a trust from God to be used for his honour. We are stewards of all that we have and of all that we are, and we will be called to account for the way we have used the one life entrusted to us. That is a terrifying prospect, for, like the manager in the parable, each one of us will be found to have fallen short, wasted and squandered our time, our opportunities, or even life itself.

Wisdom demands that we cry to the Lord God for mercy, for pardon and a fresh new start – now – before we are called to account.

Then secondly, it is a challenge to disciples to whom the parable was primarily addressed. Jesus challenged his hearers then, and present-day disciples, to note well the worldly wisdom of the dishonest manager as he made the best use of the opportunity to prepare for his future, and so learn the spiritual wisdom of looking to our eternal future and making our top priority preparation for that.

Jesus' hearers then, and we in our day, are stewards or managers of the time, the money and the opportunities that the Lord God entrusts to us. Here, our Lord teaches us to use each of these with an eye to the day when, like the manager of the parable, we shall be called to give an account, and to the days beyond that day.

By way of the parable, the Lord challenges disciples to learn from the manager and see everything in the light of eternity. This will have a very direct bearing on how we live now; it will involve our whole life and lifestyle. It is a call to a life submitted to the Lord Jesus and pleasing before our heavenly Father. The challenge is to prepare, so that when the things of earth can be enjoyed no more, there will be a joyful homecoming.

Our Lord gives us a picture of clear-sighted wisdom. Yet we can so easily fail to apply such wisdom to the opportunities we have to live to the glory of God, and to do so in the light of his calling us to account. "For the sons of this world are more shrewd in dealing with their own generation than the sons of light."

Some practical examples of the application of the parable
The parable is a challenge to use the time this short life affords wisely. In this setting of limited time, our Lord calls us to use our opportunities, our money and our abilities for the kingdom of God and to do so in the light of our own eternal destination.

Our time – The man's remaining time as manager was very short, as our time on earth may be, but he used it well. He did not let it slip away in entertainment or side issues. He did not slip idly into poverty. The people of this world, this generation, said the Lord Jesus, are, in their own situation, wiser; more clear-thinking and better at looking ahead and seizing the opportunities given them, than are many godly folk.

The parable is a challenge to learn from such worldly folk. For example, picture an athlete with an eye on a gold medal, dieting, training, resting and putting aside every other interest – all with the single purpose of winning that medal. Or, picture the self-employed business man; continually travelling, bargaining, making contacts and friends – clearly focused on getting the business off the ground and making money. The call is for disciples to be equally focused and clear with regard to the kingdom of heaven.

The apostles set us a fine example of making such godly use of the time and the opportunities given them. Enabled by the Holy Spirit, Peter stood to preach to the great crowd that had gathered because of the events of Pentecost. Peter clearly explained to them who Jesus truly is, and what they had done by his crucifixion, and he called on his fellow countrymen to repent and believe. Or take the example of the apostle Paul who never ceased to take every opportunity the Lord gave him to proclaim, persuade and implore his hearers to be reconciled with God. Paul preached in synagogues, in public places, before city leaders, governors and kings. Even in prison, he spoke of the things of God to both guards and visitors and made full use of his time of imprisonment writing the letters to the churches.

Our opportunities – For parents with children, there is just a short window of opportunity when our children listen to us and long to please us. Then in their teens, they are off and on their way in the world and, in their eyes, we are often an embarrassment and all but irrelevant – except in such matters as the giving of lifts and money, providing food and doing their washing! The challenge of the parable is that we make full use of the opportunity of those early years; making time for the youngsters, praying for them and with them, talking with them about everything and especially about the things of God. It is so easy for that godly priority to be squeezed out until it is too late, to our own and to our children's great loss.

Our homes – the manager was about to be thrown out of his home and wanted to be welcomed to other people's homes. Who do we invite into our homes and why? If we are able, could we use them for the Lord, to encourage fellow disciples or help those seeking to become disciples? Certainly, this is the New Testament pattern. Cornelius brought Peter into his home and invited him to speak to the many people gathered there. Lydia, a trader in purple goods and a lady of wealth, on believing and being baptised, opened her home to the apostle Paul and it became a meeting place for fellow believers in Philippi. Concluding his epistle to the Romans, the apostle Paul writes his greetings to Prisca and Aquila and 'the church in their house'. It seems that the New Testament churches met in homes, and the opening of homes for the Lord has been a consistent mark of times of spiritual awakening and revival.

Our Money – the manager used the money entrusted to him by his master to secure his own future. As Jesus concludes the parable, he continues to speak of our use of the wealth God entrusts to us, as our attitude to wealth is a very telling measure of our walk with the Lord God. We can gather it entirely for our own use, or we can recognise it to be the trust it is, and use it for the honour of our Lord.

'"And I tell you, make friends for yourselves by means of unrighteous wealth, so that when it fails they may receive you into the eternal dwellings . . . No servant can serve two masters, for either he will hate the one and love the other, or he will be devoted to the one and despise the other. You cannot serve God and money." The Pharisees, who were lovers of money, heard all these things, and they ridiculed him.'

The Pharisees, as the Greek has it, 'lifted their noses' in scorn and contempt, but for the true disciple, here is the challenge to be honest and faithful in all our dealings, and to use the wealth we have with an eye on eternity. Certainly, we are to take proper care of ourselves and those who depend on us, but could we also use it like the Good Samaritan to help someone in need? Could we use it to help forward the work of the kingdom of heaven, like the disciples at Philippi who sent gifts to support the apostle Paul as he proclaimed the gospel and planted churches?

In what way is wealth, 'unrighteous wealth'? Wealth in itself is neutral. God-given and honestly gained, wealth can be a great blessing to ourselves and to many others. However, gaining wealth is very addictive and can easily become the all-consuming devotion of our hearts and minds. It is also often associated with unrighteousness – the very opposite of godliness – if we defraud or cheat, overcharge or underpay to gain it, or perhaps spend it entirely on ourselves and for our pleasure, maybe, even in very ungodly ways.

Keeping an eye on heaven
By way of the parable, the Lord is challenging disciples to use the time, the opportunities and the wealth entrusted to us faithfully before the Lord, so that 'they may receive you into heavenly dwelling places'. Who are the 'they' referred to in this verse? It could be those you've helped – but it is much more likely to be a Hebrew and Aramaic way of avoiding the name of God. So 'they' means a heavenly welcome by the Lord himself.

In the parable of the talents, our Lord paints a wonderful picture of the welcome to heaven given to a faithful servant who has used well the time, the opportunities and the wealth entrusted to him. 'Well done good and faithful servant . . . enter into the joy of your lord.' Are not such words of our Lord something, for those who believe, to covet most of all, and to constantly keep our eye on? They will keep us on course in every department of life.

The Emperor Julian stumbled, the Pharisees scoffed, but let true disciples learn from the manager of the Lord's parable, not from his dishonesty, but from the ungodly man's focus on, and provision for, the future. The Lord was challenging his hearers then, and all of us now, to look ahead and prepare for eternity.

If we take it to heart, this parable will constantly help us to think clearly, with an eye on the kingdom of heaven, and to set our priorities accordingly – for each one of us will be called to give an account.

Heavenly Father, here are words of your Son our Lord Jesus Christ which the Emperor Julian found useful in rejecting Christianity and words which caused the Pharisees, who were lovers of money, to scoff. Help us to humbly read, mark, learn and inwardly digest them – for our own usefulness in this life, for our eternal wellbeing and for the glory of your name.

Questions for reflection and discussion

1. Why did the Pharisees scoff and the Emperor Julian stumble?
2. Can we learn good things from bad men?
3. What are the risks of entrusting our affairs into the hands of another?
4. To what extent are all our possessions, skills, talents and even life itself a trust from God?
5. In what ways can we be challenged by the manager's clear and forward-thinking and by his decisive action in preparing for his future?
6. In the busy-ness of life, how easy is it for eternal priorities to become blurred?
7. How can we encourage one another to effectively buy up the opportunities we have?

References

The unjust judge – Luke 18:1-8
The neighbour at midnight – Luke 11:5-8
The Prodigal son – Luke 15:13
Charging fellow Hebrews interest forbidden – Deuteronomy 23:19-20

The vineyard tenants – Luke 20:9&10
Picture an athlete – 1 Corinthians 9:25
Peter at Pentecost – Acts 2:14-41
The apostle Paul, '. . . be reconciled with God' – 2 Corinthians 5:20
Cornelius brought Peter – Acts 10:9-33
Lydia opened her home to the apostle Paul – Acts 16:14&15 and v.40
Prisca and Aquila and the church that met in their house – Romans 16:3-5
The Good Samaritan – Luke 10:25-37
The Philippians' gift – Philippians 4:10-20
'Well done good and faithful servant' – Matthew 25:21&23

The Rich Man and Lazarus

No servant can serve two masters, for either he will hate the one and love the other, or he will be devoted to the one and despise the other. You cannot serve God and money.

The Pharisees, who were lovers of money, heard all these things, and they ridiculed him. And he said to them, "You are those who justify yourselves before men, but God knows your hearts. For what is exalted among men is an abomination in the sight of God.

"The Law and the Prophets were until John; since then the good news of the kingdom of God is preached, and everyone forces his way into it. But it is easier for heaven and earth to pass away than for one dot of the Law to become void.

"Everyone who divorces his wife and marries another commits adultery, and he who marries a woman divorced from her husband commits adultery.

"There was a rich man who was clothed in purple and fine linen and who feasted sumptuously every day. And at his gate was laid a poor man named Lazarus, covered with sores, who desired to be fed with what fell from the rich man's table. Moreover, even the dogs came and licked his sores. The poor man died and was carried by the angels to Abraham's side. The rich man also died and was buried, and in Hades, being in torment, he lifted up his eyes and saw Abraham far off and Lazarus at his side. And he called out, 'Father Abraham, have mercy on me, and send Lazarus to dip the end of his finger in water and cool my tongue, for I am in anguish in this flame.' But Abraham said, 'Child, remember that you in your lifetime received your good things, and Lazarus in like manner bad things; but now he is comforted here, and you are in anguish. And besides all this, between us and you a great chasm has been fixed, in order that those who would pass from here to you may not be able, and none may cross from there to us.' And he said, 'Then I beg you, father, to send him to my father's house— for I have five brothers —so that he may warn them, lest they also come into this place of torment.' But Abraham said, 'They have Moses and the Prophets; let them hear them.' And he said, 'No, father Abraham, but if someone goes to them from the dead, they will repent.' He said to him, 'If they do not hear Moses and the Prophets, neither will they be convinced if someone should rise from the dead.'"

Luke 16:13-31, English Standard Version

The Rich Man and Lazarus – Part 1

First, the setting of the parable
There is a clear link between the two parables in this chapter. At the beginning of the chapter, Luke records Jesus' teaching concerning position, opportunity and money; teaching disciples to see these things as a trust from the Lord God to be used to bring honour to his name, and to be used with an eye to heaven. The Lord Jesus illustrates his teaching with the parable of the manager who is called to submit his accounts.

But the Pharisees, overhearing this teaching, scoffed, 'lifted their noses' in disdain. Although there were noble exceptions, the majority of the Pharisees, and certainly their high-born colleagues the Sadducees, loved money, power, position, and prestige and used these things to further their own agenda and for their own earthly pleasure.

It is easy to assume that the parable of the Rich Man and Lazarus is a challenge to disciples to give generously to those in need. The parable is often used in this way by charities seeking to raise money. But our Lord was speaking to the Pharisees, laying bare the root cause of both their ridiculing of his teaching and of their lack of compassion towards the poor and needy.

'The Pharisees, who were lovers of money . . .' despite their outward religious devotion, the key to understanding the parable is the unbelief of the Pharisees. In unbelief we are either unaware – or choose to ignore – the fact that we are accountable to the Lord God for everything he entrusts to us. Without an awareness of our accountability, it is easy to hoard wealth for ourselves, as in the parable of the rich farmer, or to squander it on ourselves, as did the rich man of this parable

As he told of the manager's use of time and money, our Lord painted a picture of genuine faith – by the way it works itself out in our lives and its heavenly consequences. Responding to the ridicule of the Pharisees, this second parable is the other side of the same coin; a mirror image of the earlier one. As he described the rich man's life and final destiny, Jesus painted a picture of unbelief – by the way it expresses itself in the way we live and its eternal consequences.

Religious devotion that can conceal actual unbelief
In the parable of the rich man and Lazarus, the Lord drew attention to three of the ways the unbelief of the scribes and Pharisees displayed itself. The first was their lack of concern for the ordinary people, the poor, the fallen and the suffering – such as the tax-gatherers and sinners of the previous chapter. The second was their assumption, fed by the relative wealth they enjoyed and the law-abiding life they pursued, that, as a matter of course, they were assured of a place with Abraham in heavenly bliss. The third was their totally blind eyes and deaf ears to those parts of the Scriptures, 'Moses and the prophets,' that challenged their traditions and current thinking. Despite their religious status and the public esteem in which they were held, each of these was an outward expression of the deep ungodliness of their hearts – their unbelief.

The Pharisees' priority was the strict keeping of the Law of Moses, as it had become interpreted over the years. However, this meticulous observance had become separated from a vital walk with the Lord God. It had become an end in itself; formal, cold and judgemental.

Instead of the love and joy of true faith and humble, obedient, godly living, their observance was a religious display overlying a very worldly pursuit of wealth. No wonder they sniffed in disdain at the Lord's teaching!

The Pharisees had become relatively rich. But spiritually they were bankrupt. Wealth and position had obscured any awareness of accountability before God and they had become, in our Lord's words, 'exalted among men and yet an abomination in the sight of God'. Although man looks on the external things, the Lord God looks on the heart.

The whole of Scripture, not just the parts that accord with our own thinking

It was to these religious, successful and highly respected men, who were confident of their place at Abraham's side, that the Lord Jesus addressed this terrifying parable. He warned them – and us – of the great danger of regarding lightly the warnings and instructions the Lord God has given us in his word.

The Pharisees were the guardians of God's word, and yet taught a human interpretation of it. Hence those brief references to God's law and to divorce which, over the years, they had 're-interpreted' to make more acceptable or, as the Lord implied, to render them empty of content; to cause 'the law to become void'.

In a religious setting, the Pharisees read and publicly expounded God's word, Moses and the Prophets, every Sabbath. However, despite their meticulous observation of some parts of the law, they did not allow the less comfortable parts to challenge their thinking or change the way they lived; their lack of love towards the Lord God and their neighbour, their failure to fulfil their God-given responsibility as under-shepherds of God's people, their assumed superiority over ordinary people and their utter disdain for those less fortunate than themselves.

Although circumstances differ, these same dangers and temptations constantly attend the leaders of God's household. Those among us called to be 'shepherds' do well to take note of the very great responsibility we have before Almighty God. We are not called to be 'esteemed persons in our society', however much that flatters our ego, but to be patterns of humble, strong and steady godly living. We are not called to be heralds of our own opinions, setting ourselves over God's word and 're-interpreting' it to comfortably fit the thinking of our age, but rather, called to be heralds of God as we submit our own lives to his word and encourage others to do the same.

The parable itself

A very rich man; the finest of food, the richest of clothes – purple dyed, the most sought-after in the ancient world. Even the Greek word used for the 'gate' of his house implies that it was a splendid gate. Rich and successful, the admiration of all; no one would condemn such a man, all would speak well of him.

There is no hint of fraud or oppression and it is no sin to be rich, to wear fine clothes or to keep a rich and generous table. Abraham, who is pictured in this parable in the joy of heaven, was a very rich man – but he walked in humble obedience to the Lord God. The snare of wealth is that we feel no need of God and so, forgetful of him and of his goodness to us, walk in self-confidence and pride, often despising or even oppressing those less fortunate than ourselves.

It was not for nothing that the writer of Proverbs prays, 'Give me neither great wealth nor poverty, lest in plenty I forget you or in poverty I steal and so take your name in vain.' The Lord Jesus did not condemn wealth – but taught that wisdom, authority, position and wealth are each an awesome trust from God to be used to bring glory to him.

'Is a man's spiritual state to be judged by his earthly condition?' asks Matthew Henry. It is a good question. Here, in our Lord's parable, was a man of prestige and plenty who everyone, including himself, would naturally assume was on his way to heavenly joy. But horror! He is actually on his way to God's just judgement and to the torment of hell. As our Lord said, it is clearly possible for that which is held in high esteem among men to be an abomination before God. We must never assume that prestige, peace and plenty here and now are the promise of heaven to come. Indeed, Psalm 73 would teach us that, while godless folk flourish, it is often the lot of some of the dearest saints of God to suffer dreadfully in this world.

But neither must we conclude that great wealth leads to God's condemnation and that poverty leads to his blessing. It is sometimes assumed, mistakenly, that those who suffer or are in poverty here on earth, automatically have a place in heaven. Heaven is equally open to believing people who have well used the good health and riches entrusted to them, or who have patiently endured the lack of them. In heaven, 'poor' Lazarus shares the company of 'rich' Abraham. The apostle Paul displays the godly pattern. He had learned to rest content in the Lord in plenty or in need.

And so to the poor man, who, unusually, is named; a fact that has caused some to question whether this is a parable. The name he is given is Lazarus, Eleazar – 'God will help' or 'God my helper'. Here is the first hint of his trust in the Lord God. He was, humanly, helpless. His friends and family had done what they could in bringing him to the gate. But here he was, a despised and hungry beggar, grateful for crumbs, full of sores which the street dogs licked. He had no possibility of earning a living, there were no public services to help, and there was no money for medical help. Yet, in our Lord's parable, there is no hint from his lips of murmuring or grumbling because of his plight. He appears patient and longsuffering. In heaven he does not gloat when he sees that the roles are totally reversed, and he offers no objection when the rich man assumes that he may be used first as his servant and then as his errand boy. Taken together, these all suggest that the Lord's picture is of a godly man who in this world was in a desperate situation. Although it was hidden from sight by his terrible circumstances, here was a man who was precious before Almighty God.

In his plight, Lazarus was laid at the gate of the rich man who was one to whom God had entrusted so much, one of 'God's treasurers'. Will he help? Well, he might send a few crumbs, the left-over scraps that neither he nor his servants want. Such action did nothing to address Lazarus' great needs. It cost the rich man nothing but in doing so he would doubtless consider that he had fulfilled his charitable duty. The Pharisees' public acts of alms-giving satisfied them in much the same way. To the rich man, Lazarus is just part of the scene; one of the many beggars. He does not have him removed but, perhaps as a way of coping with one more among so many people in need, he just does not notice him.

An ever-present danger

To avoid the pit into which the unbelieving Pharisees and the rich man of the parable had fallen, a growing and true belief will cause us to see property and wealth and everything we have as 'that part of God's total creation for which we are personally responsible,' a trust from God, to be used for his glory, and for the well-being of those around us. Not to be used to encourage dependency or idleness, but to set free those trapped by the lack of what we can provide.

Could the rich man have significantly helped this one man laid at his gate; personally brought to his attention? Although he knew him well enough to recognise him and to know his name, the rich man in his plenty does not seem to have considered it. Would we . . . ?

Questions for reflection or discussion

1. How easy is it for those of us who are spiritual leaders today to fall into the trap of relishing power, prestige or wealth for ourselves, rather than using them to further the kingdom of heaven?
2. Can those who are called to be heralds of God's truth still prefer to promote human opinions and 'interpretations' of that truth?
3. Like the Pharisees, how easy is it to be familiar with Scripture, – and yet not let it challenge or change the way we think and live?
4. Abraham was a very rich man. Can you think of wealthy men and women in more recent times who have walked humbly with the Lord God and used their wealth and position for his glory?
5. How does it help us set priorities if we see all that we have and all that we are as a trust from Almighty God, to be held in stewardship for him?
6. Do we know anything of the Christian contentment spoken of by the apostle Paul? Is it a characteristic of our society?
7. Are there people, brought to our attention; 'laid at our gate' who are in genuine need and who we could and, before the Lord God, should be actively helping?

References

The Lord God looks on the heart – 1 Samuel 16:7

The danger of wealth . . . we can trust in it and deny or ignore God – Proverbs 30 8&9

Paul content in need or plenty – Philippians 4:10-13

The Rich Man and Lazarus – part 2

'The poor man died and was carried by the angels to Abraham's side. The rich man also died and was buried, and in Hades, being in torment, he lifted up his eyes and saw Abraham far off and Lazarus at his side. And he called out, "Father Abraham, have mercy on me, and send Lazarus to dip the end of his finger in water and cool my tongue, for I am in anguish in this flame."'

Beyond this life and its circumstances

In time, Lazarus died. But so, too, did the rich man. Death is the great leveller. We all 'lie down in the dust,' says Job and that, maybe, sooner than we would like to think.

To the human eye, the poor man was just a nuisance; begging at the rich man's gate, attracting the dogs and detracting from the magnificence of the gateway. His departure would be of little interest to anyone; the rich man, however, being a jewel of society, would be greatly missed.

The Lord did not say 'The rich man died and all heaven was there to welcome him. The poor man also died and his remains were gathered to the common grave.' He said the very opposite; words to shake and awaken the unbelieving religious leaders from their proud assumptions.

'The poor man died and was carried by the angels to Abraham's side.' Lazarus was carried to recline in the place of honour beside Abraham. This is a Hebrew picture of heaven; a child of faith with the father of faith in the presence of God. No more hunger, no more sores, carried for the last time – but this time by the angels of God. Here is God's special care for those on whom he has set his love.

The rich man also died, but unlike the poor man, his body was given a fine burial. Note our Lord's words, spoken only of the rich man, '. . . and was buried.' Even in death, the rich man maintained the pride and position of his past life – but his destiny was not to be transported by angels to Abraham's side, but to find himself in Hades. In Old Testament usage, Hades was the shadowy home of the departed, but for the rich man of this parable it was clearly the place of God's just judgement.

Unlike the disposal of Lazarus' body, the rich man's burial would have been characterised by dignified ceremony; the laying to rest of one thought of by his friends as, 'a fine-living man whose table was never lacking.' Yet, hear his cries from Hades, 'I am in torment in this flame,' just 'a drop of water,' Oh, 'to warn my brothers.'

We must not press the parable too far. Our Lord was not inviting his hearers, or Luke's readers today, to pry into the mysteries of the hereafter. But he was making plain the reality of the life beyond this one, and of the absolute justice of God. The Lord God will vindicate his chosen ones – and there will be many shocks and surprises. Jesus was issuing a terrible warning of the reality of heaven and of the reality of God's final, irrevocable judgement on those who fail to honour him. Our Lord is vividly picturing the significance of our God-centred or our God-ignoring manner of life here and now, and its bearing on our eternal well-being.

Here, for the rich man, was truth learned too late – the torment, the agony, the endless, 'If only I'd . . .' but the opportunity had passed. Now, too late, he sees the reality of heaven and hell. Now, too late, he realises the terrible error of living in God's world without honouring him. And now, too late, he longs to warn others. Agonisingly clearly, he now sees the misery he has brought on himself and the glory and joy from which he has excluded himself.

His cry for a drop of water, which echoed Lazarus' earthly cry for a crumb of bread, cannot be fulfilled. 'Son, remember that you in your lifetime received your good things, and Lazarus in like manner bad things; but now he is comforted here, and you are in anguish.' As Abraham awakened them, even these memories would only serve to torment him. Despite all his earthly wealth and comfort, having forfeited God's blessing the rich man is left in utter desolation and torment. Whereas Lazarus, who had suffered so much and possessed so little, is now at Abraham's side in heaven, and has everything that really and ultimately matters.

In common with the rich man, we in our day cannot, with money or with favours given to others, 'buy' our way to heaven. We have to humble ourselves and live for the Lord God and receive the One he sent to be the way of forgiveness. There is no other way, no other door. And neither can we, even with fabulous wealth, buy our way out of hell. There is a 'great gulf' fixed.

The Rich Man's conversation with Abraham
". . . he lifted up his eyes and saw Abraham far off and Lazarus at his side. And he called out, 'Father Abraham, have mercy on me, and send Lazarus to dip the end of his finger in water and cool my tongue, for I am in anguish in this flame.'"

He who once commanded now begs! The rich man had never before been in a position where he had to beg a favour rather than demand it. Never, maybe since his childhood, had anyone ignored or refused one of his requests. Yet now, aware of the horror of his totally changed situation, the rich man begins begging and grasping for help. Seeing and recognising Lazarus far off at Abraham's side, he begins to implore and argue with all the desperation characteristic of the most determined beggar.

Just as the Pharisees constantly assumed that they could appeal to Abraham, the rich man, too, attempts to gain relief in the same way, 'Father Abraham I beg you . . .' The rich man offered no significant help to Lazarus who had suffered so terribly at his gate but, now that he is in such trouble himself, something must be done about it and done immediately! 'Send Lazarus!' With his long established superior position in society, he completely fails to recognise that Lazarus is now Abraham's honoured guest and that he is the beggar. The rich man takes it for granted that Lazarus may be used as his servant and will do whatever he wishes. But who made Abraham's honoured guest this man's servant? – Be warned, for forgetfulness of God and self-centred arrogance towards those less well-off can so easily ensnare those of us entrusted with wealth and social position.

And he said, 'Then I beg you, father, to send him to my father's house – for I have five brothers – so that he may warn them, lest they also come into this place of torment.' Let Lazarus be sent, this time as his 'messenger boy,' to warn these five brothers who were equally God-ignoring, equally living for this world only, equally in danger of sharing their rich brother's fate. The request may have sprung from a genuine concern for their eternal well-being. However, we must not build too much on the rich man's concern for them, for he shows no fundamental change of heart. Family love can be, in Alexander Maclaren's words, merely 'selfishness elongated'. The rich man shows no hint of repentance towards God for his former life-style or of remorse for the way he has consistently ignored, and now seeks to use, Lazarus. For this reason, it has been suggested that the rich man's request could have been made to spare him from the added torment of his brothers' endless anger and accusations because he himself had failed to warn them and had, by his example, led them to such a fate – just as the Pharisees were doing.

'They have Moses and the Prophets; let them hear them,' says Abraham. The rich man, in his desperation, contradicts even the one he claims to honour. 'No, father Abraham, but if someone goes to them from the dead, they will repent.' He cannot not go, '. . . between us and you,' says Abraham, 'a great chasm has been fixed, in order that those who would pass from here to may not be able,' but even if he could they would not listen. The problem is not lack of opportunity to turn and repent, to live for the Lord God – it is the lack of heart and will to do so. Indeed, says Richard Baxter, the brothers would almost certainly have persecuted the risen, returning Lazarus for daring to slur the name and memory of their magnificent brother, and for daring to suggest that he was anywhere other than among God's favoured ones in heaven. Such is the hardness of our unbelieving hearts.

The subtlety and the fierceness of unbelief

The words of Abraham, 'If they do not hear Moses and the Prophets, neither will they be convinced if someone should rise from the dead,' would have rung as a stinging rebuke in the ears of the Pharisees, to whom this parable was first addressed. The Pharisees prided themselves in being both the sons of Abraham and the experts in understanding and applying Moses and the Prophets. Through these words of Abraham, our Lord highlighted the fact that the Pharisees only heeded those parts of Scripture they found acceptable. They had no eyes to see or ears to hear those portions of Moses and the Prophets they found uncomfortable and challenging, especially those referring to the coming of the Messiah. As can happen to us, unbelief had caused them to be selective in the parts of Scripture they chose to take note of and believe.

As a terrible demonstration of the truth of the second part of Abraham's reply, '. . . neither will they be convinced if someone should rise from the dead,' the apostle John records that, right at the end of his ministry, the Lord Jesus raised a man from the dead, who also bore the name 'Lazarus'. Did the Pharisees believe? They did not! They had already resolved to kill Jesus and were now even more determined to do so – and to kill this risen Lazarus. They were in no position to deny the amazing miracle of one 'risen from the dead' but sought to be rid of the man whose risen life bore such eloquent testimony to who the Lord Jesus truly is; the Son of God, the promised Messiah.

The challenge of true faith
No matter what our outward circumstances may be, the parable spotlights the essential need of humble obedient faith, the kind of faith that informs and controls our actions in every part of life. The parable

points to the great danger of what is, in practice, an inward and hidden life of unbelief. A life hiding an inner refusal to love, honour and obey the Lord God – no matter how impressive the outward veneer may be. For the Pharisees, that veneer was religious devotion and for the rich man it was peace and plenty.

The Pharisees assumed that they, most certainly, would share the joy of heaven at Abraham's side. By this parable, the Lord Jesus challenged them to examine that assumption. In the same way the parable challenges each one of us to seriously examine the grounds of our own hope of God's favour; of heavenly joy.

From the parable, it is clearly possible to live an enviably successful life – and yet fail to walk humbly with Almighty God. It is equally painfully clear that it is even possible to have, as the Pharisees had, a highly respected public ministry – and yet fail to walk in humble obedience to Almighty God in whose hand is our breath and our eternal destiny.

The Pharisees lifted their noses in disdain at both the Lord Jesus and his teaching – as many do today. But, with regard to the consequences of such unbelief, the parable brings into sharp contrast the two destinies spoken of in the New Testament's most famous verse:

> *'For God so loved the world, that he gave his only Son*
> *that whoever believes in him should not perish . . .'*

Hear those fearful cries of the rich man from the place of the unbelieving dead, 'I am in anguish, in torment . . . send Lazarus to warn . . .' and the solemn words of Abraham, '. . . between us and you a great chasm has been fixed . . . none may cross . . .'

The verse continues,

> *'. . . should not perish but have eternal life.'*

Note well the humble trust and subsequent heavenly joy of Lazarus. For Lazarus, life on earth was very hard and harsh, but in the life hereafter he is pictured with one of the choice saints of God in the joy of heaven.

The Pharisees sniffed in unbelief. But what of our own slowness to believe the whole testimony of Scripture with regard to who Jesus really is, and, when it clashes with what we want to do, our own unwillingness to do what he said?

For believers and unbelievers alike, the parable of the rich man and Lazarus confronts us with searching questions. Our eternal destiny hangs on the answers.

Thank you, heavenly Father for this wonderful and yet terrifying parable that fell from the lips of your Son, our Lord Jesus Christ. Give us grace to heed its warnings, earnestly pray for mercy; then trust, believe, obey and lay all at your feet, for the glory of your holy name and for our own eternal well-being.

Questions for reflection or discussion

1. Do many people assume that a decent lifestyle, followed by a dignified funeral naturally leads to a place in heaven?
2. Can we, too, be selective in what we choose to 'hear' from God's word? Is this whole area of the just judgement of God often omitted from today's preaching and Christian thinking?
3. If Lazarus had been sent back, as the rich man requested, do you think his warnings would have been heeded? If not, why not?
4. What sure grounds, rather than uncertain hopes, do we have for our own eternal destiny?
5. How much do we know of love and trust toward Almighty God and his Son and a hunger to shape our lives by God's written word – even when that touches our own lifestyle, purse, wallet or bank account?

Footnotes

1. Kenneth Bailey comments that the parable is very wide ranging in its implications; if we allow it to, it will challenge and clarify our thinking concerning heaven and hell and God's irrevocable judgement. It will challenge our confidence in our earthly relationships and circumstances, and establish in our hearts the certainty of ultimate justice at the hand of God. It will pin-point the mystery of suffering and awaken compassion towards those less well-off than ourselves.

2. As with the Pharisees to whom Jesus was speaking, those of us who are parents, teachers or ministers have much to dread when we consider those we have failed to warn or have misled. However, the time to cry to God on their behalf and to do all we can to help them is now, not, as the rich man, when it is too late.

References

We all, '. . . lie down in the dust' – Job 21:23-26
Lazarus raised from the dead – John 11:38-44
The plan to kill Lazarus – John 12:9-11
In whose hand is my breath – Daniel 5:23
God so loved the world – John 3:16

The Widow and the Judge

Being asked by the Pharisees when the kingdom of God would come, he answered them, "The kingdom of God is not coming with signs to be observed, nor will they say, 'Look, here it is!' or 'There!' for behold, the kingdom of God is in the midst of you."

And he said to the disciples, "The days are coming when you will desire to see one of the days of the Son of Man, and you will not see it. And they will say to you, 'Look, there!' or 'Look, here!' Do not go out or follow them. For as the lightning flashes and lights up the sky from one side to the other, so will the Son of Man be in his day. But first he must suffer many things and be rejected by this generation. Just as it was in the days of Noah, so will it be in the days of the Son of Man. They were eating and drinking and marrying and being given in marriage, until the day when Noah entered the ark, and the flood came and destroyed them all. Likewise, just as it was in the days of Lot—they were eating and drinking, buying and selling, planting and building, but on the day when Lot went out from Sodom, fire and sulphur rained from heaven and destroyed them all — so will it be on the day when the Son of Man is revealed. On that day, let the one who is on the housetop, with his goods in the house, not come down to take them away, and likewise let the one who is in the field not turn back. Remember Lot's wife. Whoever seeks to preserve his life will lose it, but whoever loses his life will keep it. I tell you, in that night there will be two in one bed. One will be taken and the other left. There will be two women grinding together. One will be taken and the other left." And they said to him, "Where, Lord?" He said to them, "Where the corpse is, there the vultures will gather."

And he told them a parable to the effect that they ought always to pray and not lose heart. He said, "In a certain city there was a judge who neither feared God nor respected man. And there was a widow in that city who kept coming to him and saying, 'Give me justice against my adversary.' For a while he refused, but afterwards he said to himself, 'Though I neither fear God nor respect man, yet because this widow keeps bothering me, I will give her justice, so that she will not beat me down by her continual coming.'" And the Lord said, "Hear what the unrighteous judge says. And will not God give justice to his elect, who cry to him day and night? Will he delay long over them? I tell you, he will give justice to them speedily. Nevertheless, when the Son of Man comes, will he find faith on earth?"

Luke 17:20-18:8, English Standard Version

The Persistent Widow and the Unjust Judge

At a quick glance, the parable seems to illustrate the teaching, 'Show persistence in prayer and get a speedy answer.' But actually, that is not what our Lord is teaching. So, may I invite you to look a little more closely at the setting, at the parable itself and at the application that the Lord himself gave.

The setting or context of the parable
There is a similar parable in Luke chapter 11 where our Lord teaches the 'Lord's Prayer' and then tells the parable of the friend in need of bread for his guest. He shamelessly rouses his unwilling neighbour at midnight, persisting until he gets all he needs. The application the Lord gave is prayer; 'Ask and it will be given you: seek and you will find; knock and it will be opened to you.' We are urged to unashamedly plead with the Lord God, our heavenly Father, until we have all that we need to live for his glory in this world. Very specifically Jesus urged disciples, both then and now, to pray for the Holy Spirit, for God to be at work in our lives and overruling all our circumstances.

But here in Luke chapter 18 the focus is different. It is not, 'all we need day by day', but about holding fast to the justice of God in a very unjust world. It is about keeping faith when all around us men are giving up. It is about waiting, watching and being ready for the return of the Son of man; the Lord Jesus Christ.

How can we be certain of this? Well, we can because, from verse 22 of chapter 17, the Lord has been teaching his disciples about the ushering in of the kingdom of heaven, the return of the Son of man. He warns them that first he must suffer many things and be rejected. He warns them that time would pass and that men and women, totally forgetting and ignoring God, will be eating and drinking, buying and selling, planting and building – just as it was in the days of Noah or of Lot . . . until judgement fell. It will be like that on the day the Son of man is revealed.

What a frighteningly relevant warning for our own times! In secular society, men and women and their leaders imagine themselves to be totally self sufficient, with no need of God. We are taught to live our lives; buy and sell, plant and build without any reference to him at all; just as it was in the days of Noah. But – the return of the King will be sudden and dramatic and will bring judgement and the ushering in of the kingdom of heaven.

When the disciples asked, 'Where, Lord?' he said, 'Where the body is, there the eagles or vultures will be gathered together.' A very strange answer, a dark saying to our ears; he did not say where, he gave them a picture as familiar to them as maybe seagulls are to us. Throw bread in the open in winter and within a few seconds there will be a cry and a dozen seagulls will be circling and swooping, squawking, and diving for it. Or, if a farmer begins ploughing, after just a few metres, the same thing happens. Why? Because the seagulls have been alert, watching, waiting, ready – and that is how disciples are called to live as we await the Lord's return.

However, until the Son of Man returns it will not be easy; like their Lord, disciples will be despised and rejected, whipped, imprisoned and, maybe, put to death. At times disciples will find themselves in a hostile and very unjust world – hence this parable.

The parable itself – the widow and the judge

First the widow – always the most vulnerable of people in society, passed over, not noticed, ignored, open to exploitation and abuse; especially so in the days of our Lord in the Middle East. Remember the reference of the Lord to the religious leaders, '. . . devouring – gobbling up – widows' houses.'

The Lord's picture is of a widow who could not get justice. She was not seeking revenge, only justice, yet it was being denied her. Almost certainly, unlike her adversary, she had no reserve of money to bribe the judge and no powerful advocate to put pressure on him on her behalf. It was just herself, a helpless widow, and a judge who scoffed at her and ignored her plight. However, she really meant business, she would not give up, and she kept coming to him with her plea.

Then the judge – a thoroughly bad man in high office. Magistrates, judges and people in positions of authority are called before Almighty God to maintain justice, to be advocates, protectors of those who cannot protect themselves – as Wilberforce was for the slaves, as Shaftesbury was for the child labourers, widows and orphans of his day, and as the Lord God himself is described in Psalm 68 verse 5, 'Father of the fatherless and protector of widows.'

However, people with power are always vulnerable. They are at risk of being put under pressure to show a favour, to be less than impartial, and at risk of being bribed. A modern judge, just before a particular case, received a discreet message, 'You will, of course, find this man innocent.' Before God, he found him guilty. But he also found it necessary to flee the country!

They are also at risk, as the judge in the parable was, of ignoring their God-given responsibilities and simply enjoying the privileges and financial rewards of high office. (As an aside, both politicians and those chosen for Christian ministry can fall into the same trap – enjoying the privileges, the splendour and ceremony, the esteem, the political power and yet failing to fulfil their God-given responsibilities with honesty and integrity.)

As Judah's godly king Jehoshaphat appointed judges, he said to them, 'Consider what you do, for you judge not for man but for the Lord. He is with you in giving judgement. Now then, let the fear of the Lord be upon you. Be careful what you do, for there is no injustice with the Lord our God, or partiality, or taking bribes.'

Yet, the judge in the parable was a man who cared for neither God nor man, and so for whom the expressions, 'for God's sake help her,' or, 'for pity's sake help her,' would carry no weight. He neither feared God nor regarded anyone but himself. All was 'at his pleasure'. His ignoring of the woman and his subsequent attention to her case came from the same motive – selfishness. He found it troublesome to attend to her case but it became even more troublesome not to! 'She will 'wear me out,' or 'beat me down.' Literally, 'she will give me a black eye,' as the original Greek has it. Because she bothers me so much, I will vindicate her; I will secure justice for her.'

The Lord's application of his parable.
"And the Lord said, 'Hear what the unrighteous judge says. And will not God give justice to his elect, who cry to him day and night?'" Beware of equating God with the unjust judge. Our Lord is contrasting them, not likening them. It is a 'how much more' parable. If an unrighteous judge can be moved to action by the constant pleas of a widow, a total stranger, how much more will our heavenly Father hear the cries of his own chosen ones, the ones on whom he has set his love. Of course he will hear them.

Therefore, hold fast. Hold fast despite the injustices, the cold shoulders, the slurs, the persecutions, and the apparent long delay in the coming of his kingdom. He is not slack as he exercises the patience and persistence of his chosen people. He is not slack as he delays the day of his judgement out of patience with those who despitefully use us. 'He is not willing that any should perish but that all should come to repentance.' So 'pray for those who persecute you.' Though he delays long, he will vindicate his elect. He will secure justice for his chosen people.

Disciples of the Lord Jesus Christ, and the Lord himself, can be and are marginalized, laughed at, scoffed at, the butt of many jokes. But the day will come when the whole world will see him King of kings, Lord of lords and the Judge of all the earth. And on that day, his people, his chosen and elect, will be seen to be the ones most to be envied, kings and priests; the jewels of his kingdom shining like stars.

'Will he delay long over them? I tell you, he will give justice to them speedily.' 'Speedily'? – almost certainly not meaning, 'immediately,' as his chosen people had already been crying to him day and night, but meaning, at God's chosen time, they will suddenly and dramatically be vindicated by God himself.

The challenge for us, today
Have you noticed the striking opening and concluding sentences? 'And he told them a parable to the effect that they ought always to pray and not lose heart.' . . . 'Nevertheless, when the Son of man comes, will he find faith on earth?'

Those final words, '. . . when the Son of man comes will he find faith on earth?' present a challenge for every generation and for disciples in every kind of situation. Despite our sleep-inducing comfort and ease, or our being surrounded by a society that has turned its back on God and godly ways, or our great distress under oppression, will he find in us a people steadfast in faith, praying, watching and ready?

The words of our Lord were not words to entertain disciples then, or us today, but words to warn us and strengthen our backbone. They are words to prepare us and to encourage us to cry to God day and night for the coming of his kingdom. Words to challenge us to pray and hold on through difficult times, and to pray for our fellow believers crushed and oppressed by a hostile world – knowing, believing, holding fast to the fact that the Lord God is just; that he knows our situation; that he, our heavenly Father, is in control and that justice will be done; his chosen and beloved people will be vindicated.

As he told the parable of the faithful servants our Lord warned, "You also must be ready, for the Son of Man is coming at an hour you do not expect." Are we personally prepared to suddenly and unexpectedly face the return of the Son of Man, the King of kings, God's appointed Judge? Gospel singer Larry Norman used to sing of that day, 'I wish we'd all been ready.' Will we be?

In the meantime, as we watch and wait, will we grow weary and uncertain? Will we grow prayerless? Will we grow cold, lose heart and lose faith? Will we be gradually so ground down by the God-denying society all about us, that we grow to doubt the promises of God and the words of his Son?

Augustine taught that the pouring out of the heart in fervent prayer and praise builds and strengthens the heart of faith. So here is a parable to challenge us to pray, and to sing, and to encourage one another and, by God's grace, to hold fast.

'And he told them a parable to the effect that they ought always to pray and not lose heart.'

Heavenly Father, when the world grinds us down and the heavens seem unhearing of our prayers, help us to remember this parable, encourage one another and cling to the fact that our very breath and all our circumstances are in your hand. Keep us aware that ultimately justice will be done, your elect will be vindicated.

> 'Thy kingdom come O God,
> Thy rule O Christ begin,
> Break with thine iron rod
> The tyrannies of sin.'
>   Lewis Hensley

Questions for discussion or reflection

1. The parable is a challenge to persist in living for the glory of God in a world that is often unjust, and to be ready for the Lord's return. What can we learn from the widow in godly matters?

2. As our Lord prepared his disciples for hard times, can you think of any times of great difficulty that disciples down the centuries have met?

3. At home or at work, most of us – like the judge – are responsible in some measure for maintaining justice. How do we view our responsibility before God?

4. Have you ever faced pressure to make a judgement, that you knew to be wrong? How watchful do we need to be?

5. How can we best pray for those in positions of authority?

6. In what ways is God our heavenly Father entirely different from the unjust judge? What comfort and encouragement can we draw from this?

7. Why is it easier to allow injustice to embitter us and eat away at our close walk with God, rather than to entrust justice into his hands while we get on with living our lives for him?

8. How can the parable help us to come to terms with the personal injustices we will inevitably meet with in this fallen world?

9. How can the chosen people of God live in a hostile and sometimes very unjust world for the glory of God? How can we encourage and support one another and so be ready for our Lord's return, rather than become weary and ground down?

References

Friend at midnight – Luke 11:5-10
Devouring widows' houses – Mark 12:40
Jehoshaphat's charge to the judges – 2 Chronicles 19:5-7
Not willing that any should perish – 2 Peter 3:9
Pray for those who persecute you – Matthew 5:44
The ones most to be envied – Matthew 5:3-12
Kings and priests – Revelation 5:10
The jewels of his kingdom (his treasured possession) – Malachi 3:16&17
Shining like stars – Daniel 12:3
You also must be ready – Luke 12:40

The Pharisee and the Tax Collector

He also told this parable to some who trusted in themselves that they were righteous, and treated others with contempt: "Two men went up into the temple to pray, one a Pharisee and the other a tax collector. The Pharisee, standing by himself, prayed thus: 'God, I thank you that I am not like other men, extortioners, unjust, adulterers, or even like this tax collector. I fast twice a week; I give tithes of all that I get.' But the tax collector, standing far off, would not even lift up his eyes to heaven, but beat his breast, saying, 'God, be merciful to me, a sinner!' I tell you, this man went down to his house justified, rather than the other. For everyone who exalts himself will be humbled, but the one who humbles himself will be exalted."

Luke Ch. 18 vs. 9-14, English Standard Version

The Pharisee and the Tax Collector

Here, in the early verses of Luke chapter 18 is a pair parables. The first is a challenge to disciples to hold fast and not to lose heart; and to do so despite the injustice and hostility of this world, and the long wait for the return of the Son of Man and the establishment of the justice of kingdom of God. The second parable displays how true righteousness is obtained. It was a warning to those who were mistakenly confident of their own standing before God and puts before disciples a pitfall to avoid and a pattern to follow.

'He also told this parable to some who trusted in themselves that they were righteous, and treated others with contempt . . .' Like the first parable, this one also has an introduction. It was told to warn those who assumed that God would be delighted with them and their way of life, and who despised those they regarded as 'lesser men' and so held them in contempt.

I have an instinctive dislike of the proud, conceited, self-centred Pharisee. Going into the temple to pray, he just glances towards God and then congratulates himself! He reflects on how good-living and dutiful he considers himself to be and then compares himself with what he sees as 'that cringing and defiled tax collector.'

Yet, in one way, I have great sympathy with the Pharisee. He was doing his best. Like the apostle Paul before the Lord met him, this man was doing what his parents, his teachers and now his fellow Pharisees had taught him to do. From a very young age he had been taught how religious people spoke and thought and behaved. It was all part of his 'spiritual formation'. Now he was a pillar of respectability, both in society and among his fellow religious leaders. Yet he had never had cause to do as the tax gatherer did; he had never been aware of any need to do 'heart business' with God. So his fine religious appearance was very much like the large chocolate box in a shop window – actually empty; for display purposes only. Hence the quotation of our Lord from the prophet Isaiah, '. . . this people honours me with their lips but their heart is far from me.'

The Pharisee is pictured offering a public display of his impressive prayerfulness and earnestness, shown by his frequent fasting, and his generous giving – a tenth of everything. I find myself repelled by our Lord's picture of such a man. However, to my discomfort, I find that the root of the Pharisee's attitude is also here in my own heart. It is default human nature to inflate our own ego at the expense of others. With the passing of the years, godly folk can so easily slip into it; ticking religious boxes and comparing ourselves favourably with others.

Jesus did not tell this parable to warn only the Pharisees. It is a challenge to us all.

An overview of the parable

Two men went up to the temple to pray. 'Up', because the temple was on Temple Mount, and certainly you came 'up' to Jerusalem if you were coming in from the surrounding countryside. 'To pray' – to us this immediately signifies private prayer. But Jesus did not say, 'to a private place,' or, 'to a solitary place,' but, 'to the temple,' and to Jesus' hearers it simply meant, 'went up to worship.' So these two men could well have been going to join a congregation in public worship, during which – as hopefully with us – personal business with God could be done if that is truly the heart's desire.

But, as Matthew Henry points out, see how the evil one is able to bring evil out of good, as in the case of the Pharisee, and how God is able to bring good out of evil, as in the case of the tax collector. It was good that the Pharisee was not an extortioner, unjust or an adulterer. And it is good to pray seriously and to set aside money for the kingdom of heaven. Yet Satan took that which was good and pushed it to an extreme and made that man and his fellow Pharisees proud, arrogant and self satisfied, and so actually caused them to shut themselves out of the kingdom of heaven whose gateway is a humble and contrite heart.

The other man was very unpromising material indeed; a gatherer of taxes for the hated Roman overlords. It seems that tax collectors were not paid. They simply had to gather 'a little extra' from their own fellow countrymen. Some grew very rich, so it is no wonder that as a group they were hated and despised as traitors, swindlers and rogues, very much as the Pharisee described him. So, as he came to the temple to pray, others would shun him and he himself would feel filthy, unclean, and unworthy even to be there let alone to pray. Yet this man's cry from the heart for mercy, 'a gasp flung out into eternity' as Campbell Morgan describes it, was heard by Almighty God. Sometimes God has to bring us very low, until there is no room for self-confidence, self-deception or conceit, before we are willing to cry to him for mercy.

Two men went up to the temple to pray. One returned to his home feeling he had done well, even more self-satisfied and conceited – but not realising he was alienated from God. The other went home justified, declared righteous, a new-born, forgiven child of God with a fresh new start.

The world would applaud the self confident Pharisee and look with contempt on the fearful, cowering tax collector. Yet, as Richard Trench comments, at the very moment the Pharisee was viewing the tax collector as the sum total of all he despised, all heaven was rejoicing over him. It was the tax collector who went home justified.

Thank God for this example of prayer from the lips of his Son. It is a prayer we can be certain that God hears. 'God, be merciful to me a sinner!'

Putting each part of the parable under the microscope.
Kenneth Bailey makes the point of the parable even more sharply as he invites us to look closely at each aspect of it.

First the temple
He reminds us that the temple was very far from just an open space in which to pray. In front of the temple, morning and afternoon, a lamb was offered; an atoning sacrifice for the sins of the people. These two men were in the temple to worship as the lamb was being offered or as it was burning on the altar in the hours following. The sacrifice was the focus of temple worship and the whole temple area would be pervaded by the sight and sounds and subsequent aroma of the burning sacrifice.

Then the Pharisee
The Pharisee 'standing by himself, prayed thus' or 'stood and prayed thus with himself'. Scholars debate, as the manuscripts vary. If the

Pharisee 'stood by himself and prayed', what was going on was this. The Pharisee, determined to stay ritually pure and clean, did not want his clothes even to brush against those of the other people gathered for worship. He would be defiled and so he stood apart and prayed. He stood and prayed out loud as was their custom, but it was mainly for the ears of the hearers.

He seems to be imagining that he is preaching to the less fortunate people around him and offering them a glimpse of how a truly righteous person lives. In effect, 'look to me and learn from my example,' and he does so with particular reference to the 'disgusting' tax collector cowering further back. The Pharisee had his eye on him throughout his prayer. By stereotyping him and crushing him, he made his own imagined righteousness gleam even more brightly.

If, on the other hand, he 'prayed thus with himself', our Lord Jesus was using deeply perceptive satire. The Pharisee is pictured as being familiar with public worship and full of confidence as he offers his prayer. However, looking more closely, the presence of God was quite unnecessary for this man's self-congratulatory list of religious achievements and his favourable comparison of himself with those around him. Although he called on God to be witness of all his good deeds, he clearly had no sense or awareness whatever of coming into the awesome presence of the Holy One of Israel, before whom all his acts of righteousness were as filthy rags.

Could this be a warning for us as we take part in or as we lead worship? We, too, can so easily be far more aware of the people around us, than aware that we are meeting before Almighty God. We may be also so confident and familiar with godly words and phrases, that we fail to hunger after the reality of the presence of the Lord God among his people; speaking through his word, and at work in our own hearts and in the hearts of our hearers – quite unaware of the need, as the Puritans described it, of 'the felt presence of God'.

The Pharisee's outward religious zeal and enthusiasm had hidden from him his heart's condition before God, as it can for us. This is the parable's great challenge – to examine our own hearts before God.

Then the tax collector
Aware that he stood in the presence of God, the tax gatherer knew that he could come no nearer. He could see all too plainly his plight. He was not worthy to be among even the least clean of these people, let alone close to God himself. So he stood far off and, beating his chest, he just blurted out those few stumbling words from his heart, 'God be merciful to me a sinner' – 'The chief of sinners,' as the apostle Paul would later echo.

All the commentators point out that he uses an unusual word for 'mercy'. Later in the same chapter we have the ordinary word, as a blind man cries to Jesus for mercy; for his eyesight to be restored. But here it is 'propitiate me' as if he is crying, 'O God let this sacrificed lamb, this atoning sacrifice for the sins of the people cover my sin, let it be for me. God have mercy, God forgive.' Here is the man to follow. Here is the cry of the heart, not, as the other man's, a display of shallow words from the lips.

It was the tax collector, declared the Lord, who went to his house justified; forgiven, acquitted, a new man before God.

There is no specific teaching concerning the person and work of the Lord Jesus here, no specific pointing forward to the cross of Calvary and the sacrifice of the Lamb of God, and yet it is all about that cross. The sacrificial lamb of the temple pointed forward to that final, full, perfect sacrifice, the one and only way to enter the kingdom of heaven. Hence the cry of John the Baptist, 'Behold the Lamb of God, who takes away the sin of the world.' In the temple, a symbol of that which was to come; an atoning sacrifice for the sins of the people. On the cross, the fulfilment of that symbol; the perfect and final atoning sacrifice for the sins of the whole world. A sacrifice made in order that whoever approaches with a humble and contrite heart, like that of the tax collector, might be forgiven, acquitted, justified, made acceptable before Almighty God. There is no other gateway to the kingdom of heaven.

Go to the heart of the tax collector's prayer, 'God, be merciful to me, a sinner.' 'God, I am totally unworthy, a sinner, undone and ruined. Let this atoning sacrifice be for me, for my ignorance of you, for my failure to honour you, for my sin.' God laid on his Son, the Lord Jesus Christ, the iniquity of us all and yet it is only those who follow the tax collector and personally identify with that great final sacrifice, recognising that it was for them, who will benefit. Two men went up to the temple to pray; only one man benefitted.

With the apostle Paul, could we write, '. . . the life I now live, I live by faith in the Son of God who loved me and gave himself for me'?

Here in the teaching of the Lord Jesus are the roots of the apostle Paul's great teaching of justification by faith; trusting not, as Paul a former Pharisee once did, in our own religious achievement or our righteous veneer – no matter how worthy – but trusting wholly and alone in God's wonderful and merciful provision.

'He also told this parable to some who trusted in themselves that they were righteous, and treated others with contempt . . .'

Lord God, have mercy upon us; on our own wilful blindness, and our lack of mercy towards others. Show us ourselves as we really are before you the Lord, the Almighty and all holy God, and give us grace to cry to you for mercy.

> 'Just as I am, without one plea
> But that thy blood was shed for me,
> And that Thou bidst me come to Thee,
> O Lamb of God, I come.'
>
> Charlotte Elliot

Questions for reflection or discussion

1. Could you accept a 'notorious sinner' coming to a church meeting?
2. Have you been part of a group that would make you think in the way the Pharisee did?
3. Why is it so easy to compare ourselves favourably with others?
4. We can hide our heart's true condition before other people, with religious words and activity. Can we hide the true condition of our heart before the Lord God?
5. How can this parable help us, like the tax collector, to humbly approach the throne of God seeking mercy, with an honest and heartfelt awareness of how far we have fallen short before him?
6. Can you relate to the tax collector's cry from the heart and subsequent joy?

References

Honours me with their lips but . . .' – Mark 7:6
Filthy rags (polluted garment) – Isaiah 64:6
Chief of sinners – 1 Timothy 1:15
Behold the Lamb of God – John 1:29 and 35
The Son of God loved me and gave himself for me – Galatians 2:20
The iniquity of us all – Isaiah 53:6

The Ten Pounds or Ten Minas

As they heard these things, he proceeded to tell a parable, because he was near to Jerusalem, and because they supposed that the kingdom of God was to appear immediately. He said therefore, "A nobleman went into a far country to receive for himself a kingdom and then return. Calling ten of his servants, he gave them ten minas, and said to them, 'Engage in business until I come.' But his citizens hated him and sent a delegation after him, saying, 'We do not want this man to reign over us.'

When he returned, having received the kingdom, he ordered these servants to whom he had given the money to be called to him, that he might know what they had gained by doing business. The first came before him, saying, 'Lord, your mina has made ten minas more.' And he said to him, 'Well done, good servant! Because you have been faithful in a very little, you shall have authority over ten cities.' And the second came, saying, 'Lord, your mina has made five minas.' And he said to him, 'And you are to be over five cities.' Then another came, saying, 'Lord, here is your mina, which I kept laid away in a handkerchief; for I was afraid of you, because you are a severe man. You take what you did not deposit, and reap what you did not sow.' He said to him, 'I will condemn you with your own words, you wicked servant! You knew that I was a severe man, taking what I did not deposit and reaping what I did not sow? Why then did you not put my money in the bank, and at my coming I might have collected it with interest?' And he said to those who stood by, 'Take the mina from him, and give it to the one who has the ten minas.' And they said to him, 'Lord, he has ten minas!' 'I tell you that to everyone who has, more will be given, but from the one who has not, even what he has will be taken away.

But as for these enemies of mine, who did not want me to reign over them, bring them here and slaughter them before me.'"

> Luke 19:11-27, English Standard Version

The Ten Pounds or Ten Minas

The events leading up to Jesus telling this parable
The Lord Jesus was on his way to Jerusalem, by way of Jericho. On the way into Jericho, there was a blind man persistently crying to him, 'Son of David, have mercy on me!' The crowd following Jesus, with good eyesight, recognised him only as 'Jesus of Nazareth'. The blind man, with none, recognised him as God's promised Messiah, the Son of David. He was not put off by the crowd's discouragement and rebukes. He knew that the Lord Jesus, alone, could help him and, in determined faith, he continued to cry out to him for mercy. He was heard and healed by the Lord and joyfully followed him, giving praise to God.

In Jericho itself the exceedingly rich but hated chief tax gatherer, Zacchaeus, had a different but totally life-changing encounter with the Lord Jesus. Salvation came to his house. The Lord used that incident to declare what he had come to do, not to be a military leader restoring the fortunes of Israel, but to be the Shepherd King laying down his life for their rescue, '. . . the Son of man came to seek and to save the lost.' This is the setting in which the Lord Jesus told the parable. He told it for a particular reason. He was making this final journey; the seventeen miles up to Jerusalem for the Passover. The religious leaders were waiting for him – and watching for an opportunity to destroy him. At the very beginning of his journey to Jerusalem some Pharisees had warned him to escape, but Jesus had responded saying, 'O Jerusalem, Jerusalem, stoning the prophets and killing those sent to you . . .' Our Lord knew exactly what lay ahead.

However the disciples and the crowd did not. Jesus had just taken the disciples aside and warned them that he would be taken from them, and that all that was written about him would happen. He would be handed over to the Gentiles, mocked, scourged, shamefully treated and put to death. He had also told them that on the third day he would rise from death. But they had no ears to hear, or minds to understand these things.

The disciples and the people with them had a totally different expectation. Their understanding and hope was that 'this was the moment'; that at this Passover, as the promised Messiah, Jesus would spectacularly establish the kingdom, proclaim himself king, throw off the yoke of Rome and restore the nation of Israel to the peace, power and the national superiority not seen since the glory days of King David and his son, Solomon.

This thinking is reflected in the sad comment of the two walking to Emmaus and saying to the unrecognised, risen Lord Jesus, '. . . but we had hoped he was the one to redeem Israel.' Their mistaken hope had been utterly dashed by the crucifixion and the events around it. The Son of man came not as a 'conquering hero', but as the suffering servant of the Lord to 'give his life a ransom for many.'

However, false hope and euphoria had gripped both the disciples and the crowd. It had blinded their eyes and shut their ears to his warnings and was sweeping them along to think of nothing else. Hence this parable: 'As they heard these things, he proceeded to tell a parable, because he was near to Jerusalem, and because they supposed that the kingdom of God was to appear immediately.' It was a hope built on a misunderstanding of the ways of God, and a hope about to be shattered.

The significance of the nobleman seeking a kingship
Historians suggest that the parable of the minas or 'pounds' was anchored in the familiar, local history of Jericho. No one could govern

without the express permission of the Roman overlords. Any military leader who aspired to become king of a newly conquered area, had to go to Rome, to Caesar, to receive his kingship. Herod the Great had done this. On his death, his kingdom was divided between his sons, each of whom had to have their inheritance confirmed by Caesar. One of these sons, Archelaus, built a palace at Jericho. Archelaus was so dreadful that a delegation was sent to Rome to say, in effect, 'We will not have this man to rule over us.' It was in part successful, for although Archelaus was permitted to govern Judea for a time, he was never granted the title king and was eventually banished. So here is a parable that would immediately chime with local history and be well understood by the Lord's hearers.

There is a parable with very similar teaching recorded in Matthew chapter 25; the parable of the talents. It has very much the same thrust, but it is distinct; it was spoken privately to the disciples in Jerusalem in the final hours of our Lord's ministry. The talents that were given varied in value, according to each servant's ability, and there is no reference to the receiving of a kingdom or reference to those who would not have him rule over them. As Leon Morris points out, there is not a problem with our Lord using a similar story in a fresh setting to draw out different aspects of his teaching or to reinforce his previous teaching.

The parable itself

As he described a nobleman going to a far country to receive his kingship and then returning some time later, Jesus was warning them that his kingdom will not appear immediately as they had hoped, but after a lapse of time. He told the parable to prepare them for his departure, to assure them of his return and to challenge them to be faithfully about his business until that day.

J. C. Ryle describes it as a 'prophetical sketch' of Jesus himself and his kingdom. Our Lord clearly warned his disciples that he would be leaving them, that they would be given a task to fulfil in his absence, and that he will return. On his return as King, he will call them to account, and reward them according to their faithfulness, and bring the judgement of God on those who reject him and his kingly rule.

In the full light of the New Testament, those with Christian eyes can see – in the rejection of the future king and his return with full authority – glimpses of what lay ahead: The hatred of the religious establishment leading to Jesus' arrest, unjust trial and crucifixion. His resurrection, ascension and his being made the future universal Lord, as described by the apostle Paul in the letter to the Philippians, '. . . obedient to death, even death on a cross. Therefore God has raised him up and given him a name above every name, that at the name of Jesus every knee should bow . . .' And finally, his total, kingly rule as described in Revelation by the apostle John – the Lamb found worthy and given the scroll; entrusted with all authority over the whole course of world affairs.

In the parable we are given this prophetic glimpse of the crucified, risen, ascended, crowned and suddenly returning King of kings and Lord of lords. What a vision! The purposes of God for his Son are far greater than the disciples, the excited crowd – or many of us – have ever dreamed; the gathering of the whole world under the sovereign reign of the One who told this parable.

In the meantime, the parable also gives us a picture of the task, and the manner of conducting it, that should occupy his servants, until he returns.

How did the disciples come to understand this parable? What did our Lord entrust to them? What, indeed, has he entrusted to us?
The ten servants were each given a portion of the nobleman's wealth to trade with and so increase his total estate. Each 'pound' or mina was worth the equivalent of three months' wages. So, ten of them would be a very substantial sum. It was placed in their hands with the knowledge that the nobleman expected them to do their very best with

it to further his interests and that he would return and call each one of them to account.

At its widest level, like those first disciples, everything that we are and everything that we have is a trust from the Lord God to be used for his glory. This is the understanding offered by most commentators; everything is to be used to bring honour to him. So the apostle Paul in Romans chapter 12 urged his readers then, and us now, in response to God's mercy, to give our bodies, our whole lives, as 'a living sacrifice.' Our skills and abilities, our time and money, our home life and our employment opportunities are all a trust from the Lord. They are all to be brought as 'a living sacrifice' and used day by day with the aim of bringing honour to the Lord. This, argues the apostle, is the only 'logical response' if we have truly tasted the wonderful mercy of God.

The disciples did, indeed, spend the rest of their lives 'trading' in the service of their Lord. The later addition to their number, the apostle Paul, laboured most of all, devoting every part of his intellect, stamina, courage and energy to the Lord Jesus as a willing 'slave' – and counting it his joy to do so.

However, it is important and informative to ask, 'With what particular "entrusted wealth" did the apostles "trade" with the whole of their lives?'
Very specifically, as the Lord parted from the disciples, he entrusted them with a very great commission. Mark tells us that they were to go and preach the gospel to all nations. Luke records Jesus saying that 'repentance and forgiveness of sins should be proclaimed in his name to all nations, beginning from Jerusalem.' Matthew tells us that the disciples were to go and make disciples, baptising and teaching them all that he had commanded them. John writes that the Lord charged Peter to 'tend his sheep' and to 'feed his lambs'. So here is the wealth of the gospel, the whole building and caring for the kingdom of heaven, entrusted to these weak and very unstable disciples.

Yet, from the Day of Pentecost onwards, empowered by the Holy Spirit, these men, with great boldness, 'traded' with the gospel wealth entrusted to them. Peter's first sermon, in Jerusalem, under the hand of God, gathered about 3,000 new believers into the kingdom of heaven. Those who repented were baptised, and Peter with the other apostles taught them daily, aiming to build up disciples to maturity in a true Christian fellowship. In Luke's account in Acts, we read that these early disciples '. . . devoted themselves to the apostles' teaching and fellowship, to the breaking of bread and the prayers.'

This is the treasure with which our Lord's disciples 'traded' and they devoted their whole lives to it. They did this not only in Jerusalem but throughout Judea, Samaria and to the ends of the earth as our Lord had charged them. By way of the merchant shipping routes, Thomas is said to have taken the treasure his Lord entrusted to him as far as India. The area around Tiruvalla, near the South Western tip of India, is where Thomas is reputed to have preached the gospel and planted a cluster of churches in A.D 52.

True servants of the Lord Jesus, though individually 'marathon runners', are actually part of a great 'relay' down the centuries. Jesus' first disciples, joined by Paul, entrusted their Lord's wealth to faithful men. And down the centuries, faithful servants of Christ have fulfilled our Lord's charge; bringing the gospel, training disciples, creating a people of God in each place and then tending and nurturing those people. Their aim has been to bring disciples to maturity with the ability to reach out and bring the gospel to others. This is how the Lord Jesus would have his riches increase and his kingdom grow. Generation by generation, the Lord's riches entrusted to us must be faithfully invested. It is only as we are doing so, that he will fulfil his promise to be with us to the end of the age.

And the result? – Ten more, five more or no more
Noting that the master commends the first two servants for their faithfulness, Kenneth Bailey perceptively asks, 'Is the focus of the story profits, as we might easily assume, or is it also faithfulness to an unseen master in a hostile environment?' Was it a willingness to be publicly known as the servant of their absent lord, at a time when surrounded by those who hated him and did all they could to permanently undermine his authority over them? Did the servant who wrapped up his 'pound' want to keep his options open and his status as a servant secret in case his master did not return as king?

Such an understanding is certainly a challenge to us in an increasingly hostile world. Are we willing to be faithful and openly known as the servants of a despised and rejected Jesus, who is nevertheless the anointed Son of God and will return as the future King of kings?

The ten servants each received the same amount with which they were to trade. We are only told of the degree of faithfulness of three of them. The first put his whole heart to it, his effort was blessed and he gained ten more. The second did his best, and his money made five times as much. The third failed to trade at all, he just kept the money safe.

It is our turn now to play our part in contributing to the Lord's kingdom, by 'trading' with 'the whole counsel of God' entrusted to us. We, like the first disciples, are called to 'buy up' the opportunities given us to further the kingdom of God. How faithful will we be? What will we report to our Lord and Master?

Over the years some Christians, following in the steps of the apostle Paul, have been spectacularly used of our Lord to build his kingdom. To name but a few: Augustine, that early, spiritual giant of God. Athanasius, who stood 'against the world' as he guarded the truth of the divinity of the Lord Jesus Christ. John Bunyan, who spun so much rich, gospel truth into that compelling yarn, *The Pilgrim's Progress*, a book that has been a spiritual tonic and strength to Christian men and women for centuries. George Whitfield, who proclaimed the gospel so effectively in this country, and in America, in the eighteenth century. John and Charles Wesley, whose sermons, books and godly hymns still feed the church in our own day. Each of us can think of others who ought to be in that list.

In the same way there have been times when Christian men and women, working together as a team, as a church or Christian organisation, have been especially fruitful before God. They have been fruitful, first, in bringing people under the sound of God's gospel, then faithful in discipling those who truly respond and leading them on to Christian maturity. And, finally, they have been faithful in enabling them, in their turn, to be effective 'traders' of their Lord's treasure, bringing others to faith, and then on to maturity in Christ.

Then there are a great many Christian men and women who have borne a faithful, but maybe less spectacular witness. Reflect for a moment on those who have helped and encouraged you in your own spiritual pilgrimage. Maybe a teacher or a Sunday School teacher, a friend or colleague, a particular preacher or someone who just cared and 'bothered' with you.

Or it may have been a church where you first saw real Christian faith, love and forgiveness demonstrated with a quiet, ongoing, positive influence and witness in the whole community. Nothing spectacular, yet here is the bedrock of faithful 'trading'; the building of the kingdom of God.

Note the generous praise and encouragement the returning noble lord in the parable gives to his faithful servants, 'Well done, good servant! Because you have been faithful in a very little, you shall have authority over ten cities.' The reward is his master's praise and more work, greater responsibility. We might have preferred the thought of rest and retirement! However, bear in mind that his 'service is perfect freedom'; that it is our great joy and privilege to be about our Father's business – so much so that the willing 'slave' of the Lord Jesus, the great apostle Paul, counted everything else as 'dung' in comparison with this.

And finally, and very sadly, there are other Christian people and Christian churches who have just kept the treasure to themselves. 'Wrapping it up', we have kept the treasure entrusted to us uselessly 'safe', or as we would probably see it, 'pure'.

The practical encouragement and warning of this parable

The disturbing questions to ask are, where do I stand, and how does my church measure against this parable? For this parable speaks of the judgement of a Lord who will call each one of us as individuals, and each one of his local churches to account.

For those who are faithful, the Lord's parable has words of great encouragement, 'Because you have been faithful over . . . you shall be . . .' The words in the comparable parable of the talents are even more wonderful, 'Well done, good and faithful servant, enter into the joy of your lord. Since you have been faithful . . . you shall be . . .' However, the thrust of them is the same. There is great joy and reward for those who are faithful.

There is a tomb stone in a local church celebrating the business acumen and astuteness of a seed merchant who amassed a great fortune. As a result, his family could afford to bury him in the church beneath a fine memorial to himself and his efforts. But as Matthew Henry points out, it was not like that with these servants. They did not say 'my skill' or 'my industry' but 'your mina' has made so many more. God, not us, must have all the glory. Paul the apostle, returning from a great missionary journey, came back saying, 'Look what God has done.' An African pastor, telling of the complete transformation of his community, simply said, 'Look, Lord, what your gospel has done.'

However, in this parable, as in the parable recorded by Matthew, there are stern words addressed to the servant who just 'kept' the treasure; failed to trade with it himself or to give to those who would have been able to trade with it on his behalf. 'He said to him, "I will condemn you with your own words, you wicked servant! You knew that I was a severe man, taking what I did not deposit and reaping what I did not sow? Why then did you not put my money in the bank, and at my coming I might have collected it with interest?"' The words literally mean 'it should have been put on the table'. In other words, those who were able and willing should have been given the opportunity to trade with it. Hence perhaps the surprising but perfectly logical judgement on the servant who just 'kept the investment safe'. 'And he said to those who stood by, "Take the mina from him, and give it to the one who has the ten minas." And they said to him, "Lord, he has ten minas!" "I tell you that to everyone who has, more will be given, but from the one who has not, even what he has will be taken away."'

Are there 'traders' who are able to make a better use than perhaps we can of all that the Lord has entrusted to us? I suggest that there are. If we are unable, through our personal limitations or circumstances to 'trade' with the Lord's treasure there are others who will go and 'trade' on our behalf. There are men and women willing to go and bring the gospel to other groups of people – perhaps those not accessible to us – and yet to do so they need the prayerful, active and financial support of churches, Christian groups and individuals. Hudson Taylor was willing and able to carry the gospel, to 'trade' with his Lord's treasure in inland China, but a manufacturer in England 'investing' what his Lord had given him, namely wealth, quietly supported Hudson Taylor's time in China. The church at Philippi not only 'held fast', and 'held out' the gospel faith locally, it also supported and encouraged that great 'trader' the apostle Paul. They were partners with him in the gospel. They loved him, prayed for him, sent money when he asked them to help their fellow believers in Judea, and sent Ephaphroditus to visit him with gifts for his own support.

The Lord's 'trading economy' is very wide, involving more than 'front-line troops'.

Treasure 'kept safe'
In our day, are we in danger of provoking the Lord to take his treasure from our church and our land and give it to others who will value it and make better use of it? Godliness and godly ways are given us to 'trade with' not just to 'keep safe'. Despite our great Christian heritage, are we, as churches and as a society, actually coming very close to wrapping up and putting aside as 'old history' the treasure entrusted to us? Following our own opinions or the fashion of the age, we prefer not to heed his commandments, nor follow the teaching of his chosen apostles, nor walk in his holy ways. J C Ryle warns that unless, as a society, we turn, we will provoke the Lord God to give us over to our own chosen ways and allow true Biblical Christianity and godly government to fade away and even disappear from our land. As a nation we have buried the treasure entrusted to us, but surely this is only a very short step from saying, 'We will not be ruled by him.'

The Lord Jesus warned a local church that, unless it repented, he would remove its lampstand. As many a church has found, when the Lord does that, it slowly withers away. For ourselves, Matthew Henry comments, 'Many a man is happy to consider himself saved by the Lord Jesus Christ who is not willing to serve and obey him.' The apostle Paul warns of being saved, but with the loss of everything we had laboured to build.

The unfaithful servant of this parable is not punished, but he does suffer great loss – as unfaithful individual Christians, unfaithful churches and a society that turns its back on godly ways will find to their dismay.

Finally, those terrifying words, 'But as for these enemies of mine, who did not want me to reign over them, bring them here and slaughter them before me.'

On the whole, Jesus' own people, the Jews, and the religious leaders in particular, rejected him. Despite his words and mighty deeds they refused to recognise his evident divine appointment. The apostle Peter, on the Day of Pentecost, spoke of Jesus as 'a man attested to you by God with mighty works and wonders . . . you have crucified'. It was as if they had said, 'We will not have this man to reign over us.' Isn't this exactly what our leaders and modern secular society are saying in our day?

However their rejection, or ours, does not frustrate the purposes of God. Jesus has been made Lord and King, and, at God the Father's appointed time, he will return. On that day every knee will bow and judgement will be delivered upon those who fail to honour him; who reject or rebel against him, who ignore him, or for one reason or another, who '. . . will not have him reign over them.'

Rightly, we delight in the mercy, kindness and gentleness of the Lord Jesus, but here, to make sure that we do not take advantage or presume on that kindness and mercy, are some very sobering words. One of the titles given to the Lord Jesus is 'The Lion of the tribe of Judah'. He is in no sense a tame lion! All judgement has been committed to him, and on his return he will judge the world in righteousness.

We much prefer to think of 'the man of love' and, like the disciples with regard to the approaching crucifixion, we have deaf ears and blind eyes to the reality of judgement and to the terrifying justice, holiness and majesty of the One into whose hands all authority has been placed. By way of this parable, we are urgently called to recognise that we are accountable to the Son of God.

In the meantime, those who will not have him rule over them will carry on ignoring, despising and rejecting him – and, openly or covertly, little-by-little crushing and silencing his faithful servants.

Nevertheless, those who are his servants must keep about their master's business – 'buying up' every opportunity to serve him, playing their full part in his church, supporting and encouraging one another to proclaim, teach and share the gospel warnings, promises and commands; and doing their utmost to prepare themselves, and those around them, for the return of the King.

A parable to heed
For those who faithfully and diligently serve and trade with the riches he has entrusted to us – the praise of our Lord and Master and, in proportion to our ability and faithfulness, the reward of greater, joy-filled usefulness in his kingdom.

For those who fail to serve and to trade with his riches – those riches taken from us and given to those who will make better use of them.

For those who will not believe who he truly is, or accept him as Lord – one of the most terrible words in Scripture – we perish.

Let John Calvin have the last word. Here is a parable, he writes, '. . . to warn those in rebellion and to encourage his own servants to keep faithful.'

Lord God, these are stern and penetrating words from your Son. They are not comfortable; they do not fit with our imagined 'gentle Jesus meek and mild.' But they are the words and instructions of the One you have appointed 'both Lord and Christ' and who will return as King of kings and Lord of lords, the heir of the universe. Help us to hear them and heed them for the glory of your name and our own eternal joy.

Questions for personal reflection and discussion

1. Have you ever been alongside a Christian who has been greatly used of God in 'trading' with the gospel treasure entrusted to him or her?
2. Have you ever been part of a church or organisation that has been greatly used of God in gathering and equipping the people of God?
3. Can you recount personal spiritual encouragement given to you by a less spectacular but, never-the-less faithful, servant of the Lord Jesus?
4. Should we view our skills and abilities, time and money as a trust from the Lord?
5. The unique wealth specifically entrusted to the disciples was our Lord's gospel teaching, kingdom and church. What gifts, abilities and resources has the Lord entrusted to us, personally, to advance his kingdom? How could we 'trade' with them, on his behalf, more effectively?
6. Have you known Christians, or been part of a church that has, in effect, 'wrapped the gospel in a handkerchief'?
7. Can we swept along by popular false hopes and misreadings of scripture? Do the Bereans set us a fine pattern as they studied the Scriptures for themselves to see if the apostle Paul's teaching was in accord with them? Acts 17:10-12
8. Can we be unwilling to accept the 'unpalatable' aspects of the gospel?
9. Just as the disciples could not accept the thought of the crucifixion, do we shrink from believing that the Lord Jesus will return as Lord and as Judge of us, and of everyone?
10. How can we be preparing for his return?

References

Blind man – Luke 18:35
Zacchaeus and the Son of man came to seek – Luke 19:1-10

Jerusalem, stoning the prophets – Luke 13:31-34
No ears to hear or minds to understand – Luke 18:31-34
The road to Emmaus, 'But we had hoped . . .' – Luke 24:18-21
Parable of the talents – Matthew 25:14-30
'Obedient to death' – Philippians 2:8-11
The scroll given – Revelation 5:1-14
Living sacrifice – Romans 12:1
Preach the gospel – Mark 16:15
Repentance and forgiveness – Luke 24:47
Go and make disciples – Matthew 28:19
Tend my sheep – John 21:15-17
Peter's sermon and the disciples devoting themselves – Acts 2:14-42
Jerusalem, Judea, Samaria – Acts 1:8
Entrust to faithful men – 2 Timothy 2:2
To be with us to the end of the age – Matthew 28:18-20
Service is perfect freedom, see final reference
Dung in comparison – Philippians 3:8
Enter into the joy – Matthew 25:21
Look what God has done – Acts 14:27
Partnership in the gospel – Philippians 1:5
Ephaphroditus – Philippians 4:18
The church's lampstand removed – Revelation 2:4-5
Saved, but with the loss of everything – 1 Corinthians 3:15
A man attested to you by God – Acts 2:22
Lion of the Tribe of Judah – Revelation 5:5
All judgement committed – John 5:22
Judge the world in righteousness – Acts 17:31
Lord and Christ – Acts 2:36
Service is perfect freedom – *Book of Common Prayer*, Morning Prayer, Collect for peace

The Vineyard Tenants

And he was teaching daily in the temple. The chief priests and the scribes and the principal men of the people were seeking to destroy him, but they did not find anything they could do, for all the people were hanging on his words.

One day, as Jesus was teaching the people in the temple and preaching the gospel, the chief priests and the scribes with the elders came up and said to him, "Tell us by what authority you do these things, or who it is that gave you this authority." He answered them, "I also will ask you a question. Now tell me, was the baptism of John from heaven or from man?" And they discussed it with one another, saying, "If we say, 'From heaven,' he will say, 'Why did you not believe him?' But if we say, 'From man,' all the people will stone us to death, for they are convinced that John was a prophet." So they answered that they did not know where it came from. And Jesus said to them, "Neither will I tell you by what authority I do these things."

And he began to tell the people this parable: "A man planted a vineyard and let it out to tenants and went into another country for a long while. When the time came, he sent a servant to the tenants, so that they would give him some of the fruit of the vineyard. But the tenants beat him and sent him away empty-handed. And he sent another servant. But they also beat and treated him shamefully, and sent him away empty-handed. And he sent yet a third. This one also they wounded and cast out. Then the owner of the vineyard said, 'What shall I do? I will send my beloved son; perhaps they will respect him.' But when the tenants saw him, they said to themselves, 'This is the heir. Let us kill him, so that the inheritance may be ours.' And they threw him out of the vineyard and killed him. What then will the owner of the vineyard do to them? He will come and destroy those tenants and give the vineyard to others." When they heard this, they said, "Surely not!" But he looked directly at them and said, "What then is this that is written: 'The stone that the builders rejected has become the cornerstone'? Everyone who falls on that stone will be broken to pieces, and when it falls on anyone, it will crush him."

The scribes and the chief priests sought to lay hands on him at that very hour, for they perceived that he had told this parable against them, but they feared the people. So they watched him and sent spies, who pretended to be sincere, that they might catch him in something he said, so as to deliver him up to the authority and jurisdiction of the governor.

Luke 19:47 to 20:20, English Standard Version

The Vineyard Tenants

The wider setting of the parable
The parable is set in the final days of the ministry of Jesus in Jerusalem. Throughout his years of public teaching the Lord Jesus did not proclaim himself to be the long-promised Messiah. That would have been misunderstood. The people imagined and hungered for a Messiah who would be a national warrior-lord, who would throw off the bondage of subjection to the all-conquering Romans and restore Israel's pride and standing among the nations.

Jesus did not openly declare it, but by word and by deed he demonstrated, to those whose eyes were open to the things of God, who he truly was. Isaiah had prophesied some 700 years before that when the Messiah came – the time when God visited his people – the deaf would be given hearing, the blind given sight, the dead raised to life and the poor valued and given good news.

As Jesus approached Jerusalem for the final days of his ministry, he made two clear and very public statements of who he truly was. The first was the triumphal entry and the second the cleansing of the temple.

With a great crowd of followers, Jesus rode into Jerusalem, humble and riding on an ass, in exact fulfilment of the prophecy of Zechariah, 'Behold your King comes to you, just and victorious is he, humble and riding on an ass, on a colt the foal of an ass.' The people, recognising something of the significance of its fulfilment, burst out proclaiming him the Son of David, the One who comes in the name of the Lord. Waving palm branches, laying a carpet of garments, they were praising God and shouting, 'Blessed is the King who comes in the name of the Lord!'

'Rebuke them,' demanded the Pharisees. But Jesus answered, 'If they were silent, the very stones would cry out.' God's moment had come. But they had no eyes to see or ears to hear, hence the cry of the Lord over Jerusalem and the prophecy of its terrible destruction. Unlike the ordinary people, the religious leaders would not recognise the day of visitation, they were determined not to acknowledge who it was who rode into Jerusalem that day.

The clearing of the temple of those cheating and exploiting the people of God was the second, clear statement of who he truly was. No one had authority to do that except the Messiah, who, prophesied Malachi, would suddenly come to his temple and, like a refiner's fire, painfully purify all that was going on until there were offerings pleasing to the Lord God.

Signs and hallmarks of Jesus being the anointed Son of God, the true Messiah, were plainly to be seen wherever he went. The chief priests and the scribes and the principal men of the people were aware of them, but found themselves in a very difficult position. In their eyes, everything this 'unauthorised Rabbi' said and did challenged their traditions, threatened their privileged and powerful position in society and their 'working arrangements' with the Roman overlords. This they could not tolerate. They could not afford to recognise him as the true Messiah – and were therefore determined to destroy him.

Yet here he was teaching daily in the temple, and the people were hanging onto his every word. The leaders were powerless. They could not stir up a mob to stone him for he was far too popular, and they did not have the power of capital punishment. Their only option was somehow to cause him to fall foul of Rome. In this way they could secure his death; it would be a murder – but with all the trappings of apparent justice.

The particular setting of the parable – a test question
As Jesus was teaching in the temple, the chief priests, scribes and elders came upon him suddenly with the demand. 'By what authority do you do these things?' If he said, 'Of men,' they certainly had given him no such authority. If he said, 'Of God,' they could accuse him of blasphemy. He claimed neither, but rather referred them to John the Baptist, whose ministry was also recognised by the people as being of God – but was not recognised by the religious leaders as being of God. By this answer, Jesus avoided their carefully prepared trap. In effect he said, 'You already have the answer.' Jesus was not evading the question, he was saying, 'It is by the same authority, but, as with John, you are determined not to recognise it.' They were well aware that John the Baptist's ministry was of God, and that John had borne clear testimony to his own ministry being that of a herald, and to Jesus as being the promised Messiah. It was the honest answer to their question – if their question was an honest question.

The parable itself
Aware of the challenge of the religious leaders and their continued presence among those he was teaching, Jesus turned back to the people and told the parable of the vineyard tenants.

By means of this parable, the Lord shows the amazing love, kindness and patience of Almighty God – until the time comes when his justice demands judgement. The scene is a typical tenant and landlord agreement of the time. The tenants have use of the vineyard and in payment agree to give the landlord a proportion of the harvest. In patience and mercy the vineyard owner sends a succession of three servants and finally his own beloved son to collect the owner's share of the produce of the vineyard. No human landlord seeking the agreed payment of his share of the harvest would be so patient, nor, in the light of the treatment given to the servants, would he put his beloved son to such risk.

As with so many of his sayings and parables, our Lord was, as it were, holding up a mirror so that his hearers, and particularly the religious leaders, could see for themselves how greatly their judgement was mistaken and how seriously they had got things wrong.

Their forebears had rejected and ill-treated God's servants, the prophets, and these leaders were determined to put to death the beloved Son of God; Israel's glory, as aged Simeon, in that same temple, had described him years earlier. Aware of their intentions, the Lord was showing them the consequences of their deadly scheme. Almighty God will find new tenants for his vineyard, tenants who will honour him and give him the fruit of genuine worship and godly living.

The vineyard tenants, by killing the son and heir, intended to secure the vineyard for themselves. In the same way, these religious leaders, by seeking to put to death the Son of God, intended to secure their privileged and prosperous position. However, his death would actually cause the Lord God to throw them out, and so secure the very opposite of their intention. It would secure their loss of privilege, position and everything – their destruction.

The warning Jesus gave in this parable, and on two other occasions (Luke 19:41-44 and 21:20-24), was fulfilled. In A.D. 70, God gave over the city of Jerusalem to the Romans. There was great slaughter and destruction, and the whole system of temple worship ceased.

Why did the vineyard owner put his son to such risk?
Earlier in Luke's Gospel we read of a ruler of a synagogue indignant because a woman had been healed on the Sabbath. Jesus asked, '"Does not each of you on the Sabbath untie his ox or his donkey from the manger and lead it away to water it? And ought not this woman, a daughter of Abraham whom Satan bound for eighteen years, be loosed from this bond on the Sabbath day?" As he said these things, all his adversaries were put to shame . . .' The words of Jesus were an appeal to the conscience – and the leaders were ashamed of their mistaken judgement and hasty response.

In this parable of the vineyard tenants, the Lord Jesus was following the same pattern, enabling the chief priests, scribes and elders, to see for themselves:

– Who it was who rode into Jerusalem.
– Who had cleared the temple court of ungodly practices.
– What religious leaders in past generations had done.
– What they, in their generation were poised to do.
– The consequences of their action – the loss of everything and themselves destroyed.

The parable was told to warn the chief priests, the scribes and the elders that he was well aware of their murderous plans; plans that were absolutely consistent with the treatment their forebears gave to God's faithful servants and spokesmen the prophets.

Here was perhaps the last opportunity for them to consider, turn from their intended course of action and repent before they secured the crucifixion of Israel's glory; the crucifixion of God's beloved Son, the Messiah.

Kenneth Bailey notes that as the vineyard owner chose to send his beloved son, the owner reasoned, ". . . perhaps they will respect him." And then, out of respect, they would send the portion of the harvest they owed. Middle Eastern Christians translate these words differently, ". . . maybe they will feel shame in his presence" This pinpoints the reason why the father in the parable sent his beloved son. He sent him to give the vineyard tenants one last opportunity – that feeling ashamed in the presence of the owner's son, the tenants might repent and pay their fair share of the vineyard harvest. The whole parable is an appeal to the heart or conscience. One last chance for these senior religious leaders to turn, to admit that they had failed to honour God the Father or his beloved Son, and, like the vineyard tenants, were about to make a ghastly error of judgement.

Would the chief priests, scribes and elders respond to the parable with shame, as the synagogue leaders had done earlier in Jesus' ministry? Or were their hearts too hardened and their resolve to be rid of him too deeply embedded?

The response of Israel's religious leaders
'When they heard this, they said, "Surely not!" But he looked directly at them and said, "What then is this that is written: 'The stone that the builders rejected has become the cornerstone'? Everyone who falls on that stone will be broken to pieces, and when it falls on anyone, it will crush him." The scribes and the chief priests sought to lay hands on him at that very hour, for they perceived that he had told this parable against them . . .'

'Surely not!' 'It must not happen!' God forbid! The Greek is simply, 'May it not be'. But what must not happen? – That Israel's glory, the beloved Son of God should be put to death? That the terrible judgement described should fall on God's vineyard-tenants Israel for their failure to honour him? That the vineyard should be taken away from Israel and her leaders and given to others?

'Surely not!' – An expression of horror from his hearers. The religious leaders could not bear the thought of losing their position of influence, or that the judgement of God might fall on Israel. But they were unwilling to turn from their determination to be rid of our Lord. Like the rest of us, says Alexander McLaren, they were more anxious to escape the consequences than to avoid the sins. It is human nature to ignore God, but hate talk of his judgement.

The mighty building block

'The stone that the builders rejected has become the cornerstone.' These words from Psalm 118 were sung at every festival, and so would be very familiar to Jesus' hearers. In the light of the Lord God's steadfast mercy on his people, the words were traditionally taken to apply to the whole nation of Israel. Israel had often been despised and very nearly overwhelmed, and yet, time and again, the Lord God had done great things for them. For example, battles had been won against all odds, and, in Nehemiah's day, despite determined opposition, the rebuilding of walls of Jerusalem had been completed.

However, looking directly at the chief priests and scribes, Jesus applied the picture of the rejected cornerstone to Israel's true, and yet despised and rejected king – the Son of David, the Messiah. The scribes and chief priests had no intention of acknowledging that he who rode into Jerusalem, cleared the temple and was now teaching the truth of God in the temple courts, was none other than the Son of God. They had no desire to see how the words spoke of the 'glory of God's people Israel,' the Lord Jesus himself.

'The stone that the builders rejected has become the cornerstone. This is the Lord's doing: it is marvellous in our eyes. This is the day that the Lord has made: let us rejoice and be glad in it.' The people surrounding our Lord 'saw' and 'rejoiced'. The scribes and chief priests who had joined them had no intention of doing either.

'Everyone who falls on that stone will be broken to pieces.' For the religious leaders of Jesus' day and for ourselves, it is to our own present serious hurt and loss if we fail to honour God's Son, the chosen and anointed King.

'And when it falls on anyone, it will crush him.' Here is God's final judgement on those who refuse to honour his 'beloved Son.' He, the Son of God, the one to whom all power and authority has been committed, will crush them in judgement.

The chief priests, scribes and elders were not moved to shame and repentance. They were enraged and '. . . sought to lay hands on him at that very hour, for they perceived that he had told this parable against them, but they feared the people. So they watched him and sent spies, who pretended to be sincere, that they might catch him in something he said, so as to deliver him up to the authority and jurisdiction of the governor.'

A warning for us today
The parable was addressed to the scribes and chief priests, but it also stands as a call to examine our own lives, our own tenancy, for we are only 'tenants' in God's world. Satan's temptation is always to cause us to assume that we can own it and – just like the non-paying vineyard tenants – to suppress or blot out any consideration of our accountability to Almighty God from our thinking.

The temptation is then to ignore, or, for some more determined people, attempt to silence those faithful servants of God whose preaching calls us to 'pay our dues'; to turn, and in obedience live to the honour of the Lord God and his beloved Son. For this reason, Matthew Henry notes that the very best of God's prophets and Christ's ministers have consistently received the harshest treatment from the world and especially from the established religious leaders. Those who hold fast to the teaching of the Scriptures do well to take note of his warning and not be taken by surprise.

The vineyard given to others
Europe, North America and the rest of the English speaking world have been 'favoured tenants' of the Lord's vineyard for centuries. J.C Ryle asks if the principle of 'taking away and giving to others' is a warning to us? He writes, 'It is a mournful fact that in hardness, unbe-

lief, superstition and self righteousness the Christian Churches as a whole are little better than the Jewish church of our Lord's time.' Will the gospel vineyard be taken from us and given to the new tenants eagerly flocking into the kingdom and joyfully giving glory to God in Africa, Asia, India and China? If we heed the serious warning of this parable, we will pray earnestly for revival; for fruit-yielding churches in every city, town and village of our land, and for godly living, thinking and speaking to be welcomed and encouraged at every level of our society.

The Lord God has sent his servants. Finally, he sent his beloved Son. As our Lord challenged his hearers that day to pause and consider who he truly is, we do well to do the same. We ignore or reject the beloved Son of God – and in doing so fail to honour the One who sent him – to our great hurt and ultimately to our eternal peril. Here is the great application of this parable. It is the Lord's own application of it.

Will we be moved to 'feel shame in his presence'?
The promise of God to Solomon was true for the nation and leaders of Israel in the days of our Lord, and it still holds true for the Christian church today. 'If my people , who are called by my name, will humble themselves and pray and seek my face and turn from their ungodly ways; then I will hear from heaven , and will forgive their sin and heal their land.' If non-Jewish Christians, who have been 'grafted into' the Lord's people, can take hold of this wonderful promise today, how much more can God's ancient people Israel, even now, if they choose to do so.

In hardness of heart, the chief priests, scribes and elders leading the nation of Israel would not humble themselves. Will we as individuals, church and nation, 'humble ourselves and pray and seek God's face?' Will we, by God's enabling and grace, 'turn from our ungodly ways'?

'The stone that the builders rejected has become the head of the corner.' Here, set before us in this parable, is the beloved Son of God, the heir of the universe, the One to whom every knee will one day bow.

Heavenly Father, by the grace of your Holy Spirit, humble our proud, stubborn and self-centred hearts that we may recognise how little we have repaid of the honour that is due to you and how little we have respected the authority of your Son, the Lord Jesus. Son of God, have mercy upon us and give us hearts to gladly submit, obey and honour you. Soften our hardened hearts, revive your church and glorify your holy name in our day.

Questions for reflection and discussion

1. Who did the vineyard tenants represent? What can we learn from them?
2. Who do the servants represent? Do we have cause to thank God for sending modern servants of God?
3. Who does the beloved son represent? To what extent have we grasped who the Lord Jesus truly is? What power and authority does he hold?
4. Who does the owner of the vineyard represent? What do we owe him?
5. 'No human landlord seeking justice would be so patient.' How many of us have cause to stand back in amazement and gratitude for the incredible mercy and patience of our heavenly Father?

Some harder questions
6. To what extent are and should our churches be 'houses of prayer'? (See Luke 19:45-48)
7. Why should the Lord's practice of 'preaching and teaching the gospel' be absolutely central to Christian ministry?
8. 'By what authority' should disciples be 'preaching the gospel,' 'teaching all that Jesus commanded,' and 'making disciples'?

9. How can 'outward religion' take the place of inward belief and godly living?

10. The vineyard tenants refused to pay their 'rent'. As modern 'tenants', what do we owe the Lord God as churches, and as a nation?

11. What could 'being turned out of God's vineyard' mean for us as churches and as a nation?

Some questions for personal reflection

1. What is the proper place of 'Christ the Cornerstone' in our thinking and in our living?

2. What are the personal consequences of rejecting him now, and hereafter?

3. If 'Surely not!', 'God forbid!', 'It must not happen!' is only a wish to escape judgement, rather than to change our thinking and practice, what would be a far more appropriate response to the warning of God's judgement?

4. The religious leaders were settled and determined in their course. How hard is it for us to recognise and then be willing to turn from our settled ways of behaviour? What can make it possible?

5. By God's grace, can an overwhelming sense of shame before Almighty God and his Son be the key that enables us to come in true repentance and find the depth and wonder of forgiveness?

References

Sight and hearing restored – Isaiah 29:18&19, 35:4-6
'Behold your King' – Zechariah 9:9
The triumphal entry – Luke 19:28-40, Mark 11:1-11
Son of David – Matthew 21:9
Blessed is the King – Luke 19:38
The cry over Jerusalem – Luke 19:41-44
Cleansing of the temple – Luke 19:45-48

'Refiner's fire' – Malachi 3:3&4
John the Baptist's witness – John 1:29-37
Israel's glory – Luke 2:32
His adversaries put to shame – Luke 13:15-17
The stone that the builders rejected – Psalm 118:22 (23&24)
'Everyone who falls on that stone . . .' Words in accord with Isaiah 8:13-15 and Daniel 2:34-35
'Humble themselves and pray' – 2 Chronicles 7:14
Christians 'grafted in' – Romans 11:17-24

The Budding Fig Tree

"And there will be signs in sun and moon and stars, and on the earth distress of nations in perplexity because of the roaring of the sea and the waves, people fainting with fear and with foreboding of what is coming on the world. For the powers of the heavens will be shaken. And then they will see the Son of Man coming in a cloud with power and great glory. Now when these things begin to take place, straighten up and raise your heads, because your redemption is drawing near."

And he told them a parable: "Look at the fig tree, and all the trees. As soon as they come out in leaf you see for yourselves and know that the summer is already near. So also, when you see these things taking place, you know that the kingdom of God is near. Truly, I say to you, this generation will not pass away until all has taken place. Heaven and earth will pass away, but my words will not pass away.

"But watch yourselves lest your hearts be weighed down with dissipation and drunkenness and cares of this life, and that day come upon you suddenly like a trap. For it will come upon all who dwell on the face of the whole earth. But stay awake at all times, praying that you may have strength to escape all these things that are going to take place, and to stand before the Son of Man."
    Luke 21:25-36 English Standard Version

For us, this is a sharply relevant parable for days of unrest, pandemic and potentially devastating climate change.

The Parable of the Budding Fig Tree and All the Trees Coming into Leaf

The parable of the fig tree coming into leaf and the teaching around it is recorded by each of the first three gospel writers.

The setting – an overview
'Jesus looked up and saw the rich putting their gifts into the offering box, and he saw a poor widow put in two small copper coins. And he said, "Truly I tell you, this poor widow has put in more than all of them. For they all contributed out of their abundance, but she out of her poverty put in all she had to live on." And while some were speaking of the temple, how it was adorned with noble stones and offerings, he said, "As for these things that you see, the days will come when there will not be one stone upon another that will not be thrown down." And they asked him, "Teacher, when will these things be, and what will be the sign when these things are about to take place?"' (Luke 21:1-7) In answer to this two-fold question, Jesus spoke of all that was to come.

Living as we do nearly two thousand years later, we can see something of the beginning of the outworking of Jesus' prophetic words.

The first thing Jesus warned against was the succession of people who would falsely claim to be the Messiah, or to speak on his behalf. "See that you are not led astray. For many will come in my name, saying, 'I am he!' and 'The time is at hand!' Do not go after them." (Luke 21:8)

Looking far ahead, Jesus told of great international commotions, "Nation will rise against nation, and kingdom against kingdom. There will be great earthquakes, and in various places famines and pestilences. And there will be terrors and great signs in heaven." (Luke 21:10&11)

Looking to the immediate future, he warned the disciples, "But before all this they will lay their hands on you and persecute you, delivering you up to the synagogues and prisons, and you will be brought before kings and governors for my name's sake. This will be your opportunity to bear witness . . ." (Luke 21:12&13)

Looking some 40 years ahead, Jesus warned, "But when you see Jerusalem surrounded by armies, then know that its desolation has come near . . . there will be great distress upon the earth and wrath against this people. They will fall by the edge of the sword and be led captive among all nations, and Jerusalem will be trampled underfoot by the Gentiles, until the times of the Gentiles are fulfilled." (Luke 21:20& 24)

Finally, Jesus speaks of his return. ". . . And then they will see the Son of Man coming in a cloud with power and great glory. Now when you see these things begin to take place, straighten up and raise your heads, because your redemption is drawing near." (Luke 21:27-28)

It is in the setting of these words of warning and prophecy that our Lord tells the parable of the fig tree and the trees coming into leaf.

And he told them a parable
"Look at the fig tree, and all the trees. As soon as they come out in leaf you see for yourselves and know that summer is already near. So also, when you see these things taking place, you know that the kingdom of God is near."

Why did our Lord specifically draw attention to the fig tree? The fig was a very common and familiar local sight, and it could be that our Lord was drawing attention to a particular tree as an example. The fig tree has very large leaves and so when the swollen buds burst into leaf the change is particularly dramatic. Only Luke records Jesus mentioning all the other trees, from which the same great lesson can be learnt.

The parable was told as Jesus was approaching Passover and the cross of Calvary. It was springtime and, with the arrival of the warmer weather, the swollen buds on the trees were bursting into leaf. So it was a very natural, seasonable and clear parable.

'Now when these things begin to take place'
These words of Jesus introduce his telling of the parable, and are therefore the key to understanding it. They also give us the key to understanding the times in which we are living.

If disciples then, and now, watch and pray and take note of the great happenings of the times in which they are living, and compare them with the signs the Lord had just described, they will be able to judge, writes Matthew Henry, 'with as much certainty and assurance as they could judge the approach of summer by the budding forth of the trees.'

In order to read the times in which disciples are living, it has always been essential to pay close attention to the signs Jesus spelled out.

The fulfilment of the signs that Jesus outlined

False claims and false prophets
And he said, "See that you are not led astray. For many will come in my name, saying, 'I am he!' and, 'The time is at hand!' Do not go after them" (Luke 21:8)

Despite Jesus' warning, "Do not go after them," over the centuries among Hebrew people charismatic leaders have arisen who falsely claim to be the long awaited Messiah – and they have gathered followers.

Throughout the Gentile (non-Jewish) world, a great many people who have tasted something of Christianity have been led astray. They have followed religious leaders whose teachings have caused them to wander very far from the teachings of our Lord and his chosen apostles.

The persecution and the wonders that so closely followed the birth of the church at Pentecost

"But before all this they will lay their hands on you and persecute you, delivering you up to the synagogues and prisons, and you will be brought before kings and governors for my name's sake. This will be your opportunity to bear witness." (Luke 21:12-13)

Initially, as the apostles taught daily in the temple, they, and those whom the Lord added to the new-born church, found favour with all the people. But all too soon the religious authorities stepped in. They first arrested Peter and John and threatened them. Later, they were again arrested and put in prison. 'But,' Luke records, 'during the night an angel of the Lord opened the prison doors and brought them out, and said, "Go and stand in the temple and speak to the people all the words of this Life."'

Stephen, 'full of grace and power' and 'doing great wonders and signs among the people' was seized and brought before the council who, hearing his faithful witness, ground their teeth and stoned him in rage. On the day of Stephen's death, there arose 'a great persecution against the church in Jerusalem, and they were all scattered throughout the regions of Judea and Samaria, except the apostles.'

The young man Saul, who had approved the stoning of Stephen, set about 'ravaging the church, and entering house after house, he dragged off men and women and committed them to prison.'

Herod the king 'laid violent hands on some who belonged to the church. He killed James the brother of John with the sword and, when he saw that it pleased the Jews, he proceeded to arrest Peter also.' Despite chains and guards, the Lord sent an angel and Peter was yet again miraculously set free.

After his dramatic conversion on the road to Damascus, Saul became the great apostle Paul, and also suffered almost endless persecution for the gospel. Brought before leaders, governors and kings, Paul fearlessly and tirelessly proclaimed 'Jesus Christ and him crucified' first to his own people, the Jews, and then on their rejection of it, to the Gentile world. As he did so, the Holy Spirit honoured the apostle's words with God-given power and effectiveness.

The fall of Jerusalem and the temple reduced to rubble

"But when you see Jerusalem surrounded by armies, then know that its desolation is near. Then let those who are in Judea flee to the mountains, and let those who are inside the city depart, and let not those who are out in the country enter it, for these are days of vengeance, to fulfil all that is written. Alas for women who are pregnant and for those who are nursing infants in those days! For there will be great distress upon the earth and wrath against this people. They will fall by the edge of the sword and be led captive among all nations, and Jerusalem will be trampled underfoot by the Gentiles, until the times of the Gentiles are fulfilled." (Luke 21:20-24)

Within the lifetime of many of those listening to Jesus, these words were fulfilled. The unthinkable happened. Jerusalem, the strong and secure city of David, was surrounded, overthrown and razed to the ground by the all-conquering Roman army under Titus.

Luke records Jesus saying, ". . . when you see Jerusalem surrounded by armies, then know that its desolation is near. Then let those who are in Judea flee to the mountains . . ." Matthew and Mark refer to our Lord giving warning to escape when they see the 'abomination of desolation standing in the holy place' or 'where it ought not to be'. Matthew and Mark are alluding to the prophecies of Daniel, but these prophecies are not mentioned by the Gentile writer Luke. He simply records our Lord saying 'surrounded by armies' and warning of desolation, but the prophecy of Daniel would exactly fit the vast, ruthless Roman army surrounding Jerusalem with their Eagle standards, and emperor-worshiping banners.

Eusebius (c. 260-340, the 'Father of Church History') records that when they saw the city beginning to be surrounded by the Roman armies, many believers, aware of our Lord's warning, fled and during the siege took refuge in Pella, a city on the eastern side of the Jordan valley, a little under twenty miles south of the Sea of Galilee.

As it was the Passover season when the Romans began their offensive, the city was packed with people who had come up to the city for the feast. After a brief siege from without and many self-inflicted tragedies within, the city fell in August A.D. 70 with the loss of over a million lives. Over ten thousand survivors were taken prisoner and sold into slavery.

The temple, considered to be the very seat of God's presence among his people, was reduced to rubble, 'not one stone left on another.' This was certainly not the intention of Titus, who had ordered the temple to be spared, but it was totally destroyed; burned down by fire which the defeated people of Jerusalem first started. It is possible that Titus' aim of placing the Roman standard, the symbol of conquest and worship of the Emperor, at the heart of the temple, would so desecrate it in the eyes of the defeated people that it provoked them to destroy their own temple.

So strong did the city first appear to Titus, that the Jewish historian Josephus (c.37-100) quotes him exclaiming, "We certainly had God on our side in this war; and it was God alone who ejected the Jews from these fortifications." Titus is also said to have declined the wreath of victory, saying that the victory was not his, he only served as an instrument of divine wrath.

There could well be a further fulfilment of Jesus' words concerning armies surrounding Jerusalem, for at the return of the Son of Man,

The times of the Gentiles and the desolation of the Jewish people

". . . there will be great distress upon the earth and wrath against this people. They will fall by the edge of the sword and be led captive among all nations, and Jerusalem will be trampled underfoot by the Gentiles, until the times of the Gentiles are fulfilled."

Jesus, writes Matthew Henry, 'foretells the terrible havoc that should be made of the Jewish nation . . . after days of patience long abused, there will come days of vengeance; for reprieves are not pardons.'

With the fall of Jerusalem in AD 70 temple worship ceased and the Jewish people were dispersed throughout the Roman Empire. This was to be the beginning of many centuries of great difficulty. Scattered throughout the nations, they have been hated, hounded, falsely accused, oppressed, robbed and despised. More than one attempt has been made to completely wipe the Jewish nation from the face of the earth, and yet under the hand of God they have survived. Although they have been scattered, persecuted, and, until recently, homeless, their continuing existence as a distinct people must surely be a clear sign of the reality of God and of his sovereign control of human history.

These first four signs spoken of by Jesus have been fulfilled: false leaders have arisen leading many astray; terrible treatment and yet wonderful opportunities to witness for their Lord were given to the disciples; the fall of Jerusalem with the destruction of the temple has taken place; and the centuries of oppression, dispersion and dreadful treatment of the Hebrew people together with present day anti-Semitism continue to be a shameful blot on world history.

Jerusalem has been trampled on, neglected, desecrated and fought over by Gentiles for approaching 2,000 years. Have the times of the Gentiles been all but fulfilled? The non-Jewish nations have been given ample opportunity to receive and to share the gospel message and, in recent decades, the people of Israel have been able to return to their land. Are the times of the Gentiles coming to their end – or perhaps coming to their devastating climax?

The Trees Coming into Leaf – the Budding Fig Tree, continued

The Coming of the Son of Man

"And there will be signs in sun and moon and stars, and on earth distress of nations in perplexity because of the roaring of the sea and the waves, people fainting with fear and with foreboding of what is coming on the world. For the powers of the heavens will be shaken. And then they will see the Son of Man coming in a cloud with power and great glory. Now when these things begin to take place, straighten up and raise your heads, because your redemption is drawing near." (Luke 21:25-28)

Norval Geldenays comments that the fall of Jerusalem affected one small region and one people. The return of the Son of Man will 'embrace the whole world and finally and forever determine the eternal fate of every individual.'

"Immediately after the tribulation of those days the sun will be darkened, and the moon will not give its light, and the stars will fall from heaven, and the powers of the heavens will be shaken. Then will appear the sign of the Son of Man, and then all the tribes of the earth will mourn, and they will see the Son of Man coming on the clouds of heaven with power and great glory. And he will send out his angels with a loud trumpet call, and they will gather his elect from the four winds, from one end of heaven to the other. From the fig tree learn its lesson . . ." (Matthew 24:29-32)

William Barclay notes that the coming of the Son of Man will be associated with all the distress and confusion God's faithful prophets, Isaiah, Joel, Amos and Zephaniah had foretold concerning the 'Day of the Lord.' Isaiah spoke of the Day of the Lord in the same terms as our Lord; the sun, the moon, the stars; the whole created order in great confusion and commotion.

As Jesus warned, men and women will be filled with overwhelming apprehension; fainting for fear of the future. (Luke 21:26)

These great upheavals, writes John Calvin, are signs to summon humanity to turn to the Lord God and to honour both him and his anointed Son; to repent. But – will we acknowledge our failure to honour the God in whose hand is our very existence? Or will we treat our Maker with contempt until the last day?

Until the Lord Jesus returns, the kingdom of God continues to be ignored and despised by the world. But on that day every eye will see him, God's anointed Son. The Son of Man, who lived on earth as one despised and rejected, will then be seen in great glory and majesty.

To those who have ignored and failed to honour him, and so face his just judgement, his appearance must inevitably bring great terror. But to those who have received him, and continue to serve him as his faithful servants, the return of the Son of Man will bring awe and wonder, and great joy.

The nearness of the kingdom of God
"Now when these things begin to take place, straighten up and raise your heads, because your redemption is drawing near." (Luke 21:28)

Illustrated by this parable of the fig tree and its leaves, disciples are solemnly called to take careful note of the signs of human history and so be prepared for what the Lord Jesus warned would be the terrifyingly violent and fearful end of this present evil age. These awesome and awful world-wide happenings are the birth pains that will herald the approach of the beginning of the Messiah's glorious reign.

". . . when you see these things taking place, you know that the kingdom of God is near. Truly, I say to you, this generation will not pass away until all has taken place. Heaven and earth will pass away, but my words will not pass away." (Luke 21:31-32)

The words 'this generation' could refer to the disciples and those who were present and physically hearing his words, many of whom saw glimpses of the glory of the kingdom of God at Pentecost and in the days of the early church, and some of whom lived to also witnessed the fall of Jerusalem and the destruction of the temple.

However, the word 'generation' can also be translated 'nation' or 'people', and so Jesus could have been speaking of the amazing continuity of the Jewish people. Despite being dreadfully mistreated and having no homeland for nearly 2,000 years, they are still a distinct people. Or, as a third possibility, he could have been speaking of an ongoing strand or 'remnant' of faithful believers, scattered throughout the world, a people watching, waiting, holding the faith, about his business and ready for his return.

Several passages in our Lord's teaching make it plain that he did not indicate that his return would be in a very short span of time. Even in this chapter, Jesus had taught, "And when you hear of wars and tumults, do not be terrified, for these things must first take place, but the end will not be at once." (Luke 21:9) And the words 'the times of the Gentiles' suggest several different Gentile nations ruling over Jerusalem, and therefore the elapse of quite some time. (Luke 21:24)

J. C. Ryle draws attention to the words of our Lord, "Heaven and earth will pass away, but my words will not pass away." The words are very strong and solemn. The Lord Jesus does not speak as the prophets did, 'Thus says the Lord,' but speaks with all the authority of the Godhead, '. . . my words will not pass away.' Although there are manuscripts which give scholars occasion to challenge these words, the words of Jesus will stand because, as the gospel writers make plain, he is Emmanuel, God amongst us.

The great significance of Revelation chapter five is that the scroll of future human destiny has been placed in the hands of 'the Lamb who was slain.' Into the hands of the One who told this parable has been committed all authority, and so he who gave these warnings will oversee the fulfilment of his own word. Our Lord's words will neither fail nor pass away.

The significance of our Lord's words and of this parable

The parable of the fig tree and all the trees bursting into leaf is as sharp and relevant for us in our day as it was to our Lord's first hearers. It is clear from the New Testament, that the church in its early years lived in eager expectation of the fulfilment of Jesus' promised return within their own lifetime. Two thousand years later we are still called to heed our Lord's words and to be constantly on our watch and prepared.

Our natural modern human assumption is that the kingdom of heaven will be ushered in by universal peace among people, but that is not what our Lord said. The Lord Jesus uses very dramatic language to speak of wars and confusion, perplexity and great distress. There will be famines, earthquakes, international wars, and a general hatred and persecution of Jews, God-fearing Gentiles and believing Christian people. All these things will be taking place in such a spiritually-freezing and increasingly godless atmosphere, that the love of many both for the Lord and for one another will grow cold. Could we be living at the beginning of days like these?

'For nation will rise against nation, and kingdom against kingdom, and there will be famines and earthquakes in various places. All these are but the beginning of the birth pains. Then they will deliver you up to tribulation and put you to death, and you will be hated by all nations for my name's sake. And then many will fall away and betray one another and hate one another. And many false prophets will arise and lead many astray. And because lawlessness will be increased, the love of many will grow cold. But the one who endures to the end will be saved. And this gospel of the kingdom will be proclaimed throughout the whole world as a testimony to all nations; and then the end will come.' (Matthew 24:7-14)

Godless men 'will be perplexed and fearful,' writes Leon Morris, 'they will know that strange things are happening but will not understand what is about to befall them.' J. C. Ryle comments, 'The second coming of Christ will be attended by everything which can make it alarming to the senses and heart of man.'

It is during world-wide and overwhelming human disasters like these, that we are to hold fast and look for the sudden appearance of the Son of Man.

The unbelieving world will always regard Jesus' warnings as 'fairy tales', but despite clever weaving of words or sneers, it is clearly essential for believers to hold fast to our Lord's words, for only then shall we be prepared.

The ongoing call to be ready

The parable of the budding fig tree together with these warnings of the Lord surrounding it, come starkly into focus in days like our own; days of global unrest, pandemic and potentially devastating climate change.

"But watch yourselves lest your hearts be weighed down with dissipation and drunkenness and cares of this life, and that day come upon you suddenly like a trap. For it will come upon all who dwell on the face of the whole earth. But stay awake at all times, praying that you may have strength to escape all these things that are going to take place, and to stand before the Son of Man." (Luke 21:34-36)

These words summon us to walk closely with the Lord, and not to let the all-consuming cares, concerns and pleasures of this world make us like drunken people; dull-headed and sleepy. They call us to beware of all that would quench our spiritual discernment and alertness. The earth-shaking days of which Jesus had been speaking are clearly not local events, but the final days of the world as we know it. We are to keep alert, pleading for strength and godly wisdom that we may be found watching and ready, rather than overtaken and trapped. Our ultimate joy and aim should be to 'stand before the Son of Man.' The meaning here is not 'to bow in his presence and receive his judgement,' – as we all must, either to be honoured by him, or to be dismissed by him to our endless regret. The meaning here is to stand before the Son of Man as a faithful servant, standing in the Master's presence and ready to be of further service to him.

In every succeeding generation, we are called to live with an eye to the signs of the times and to be constantly prepared. Kenneth Bailey notes that, 'Some believers in every century have held the firm conviction that they were living in the last days . . . Christians in every age are encouraged to live expectantly and at the same time never to presume to read the mind of the Father as regards the timing of the end of all things.' Disciples are nowhere encouraged to work out a timetable for the return of the Son of Man.

In every generation there have also been good folk who, touched by war, epidemic, fire or flood, conclude and proclaim that 'this is the end.' But, again, the Lord did warn, "And when you hear of wars and tumults, do not be terrified, for these things must first take place, but the end will not be at once." (Luke 21:9) Rather, our Lord warned us to take careful note of the coming together of many world-wide and world-convulsing events and disasters that together present an overwhelming threat to humanity's very existence. When these come, be prepared. "Now when these things begin to take place, straighten up and raise your heads, because your redemption is drawing near."

As the trees bursting into leaf are a clear sign that summer is near, so disciples then, and now, are called to watch the signs, and to be ready for times of great testing, and ready for the return of the Son of Man.

The Lord Jesus had earlier warned his disciples to be constantly prepared, ". . . for the Son of man is coming at an hour you do not expect." But will we be ready? Will I, will you, be prepared?

Heavenly Father, give us ears to hear and minds and hearts to heed these words of your Son.

We pray for Jewish people, both scattered throughout the nations and gathered in their homeland, to whom these words were first addressed.

We pray, too, for the people of the Gentile nations, the vast majority of whom are completely unaware of the seriousness of warnings such as these.

Father, it is not your will that any should perish but that all should come to repentance. We plead with you to send a world-wide spiritual revival. Cause us to turn, repent, believe, take heed, watch, pray and be faithfully about your business – and so be found ready for the return of your glorious and anointed Son.

Questions for personal reflection or discussion

1. Our Lord's first disciples were hated and hounded, are there situations and places where this is still the case? How might we support and encourage our fellow disciples?

2. Jerusalem has been trampled on and fought-over for centuries by non-Jewish nations. Are there signs that the 'times of the Gentiles' could be nearly over; signs that call us to be alert in our day to the return of the Son of Man?

3. In what ways is the parable of the bursting out of the leaves in the spring a warning to those who have yet to heed our Lord's words and believe, and a call to believers to wake up and be alert?

4. Why will the final times leading up to the return of the Son of Man be very difficult days in which to live?

5. In times of great personal or national crisis, why can the attitude of true believers be so different from that of those around us?

6. How can we best encourage one another to hold fast and be ready?

7. In what ways can the words of our Lord help us to stand firm?

References

Found favour with all the people – Acts 2:47

Arrested Peter and John and threatened them – Acts 4:3&21

Speak to the people all the words of this Life – Acts 5:18-20

Stephen, 'full of grace and power' and 'doing great wonders and signs' – Acts 6:8

Stephen, brought before the council who stoned him – Acts 7:54-58

A great persecution against the church in Jerusalem – Acts 8:1

The young man Saul . . . 'ravaging the church' – Acts 7:58-8:3

Paul's conversion on the road to Damascus – Acts 9

Herod the king . . . Peter miraculously set free – Acts 12:1-11

Paul preaching 'Jesus Christ and him crucified' – 1 Corinthians 2:1-2 and Luke's account of Paul's life of faithful witness, particularly Acts chapters 22-28

Abomination of desolation – Matthew 24:15-21 and Mark 13:14-19

The prophecies of Daniel – Daniel 9:27 and 11:31

The fall of Jerusalem and the temple – Luke 19:41-44 and 21:6

The day of the Lord – Isaiah 13:9-13, Joel 1:15 and 2:11, Amos 5:18-20, Zephaniah 1:14-18

Every eye will see him – Revelation 1:7
Heaven and earth will pass away – Luke 21:31-33
The 'Lamb who was slain' – Revelation 5:1-14
All authority – Matthew 28:18
That all should come to repentance – 2 Peter 3:9
The Son of man is coming at an hour you do not expect – Luke 12:40

Footnotes

1). Matthew and Mark record the teaching of the twenty first chapter of Luke's gospel as a conversation with the disciples on the slopes of the Mount of Olives, overlooking the temple and the city of Jerusalem. But from Luke's account, it could have taken place there, overlooking Jerusalem, or it could have been part of Jesus' public teaching in the temple.

In chapter twenty, Jesus was teaching in the temple, 'And in the hearing of all the people he said to his disciples, "Beware of the scribes . . ."' (Luke 20:45&46) Then chapter twenty one continues as Jesus noticed people contributing to the temple treasury. The chapter concludes with the words, 'And every day he was teaching in the temple, but at night he went out and lodged on the mount called Olivet. And early in the morning all the people came to him in the temple to hear him.' (Luke 21:37&38)

2). Our Lord's teaching in Luke chapter twenty one is full of prophecy; a looking ahead to future events. Looking at the horizon, the foothills and the great mountain ranges beyond are all 'on the horizon', with little or no reference to their order or indication of what lies between them – which could be great distances. So in speaking of future events there is a compression of the events so that they are all 'on the horizon'. This is sometimes known as 'prophetic fore-shortening'.

3). Matthew and Mark record our Lord giving warning to escape from Jerusalem when they see 'abomination of desolation standing in the holy place' or 'where it ought not to be'. Matthew and Mark are alluding to the prophecies of Daniel, 'on the wing of abominations comes one who makes desolate' (Daniel 9:27) and 'Forces from him shall appear and profane the temple and fortress, and shall take away the regular burnt offering. And they shall set up the abomination that makes desolate.' (Dan 11:31) Luke does not draw attention to these prophecies.

Three Striking Sayings or Short Parables Spoken by Jesus at the Very Beginning of his Ministry

The New Patch and the New Wine

On one of those days, as he was teaching, Pharisees and teachers of the law were sitting there, who had come from every village of Galilee and Judea and from Jerusalem. And the power of the Lord was with him to heal. And behold some men were bringing on a bed a man who was paralysed, and they were seeking to bring him in and lay him before Jesus, but finding no way to bring him in, because of the crowd, they went up on the roof and let him down with his bed through the tiles into the midst before Jesus. And when he saw their faith, he said, "Man, your sins are forgiven you." And the scribes and the Pharisees began to question, saying, "Who is this who speaks blasphemies? Who can forgive sins but God alone?" When Jesus perceived their thoughts, he answered them, "Why do you question in your hearts? Which is easier, to say, 'Your sins are forgiven you,' or to say, 'Rise and walk'? But that you may know that the Son of Man has authority on earth to forgive sins" – he said to the man who was paralysed – "I say to you, rise, pick up your bed and go home." And immediately he rose up before them and picked up what he had been lying on and went home, glorifying God. And amazement seized them all, and they glorified God and were filled with awe, saying, "We have seen extraordinary things today."

After this he went out and saw a tax collector named Levi, sitting at the tax booth. And he said to him, "Follow me." And leaving everything, he rose and followed him.

And Levi made him a great feast in his house, and there was a large company of tax collectors and others reclining at the table with them. And the Pharisees and their scribes grumbled at his disciples, saying, "Why do you eat and drink with tax collectors and sinners?" And Jesus answered them, "Those who are well have no need of a physician, but those who are sick. I have not come to call the righteous but sinners to repentance."

And they said to him, "The disciples of John fast often and offer prayers, and so do the disciples of the Pharisees, but your disciples eat and drink." And Jesus said to them, "Can you make wedding guests fast while the bridegroom is with them? The days will come when the bridegroom is taken away from them, and then they will fast in those days." He also told them a parable: "No one tears a piece from a new garment and puts it on an old garment. If he does, he will tear the new, and the piece from the new will not match the old. And no one puts new wine into old wineskins. If he does, the new wine will burst the skins and it will be spilled, and the skins will be destroyed. But new wine must be put into fresh wineskins. And no one after drinking old wine desires new, for he says, 'The old is good.'"

Luke 5:17-39 English Standard Version

The New Patch and the New Wine

The events that led to Jesus telling the parables
The parables are set in the very earliest days of Jesus' ministry. Returning from the time in the wilderness, where he had been fasting, praying and preparing for his days of public ministry, Jesus spoke in the synagogue at Nazareth, his own home town. People were both amazed by his words – and very seriously offended by them. They

threatened to kill him, but safely leaving Nazareth, he began preaching and teaching around Galilee.

The call of the first disciples
Great crowds followed him to the extent that on one occasion he taught from Peter's boat a little way from the shore. When he had finished, Jesus asked Peter to let down his net for a catch. And Peter responded, 'Master we have toiled all night and caught nothing.' (How many missionaries and ministers, Sunday school teachers and youth leaders have echoed those sad words of Peter!) However, Peter's next words are there for our encouragement. 'Nevertheless, at your word . . .' and he let down the net and enclosed so great a catch of fish that he needed to call his fishing partners to help land them. It was following that incident of the great catch of fish safely landed, that Jesus challenged them to leave their nets, and to follow him; to become fishers of men for the kingdom of heaven.

The scribes and Pharisees begin to question
And yet what is this? 'Pharisees and teachers of the law were sitting there, who had come from every village of Galilee and Judea and from Jerusalem.' The Lord Jesus had hardly begun to gather his disciples, and yet the Pharisees and their scribes were already coming from all over the country, to examine, challenge and increasingly to confirm one another in their rejection of him.

A paralysed man's friends longed to beg Jesus to have mercy on him. However, there was no chance of bringing him anywhere near him, because of the crowd. Showing great faith and determination, their answer was to let him down at Jesus' feet – through the roof.

When Jesus saw their faith, he said, 'Man, your sins are forgiven you.' The Pharisees immediately murmured, 'Who is this who speaks blasphemies? Who can forgive sins but God alone?' They were absolutely right, only God can forgive sins. But to show them who he really was, and that he had such authority, he said to the man who was paralysed – 'I say to you, rise, pick up your bed and go home.' At Jesus' command, the paralysed man stood up, took up his mat and walked home, glorifying God. Jesus had compassion on this totally disabled man, and by this dramatic sign, very clearly demonstrated who he was. Luke concludes, 'And amazement seized them all, and they glorified God and were filled with awe, saying, "We have seen extraordinary things today"'

The people were amazed and glorified God, but the scribes and Pharisees were somewhat less inclined to do so. They did not wish to draw the conclusion the mighty miracle demanded. Their eyes had seen, their ears had heard, but they were unwilling to perceive that here before them was Emmanuel, the long promised Messiah, God amongst them.

The call of Levi, also known as Matthew
'Those who are well have no need of a physician, but those who are sick. I have not come to call the righteous but sinners to repentance.'

Levi was one of the many tax collectors who were extracting money from their fellow countrymen – the taxes and custom charges demanded by the ruling Roman conquerors. These collectors often grew very wealthy by a fee they added for themselves. The fee was the way the Romans paid them for tax collecting. Not surprisingly, they were hated and regarded as traitors and thieves. Yet Jesus chose one of them, Levi, to be his disciple.

Calling together many of his tax-collecting friends, Levi held a feast with Jesus and his disciples. Again the Pharisees and scribes were present to 'critically assess' the scene. They did not miss the opportunity. Perhaps trying to drive a wedge between Jesus and his disciples, the Pharisees and their scribes grumbled to his disciples, saying, 'Why do you eat and drink with tax collectors and sinners?'

Were they implying by their question, 'What kind of "Messiah" is this you are following, who leads you to be eating and drinking with such fallen, soiled wretches?' They themselves would never dream of mixing, let alone eating, with such 'unrighteous sinners'.

Luke does not record a response from the disciples. Jesus answered for them. He had not come to call those who considered themselves righteous. He had come to call to repentance those who had fallen.

Can you make wedding guests fast while the bridegroom is with them? The Pharisees changed direction but persisted, asking Jesus why he and his disciples were not conforming to the times of fasting and prayer which both the Pharisees and the disciples of John the Baptist observed. In the light of Mark's account, they might have asked, 'John the Baptist's disciples and ours are fasting and praying, so how is it that yours are eating and drinking?' Implying, 'If you don't keep the traditional rules how can you possibly be a man of God, let alone the Holy One, God's promised Messiah?'

'The days will come when the bridegroom is taken away from them, and then they will fast in those days.' Most certainly, there is a time to fast and pray, as Jesus himself had been doing in the wilderness not many days earlier, and by his example and his teaching, our Lord clearly taught his disciples to both fast and to pray. However, there is also a time to feast, and for the disciples this was such a time. This was the wedding feast and the bridegroom was with them.

William Hendriksen suggests that Jesus' answer with his reference to himself as 'the bridegroom,' – which was a constant Bible picture of the Lord and his people – and the reference to his being 'taken away', could have been a pointer to his being the Suffering Servant of the Lord, spoken of by Isaiah. If that is so, for those with ears to ear, here was yet another confirmation that he was indeed the promised Messiah.

An overview of the two parables

To his hearers, the teachings of Jesus were completely 'new', and so Jesus compared them with things that are new. In fact, his teachings were a 'new' uncovering of the unchanging ways of God, which had become obscured and smothered by human traditions.

'No one tears a piece from a new garment and puts it on an old garment. If he does, he will tear the new, and the piece from the new will not match the old. And no one puts new wine into old wineskins. If he does, the new wine will burst the skins and it will be spilled, and the skins will be destroyed. But new wine must be put into fresh wineskins. And no one after drinking old wine desires new, for he says, "The old is good."' (Luke 5:36-39)

In these two parables, Jesus gave examples of things that no sensible person would mix, simply because they cannot be put together without the result being ruin and loss. And Luke, alone, records the reason why we, as human beings, persist in doing such things. The reason is our preference for the familiar things that we are used to. Jesus illustrated this by our preference for the 'old wine'.

Mixtures that end in destruction

Teaching continuously and in different situations, Jesus sometimes used very similar parables and word pictures to draw out different points. Matthew and Mark in their gospels record a telling of the parable of the sewn patch, in which Jesus said, "No one puts a piece of unshrunk cloth on an old garment, for the patch tears away from the garment, and a worse tear is made." As it is washed and worn, the new patch shrinks, and being stronger tears away. Jesus was showing that, just as a new piece of cloth sewn to an old garment will tear away, so true godliness and human tradition will inevitably tear themselves apart. (The New Testament record of the dealings of the religious leaders with our Lord and his apostles, and of their dealings with those who came to believe through their testimony, taken together with church history over the centuries, has very painfully demonstrated the truth of Jesus' words.)

Luke records a slightly different telling of the parable, "No one tears a piece from a new garment and puts it on an old garment. If he does, he will tear the new, and the piece from the new will not match the old." Jesus was making a different point. The newer cloth torn from a new garment ruins that garment, and as a patch on an older garment, it is useless as it does not match the old. Both garments, the new one from which it was torn, and the old one onto which it was sewn, will be rendered good-for-nothing rags.

(i) *Combining:* The parable of the cloth torn from the new and sewn onto the old, was a warning to those who, like the Pharisees, would attempt to 'sew' the glorious liberty of true godly ways, as Jesus taught and displayed them, onto traditional systems of religion. The 'new garment' of his teaching is ruined by tearing out a portion, and, sewn onto an old garment, the patch never matches. It becomes clear that attempting to create a mixture of human thinking and Jesus' teaching, detracts from, dilutes and, in a real sense, ruins the true message of the gospel.

(ii) *Containing*: In the parable of the new wine put into an old wineskin, Jesus was illustrating what happens when true godly liberty and freedom are confined within human religious traditions, rules and regulations. Putting new wine into an old wineskin, although unfamiliar to us, would have been a familiar picture in those days. Wineskins were made from the skins of sheep or goats, shaved and turned inside-out. A fresh skin would be flexible and able to accommodate the completing of the fermentation process. New wine put into an old brittle skin, as it completes fermentation and matures, will weaken, stretch and burst the old skin, and so both the wine and the wineskin will be lost; '. . . new wine must be put into fresh wineskins.' Our Lord was showing that just as new wine will burst an old wineskin and so be lost, so true godliness cannot be restrained, let alone contained, within our human traditions without leading to tensions, difficulties and great loss.

Each of these parables seems to have two aspects. The first is the loss of the true teaching of our Lord Jesus – pictured in the parables as the new garment being torn and ruined, and by the new wine being totally lost. The second aspect is the futile, human attempts to 'incorporate' or 'contain' his teaching within human thinking and traditions – pictured as sewing onto an old garment a new and unmatching patch, and putting the new wine into an old wineskin and so causing it to burst.

Nevertheless, the Pharisees desired to achieve just such a mixture; our Lord's teaching contained within their own traditions.

'And no one after drinking old wine desires new, for he says, "The old is good."'
At an everyday level, in our work place or in our home, many of us tend to resist change; we regard the old and familiar as 'good'. Our well-established and comfortable ways seem 'better' than some newly introduced approach or system. We find ourselves challenged, and so regard our familiar ways as preferable. 'The old is good.' Or, as some manuscripts have it, 'The old is better.'

Here is the reason why the Pharisees were insisting that their established times of fasting and other regulations were kept, and the reason why we continue to try to contain vital Christianity in structures and systems of our own human devising. However, as we attempt to incorporate the Lord's teaching into our thinking and traditions, we tear portions from Christ's new and perfect garment and so spoil or ruin it. And as we attempt to contain his teaching within our traditions and thinking we spill or lose the treasure entrusted to us; the new wine of the apostolic gospel. The end result is patches that do not match and wine skins that burst and lose everything. As our Lord was making plain, combining or containing his teaching within human thinking and traditions, will inevitably prevent the message of the gospel shining forth or being clearly understood.

The fulfilment of our Lord's warning
The religious leaders, in New Testament times, clung to their comfortable position in society, their rituals and their established ways, and rejected the challenge of the gospel of God. On the basis of their preference for their traditional ways, the scribes and Pharisees could not comprehend why Jesus and his disciples were mixing and eating with tax collectors. They could not comprehend why he and the disciples were failing to keep the appointed fasts. And what was the final outcome? Clinging to their preferred, carefully regulated religious ways, and blinded to what the Lord God was actually doing before their eyes, they finally secured the death of Israel's glory, their own long-promised Messiah, the very Son of God.

The apostles and the people in the churches they founded did not fare better than their Lord. They were hunted, hounded, stoned and imprisoned, just for their faithfulness to the Lord God and to his Son, and for their refusal to follow either the traditions of Judaism or the current way of life of the cities in which they preached.

The apostle Paul's teaching, just like the piece of cloth, did not 'match' pagan ways, neither did it match Judaism – and the reaction of each of them was sometimes violent as it was at Philippi and Ephesus and as it was at the end of Paul's ministry, in Jerusalem.

Even within the newly founded Christian churches, Paul constantly found that he had to defend the true faith from Jewish believers who were determined to pour Christianity into the old wineskin of Jewish traditions, and so keep it within Judaism. They were insisting that all believers, Jewish and Gentile alike, must submit to Jewish traditions and rituals.

Throughout the history of the church, can we see the out-working of these parables?

Whenever the teaching of our Lord and his chosen apostles has been rediscovered and upheld, the reaction of church leaders has been very much like that of the Pharisees. Like them, the church leaders may have meant well, but have come to regard the apostolic teaching as 'not matching' the current teachings and traditions of the church, and, therefore, in need of being contained or excluded.

Down the centuries, the cry of the crowd in Jerusalem, condemning the apostle Paul, has often been echoed against those who closely follow the teaching of our Lord and his apostles, 'Away with such a fellow from the earth!'

Athanasius, the Bishop of Alexandria (c. 296-373), found himself standing 'against the world' as he upheld the clear teaching of the apostles concerning the divine origin and nature, the deity, of the Lord Jesus. Like the piece of new cloth, the Bishop's faithful teaching clashed completely with the thinking of his day. As a result he suffered exile on several occasions.

When the teaching of our Lord and his apostles was rediscovered towards the end of the Middle Ages, the church rejected it. It was a patch that not only did not 'match' the teachings and traditions the church had developed over many years – there was a 'clash'. Many of those rejoicing in and proclaiming the newly re-discovered faith, later known as the Reformers, were hounded and often violently silenced. Throughout Europe the church was determined to contain it, and yet, as our Lord warned, it could not be contained and the result was a terrible tearing and bursting apart at great cost.

In our own land, godly people and leaders alike were imprisoned and many burned at the stake during the reign of Queen Mary, who was determined to hold fast to the old and traditional ways, and to contain or suppress the new.

In today's world, many of our religious leaders seem determined to contain the teaching of our Lord and his chosen apostles within the 'wineskin' of current secular thinking and political correctness. So we find the church tearing itself apart over some of the apostolic teachings that lie at the heart of Christian faith; the person and work of the Lord Jesus Christ, his deity and the significance of his cross and resurrection. And it is tearing itself apart over practical issues such as the spiritual headship of women, and matters of holiness of living such as the acceptability of homosexual practice.

Just as the Pharisees attempted to put pressure on Jesus' disciples to fit in with their traditions, here are the church leaders attempting to 'blend' or 'contain' the word of God so that it fits within 'modern enlightened thinking'. The result is at best, an uncomfortable but tolerated mismatch and at worst, exclusion or a bursting and tearing apart.

It is salutary to ask, 'Would those holding to the teaching of the Bible, and unwilling to accept current politically correct views concerning gender, be appointed ministers?' Sadly, in the mainstream churches, this seems to be increasingly unlikely.

What of those ministers and churches still 'devoting themselves to' and holding fast to the Apostles' teaching? In the American Episcopal Church, many of them have found themselves compelled to leave both their denomination and their buildings, as, nearer to home, have some churches in Scotland.

Despite these discouraging signs, it is so encouraging to hold fast to our Lord's words to Peter, '. . . I will build my church'. The Lord can use human organizations while they keep close to him and do his will, but he is not dependent on them. He is well able to build the true people of God as, and where, and how he chooses.

Some more, subtle modern patchwork in our churches
You have probably noticed how often you find echoes, reflections and phrases of the Bible sewn onto or into the fabric of sects and offshoots of true Christianity. These echoes and phrases give them a familiar

and authentic ring and yet, you can see from this parable what they really are. They are simply attractive pieces torn from the true apostolic gospel and sewn onto, or sometimes subtly woven into, a garment of human devising.

Many new churches have sprung up, each claiming to follow 'the new wine' of the true teaching of our Lord and his apostles. However, in so many cases they have soon developed their own distinctive traditions. Human thinking and psychology constantly tend to creep back in.

You can see exactly the same pattern working itself out over the decades in theological colleges initially established for the training of ministers of the gospel. Human thinking and the true teaching of our Lord and his apostles do not match, and the new wine of the apostolic gospel is easily lost.

Subjected to the searchlight of these parables, how many of our churches are, at root, patches of Biblical colour and texture torn from our Lord's teaching and sewn onto attractive human tradition and thinking? At one end of the scale they are sewn onto magnificent and dignified ceremony, and at the other end onto lively presentations offering 'life skills' and popular psychology. In each case, the teaching of the Lord and his apostles is acknowledged. And yet it is salutary to ask, Is it truly the foundation on which the church is built? To our great loss, have we torn the new garment, sewn on unmatching patches, and attempted to contain the new wine?

The Lord's thoughts and ways are so very different from the ways and thinking of human nature. 'For my thoughts are not your thoughts, neither are your ways my ways, declares the Lord.'

Here in these parables is strong encouragement to church leaders and their congregations to be vigilant. From the letters of the apostle Paul and from the churches spoken of in the opening chapters of Revelation, it is clear that no church is perfect. However, we must be constantly striving to defend the church from human ideas, and striving to uphold the God-honouring ways of thinking and of living taught by the Lord Jesus' own chosen apostles.

In the light of these parables, do we need to step back and examine ourselves?

With regard to the patch, are we tearing, from the truly apostolic gospel, portions of cloth we like, and sewing them onto dearly held opinions of our own, or onto our established traditions?

With regard to the wine, are we restricting truly apostolic teaching, by attempting to contain it within our own preferred lifestyle choice or pattern of worship?

With regard to the judgement that 'the old is better', are we rejecting the full apostolic gospel, clinging onto our familiar traditions and ways of thinking and living?

Each of these allows us to maintain our familiar ways – while ignoring or discounting the gospel's life-changing challenges.

Our response to such questions might initially lead to discouragement, but honestly confessed before the Lord, they can set us free and spur us on to obey the teaching of our Lord and his apostles – to take his yoke upon us and learn from him.

J.C. Ryle wrote: 'May God give us an honest, self-inquiring spirit, and show us what we are!'

Heavenly Father, these parables are an uncomfortable challenge to us, as members of a church, and as individuals. By your Holy Spirit, cause us to be stirred and warned by them, in order that we may be discerning. In matters of Christian faith and living cause us to cling solely to the truth of the teaching of your Son and of his chosen apostles, given to us in your holy word.

Questions for reflection or discussion

1. In what circumstances might it be right to fast and pray?
2. It can be very painful to be part of a church with teaching from some of the leaders that does not match the teaching of our Lord and his apostles. It may end up tearing itself apart. Why did the Reformers encourage us to pray, that we may 'agree in the truth of thy holy Word and live in unity and godly love.'? What is the only true foundation of Christian unity?
3. In what ways can these two parables offer us an opportunity to look carefully at the teachings and traditions we are being given, in order to measure them against the teaching of our Lord and his apostles?
4. Do we naturally find our own way of thinking and doing things 'good' or 'better'? In what ways can that hinder us from closely following the teaching of our Lord and his apostles?
5. Would we be willing, in each part of our lives, to pray – and really mean – 'Thy will be done'?

Footnote

A fairly recent, non-matching 'patch'
In Britain, although many of our schools were founded on Christian foundations, are we now rearing a generation without any awareness at all of the Lord God or of our accountability toward him – a whole generation of 'state-nurtured atheists'?

In this postmodern world, children are taught in school from the youngest of ages 'It does not matter what you believe; you can follow any religion or none. You can choose any lifestyle you want. Do what is right for you.' If, like so many children, you have grown up with this, there is a choice to be made. We can accept this godless teaching with its apparent freedom, yet with all its negative implications for our personal lives and the well-being of our society. Or we can follow the very different teaching of the Lord Jesus and his apostles. It is this godly teaching that has built the English-speaking world; it clearly spells out wholesome relationships with the Lord God, with one another, and with our society as a whole.

References

Earliest days of Jesus' ministry – Luke 4:14-32
Peter and the great catch of fish – Luke 5:1-11
Ears to hear and eyes to see – Isaiah 6:9-10
The fasting disciples of the Pharisees and of John – Mark 2:18
Fasting and Praying, Jesus' time in the wilderness – Matthew 4:1-2, and his teaching, Matthew 6:5-18
Suffering Servant of the Lord – Isaiah 52:13 to chapter 53:12
The new cloth tears away – Mark 2:21 and Matthew 9:16
Philippi – Acts 16:19-24
Ephesus – Acts 19:23-34
Jerusalem – Acts 21:27 and 22:22-24
Devoting themselves to the apostles teaching – Acts 2:42
Challenge of fresh thinking, God's thoughts and ways are very different from ours – Isaiah 55:8
Take his yoke upon us and learn from him – Matthew 11:28-30
Agree in the truth of thy holy Word – *Book of Common Prayer*, the Prayer for the Church Militant in the Communion Service.

The Blind Leading the Blind

"Judge not, and you will not be judged; condemn not, and you will not be condemned; forgive, and you will be forgiven; give, and it will be given to you. Good measure, pressed down, shaken together, running over, will be put in your lap. For with the measure you use it will be measured back to you."

He also told them a parable: "Can a blind man lead a blind man? Will they not both fall into a pit? A disciple is not above his teacher, but everyone when he is fully trained will be like his teacher. Why do you see the speck in your brother's eye, but do not notice the log that is in your own eye? How can you say to your brother, 'Brother let me take out the speck that is in your eye,' when you yourself do not see the log that is in your own eye? You hypocrite, first take the log out of your own eye, and then you will see clearly to take out the speck that is in your brother's eye."

Luke 6:37-42 English Standard Version

The Blind Leading the Blind into a Pit

He also told them a parable: "Can a blind man lead a blind man? Will they not both fall into a pit?

To whom were the words addressed? Who were these guides who were blind?
Luke records that our Lord had spent a night on a mountain praying. At daybreak he had chosen the twelve who were to become his apostles, 'And he came down with them and stood on a level place, with a great crowd of his disciples and a great multitude of people from all Judea and Jerusalem and the sea coast of Tyre and Sidon,

who came to hear him and to be healed of their diseases.' (Luke 6:12-17) From that 'level place' our Lord preached to this large and very mixed company of people. Towards the end of this sermon, he told the parable of the blind leading the blind.

This brief parable is the first of a series of striking sayings. Luke describes this first one as 'a parable,' although the description could apply to the whole series of sayings. The parable is often hardly noticed, as it is all but overshadowed by the well known picture of someone attempting to remove a 'speck' from another's eye while having a 'log' in their own.

We do not know whether Jesus taught in the way many of the Rabbis did, moving rapidly from one memorable saying to the next, or whether Luke has given us the sermon in outline or summary form. Neither are we told how the Lord applied this parable to his hearers. For, typical of his parables, the Lord left it with those who had 'ears to hear,' to think it through and apply its teaching to their own lives.

However, the gospel writers record that our Lord echoed or alluded to this parable many times during his teaching ministry. On each occasion it was with reference to the religious leaders. He was warning both them and those who heard them that, well-meaning as they may have been, they were nevertheless blind guides.

Although our Lord applied his words particularly to the Pharisees as Israel's religious leaders, his words would also apply to their scribes and to their fellow religious leaders, the Sadducees, who held high positions in both government and religious matters.

To what kind of blindness was Jesus referring?
There was nothing wrong with the Pharisees' eyesight, it was perfectly good. They were constantly in attendance during Jesus' public ministry and they carefully and critically watched him.

However, Matthew records a conversation Jesus had with his disciples as they let him know how offended the Pharisees had become by his teaching. (Matthew 15:12-14) Jesus took the occasion to warn the disciples of the spiritual blindness of the Pharisees. As they clung to their own rigid rules and traditions, the Pharisees were actually over-ruling the word of God they claimed to be carefully keeping.

Our Lord warned the Pharisees, "So for the sake of your tradition you have made void the word of God. You hypocrites! Well did Isaiah prophesy of you, when he said: 'This people honours me with their lips, but their heart is far from me; in vain do they worship me, teaching as doctrines the commandments of men.'" Rather than teaching and making clear to the people the plain truths of the word of God, the religious leaders were proclaiming – as if it was from the Lord – their own opinions and the current thinking of the day. It is a very painful question, but how many modern church leaders are doing exactly the same thing?

Despite their spiritual blindness, the scribes and Pharisees were the established and trusted religious leaders of God's Israel. The spiritually blind were leading the spiritually blind . . . to disaster.

What hindered the Pharisees from seeing the great principles of the Scriptures?
Over many years, the Pharisees had searched the Scriptures and identified some 613 commandments of God. They had gathered these, added their own interpretations to them, and continued to debate which of them took priority over others, and how they should be applied. They had learned the rules and kept the traditions scrupulously, and yet it seems that very few of them knew a vital closeness to the One they claimed to serve. Being blind to the kingdom of God themselves, how could they safely lead the people to it, or guide the people in it?

By concentrating on the details of the application of the law, the Pharisees had restricted their vision. It led them to hold a very unbalanced view of Scripture. They could no longer see its great message or its governing principles, as their traditional interpretations obscured or overruled them.

The prophet Micah lays down this great principle: 'He has told you, O man, what is good; and what does the Lord require of you but to do justice, and to love kindness, and to walk humbly with your God?'

However, to the Pharisees, our Lord was compelled to deliver stern warnings like these:

"But woe to you Pharisees! For you tithe mint and rue and every herb, and neglect justice and the love of God. These you ought to have done without neglecting the others."

"Woe to you, scribes and Pharisees, hypocrites! For you tithe mint and dill and cumin, and you have neglected the weightier matters of the law: justice and mercy and faithfulness. These you ought to have done, without neglecting the others. You blind guides, straining out a gnat and swallowing a camel!"

Jesus in no way encouraged his hearers to abandon God's law, (Matthew 5:17), but to beware of the spiritual blindness and great imbalance in understanding of the Scriptures that dedication to human traditions can bring.

What hindered the Pharisees from seeing who Jesus was?

Their expectation: Surely the true Messiah, being a descendent of King David, would be of clear and incontestable royal descent. Surely he would be drawn from the class of great ones. Either he would be drawn from among the military leaders, someone who could throw off the burden of the Roman occupation and restore Israel to the former days of national glory, or he would be drawn from among religious leaders and so be one of themselves, either a Pharisee or a Sadducee.

But Jesus did not fit. In their eyes, he was not a 'recognised' religious leader. He grew up and began his public ministry in Nazareth, rather than in David's cities of Bethlehem or Jerusalem. He had, and he sought, no military power. He was not one of this world's 'great heroes' but a humble preacher and teacher with an apparently insignificant ministry based in Galilee.

Their established position in society: The religious leaders in Israel had adapted well to the unwelcome rule of Rome. They had established a satisfactory working relationship with their Roman overlords, and had become a privileged and relatively wealthy class. As such, they had come to despise the poor – the very class from which our Lord himself was drawn, and the very people he especially mixed with and cared for.

Their pride: The wealthy ruling class of Sadducees was essentially composed of able statesmen and politicians. They held high state and religious office but believed very little; rejecting as of passing value all but the five books of Moses. They were the equivalent of modern rationalists and could not be said to 'walk humbly with the Lord'. The Pharisees were very much more serious in their beliefs, accepting the writings of the prophets and believing in life beyond the grave, the existence of angels and the reality of God-given visions. Nevertheless, their established position in society also led to pride.

Their traditions: The Pharisees' approach, guided by their traditions, not only affected the way in which they kept, or failed to keep, the word of God, it also affected the way they responded to other people. The Pharisees judged others, including our Lord, only by the extent to which they kept 'the traditions of the elders'. However, using the narrow measure of 'the traditions of the elders' had blinded the Pharisees' eyes to the God-given signs of his presence among his people.

Over seven hundred years earlier God had spoken through his prophet Isaiah clearly describing the marks of the presence of God among them. Isaiah prophesied, "Behold your God will come with vengeance, with the recompense of God. He will come and save you. Then the eyes of the blind shall be opened, and the ears of the deaf unstopped; then shall the lame man leap like a deer, and the tongue of the mute (the dumb) sing for joy."

The first part of the prophecy – concerning the judgement of God – will be, but has yet to be, fulfilled. The second part of the prophecy gives a clear indication of the marks that accompany the presence of God among his people. For those with eyes to see, these were to be the signs of the true Messiah's ministry.

At the beginning of his ministry, in the synagogue at Nazareth, Jesus read another portion of the prophecy of Isaiah. "The spirit of the Lord is upon me, because he has anointed me to proclaim good news to the poor. He has sent me to proclaim liberty to the captives and recovering of sight to the blind, to set at liberty those who are oppressed, to proclaim the year of the Lord's favour." Then he said to the people, "Today this Scripture has been fulfilled in your hearing."

It was to these defining acts of mercy and compassion that Jesus drew attention, in the reply he gave to the messengers of John the Baptist, "Go and tell John what you have seen and heard: the blind receive their sight, the lame walk, lepers are cleansed, and the deaf hear, the dead are raised up, the poor have good news preached to them."

The Pharisees' concentration on detail and tradition gave them a blindness to the word of God as a whole. They could not see the great panorama of the fulfilment of the word of God unfolding before their eyes. They were unable to recognise their own longed-for Messiah. They could only see how our Lord broke their traditions. He mixed with sinners; he ate with hands that were ritually unwashed, and even on the Sabbath, he healed those distressed in body or mind.

Blinded by their traditions, the Pharisees were unable see the great prophecies of Scripture he fulfilled.

In the saying that immediately follows this short parable, Jesus clearly showed and warned the Pharisees what they were doing. As they searched for specks and apparent imperfections, they were completely blind to their own gross failures, "Why do you see the speck in your brother's eye, but do not notice the log that is in your own eye? How can you say to your brother, 'Brother, let me take out the speck that is in your eye,' when you yourself do not see the log that is in your own eye? You hypocrite, first take the log out of your own eye, and then you will see clearly to take out the speck that is in your brother's eye."

Their determined blindness: Coupled with all this, there was a wilful blindness. The religious leaders were determined not to recognise the fulfilment of their own Scriptures: that Jesus was, and is, the Lord's anointed, the long-promised Messiah. Both his existence and his teaching were a threat to their established position, and so they did not wish to see. However, he demonstrated again and again that he, the Son of Man, is the One to whom all authority has been given; over sin and sickness, over spiritual and mental suffering, over nature, and even over death itself.

"You search the Scriptures because you think that in them you have eternal life; and it is they that bear witness about me, yet you refuse to come to me that you may have life."

"But woe to you, scribes and Pharisees, hypocrites! For you shut the kingdom of heaven in people's faces. For you neither enter yourselves, nor allow those who would enter to go in."

On a later occasion, after healing a man born blind, Jesus said, "For judgement I came into this world, that those who do not see may see, and those who see may become blind." Some of the Pharisees near him heard these things, and said to him, "Are we also blind?" Jesus said to them, "If you were blind, you would have no guilt; but now that you say, 'We see,' your guilt remains."

The Scriptures consistently warn that to mislead the people of God, to conceal from them a known truth or warning, to give them a false hope, or to give them false comfort, is a very serious offence before Almighty God. The prophet Jeremiah pinpoints the seriousness of it, as he warns a false prophet, 'Listen, Hananiah, the Lord has not sent you, and you have made this people trust in a lie. Therefore thus says the Lord: "Behold I will remove you from the face of the earth . . ."' An equally severe judgement was given by our Lord, as he said of the Pharisees, 'Every plant that my heavenly Father has not planted will be rooted up. Let them alone; they are blind guides. And if the blind lead the blind, both will fall into a pit.'

The Blind Leading the Blind into a Pit – continued

Could such things be happening in our day?

The sharp challenge of this short parable is that it brings to light the uncomfortable truth that, like the Pharisees before us, those of us who are leaders can convince ourselves that we are capable and well-qualified guides of the Lord's people, when in fact, before God, we may be spiritually blind.

Nationally

In the Israel of our Lord's day, the Sadducees were able but ungodly leaders. They worked with – yet under – the rule of Rome. In our own day, we have cause to be very grateful to the Lord God whenever and wherever he raises up godly national leaders. However, so many of our modern nations have yielded power to people who are totally without a godly perspective – to atheists, secularists and postmodern humanists. Some of these will respect the history of a nation, but others come with a determination to undermine and be rid of our

Christian heritage, and often have agendas to make ungodly ways normal throughout society. These can be coupled to educational policies and thought-controlling political correctness – enforced by law.

Has the Lord God 'given us up' or 'given us over' as the apostle Paul describes in the first chapter of his epistle to the Romans? One sign of the judgement of God on a nation turning from godly ways, is to be ruled by spiritually blind leaders. But for his mercy in sending a revival of true godliness and turning us from such ways, are we are in great danger of being 'swallowed up' under the judgement of God? Will we be led into a pit?

In the church
The practical application of this parable in our own day is painfully clear to see. In so many of our churches we have leaders who, in Matthew Henry's telling words, are '. . . called to lead us to Christ, but are strangers to him.' And the result – good people who faithfully attend our churches are neither presented with the apostolic faith nor able to grow in it. J.C. Ryle spelled it out very clearly. He wrote, 'The teaching of human traditions and thinking has done great damage to Christ's church in every age . . . If a man will hear unsound instruction, we cannot expect him to become otherwise than unsound in the faith himself.'

The prophet Jeremiah warned in his day, 'An appalling and horrible thing has happened in the land: the prophets prophesy falsely, and the priests rule at their direction; my people love to have it so, but what will you do when the end comes?' and, 'My people have been lost sheep. Their shepherds have led them astray . . .' Could this be happening in our day? Are we, too, being led into a pit?

A parable for those of us appointed to be spiritual guides

The Lord Jesus alone has seen the Father, and he has made him known. There is a day coming when we shall each appear before our Lord. Hence the importance of heeding God the Father's instruction, 'This is my beloved Son; listen to him,' and the relevance of the opening lines of the letter to the Hebrews, 'Long ago, at many times and in many ways, God spoke to our fathers by the prophets, but in these last days he has spoken to us by his Son..'

This parable is a challenge to those of us, entrusted with any kind of spiritual leadership, to humbly examine ourselves before Almighty God. The Lord God has spoken – have we listened?

Priorities for church leaders

Our expectations: What is our vision? Are we appointed primarily to encourage good relationships among people, to facilitate community activities, to raise funds to keep the church in good repair and solvent, and to play our part in the wider church as we run or sit on committees? Some or all of these may fall to us to fulfil, but can we, like the first apostles and later the apostle Paul, hold fast to a higher priority? Can we delegate or share these practical and administrative matters with others and see ourselves as primarily servants of the Lord Jesus and of his people, called to walk closely with him and to take every opportunity to live and speak for him?

Our natural human pride: The constant temptation in matters of godliness and spiritual leadership, for minister and people alike, is to trust in our own wisdom and abilities and in our own discernment of a situation. Like the Pharisees, we can enjoy doing many of the practical tasks of religious leadership in our own strength and by the application of our own natural abilities. To fulfil these tasks, we may be unaware of any need to walk humbly with the Lord God

Like the Pharisees, too, we can so easily set ourselves as judges of our Lord and of his recorded teaching, and as judges of the teaching of his chosen apostles. We like to measure and assess, and we do so according to our own opinions and traditions. Considering ourselves 'more enlightened,' we may feel that we can safely dismiss certain aspects of our Lord's teaching – his deity, his exclusive claims, and his warnings concerning judgement, heaven and hell, together with some of the teachings of his apostles concerning practical holiness of living.

However, we do well to beware lest we be found at the last to have been, like the Pharisees, blind guides, leading both ourselves and those we have been called to lead, into an eternal pit. For, like the Pharisees, we shall be judged, not by our opinions, but by whether we acknowledged our Lord to be all that the Scriptures show him to be, and whether or not we 'did what he said'.

In the words of our Lord's own solemn warning, 'Not everyone who says to me, "Lord, Lord" will enter the kingdom of heaven, but the one who does the will of my Father who is in heaven.'

Our traditions: In our own day, some of our traditions are helpful. Some traditions are neutral; they neither help nor hinder true godliness. Some traditions are quaint and long out-dated and obscure godly truth and make it inaccessible to the mind of our generation. Lastly, like those to which the Pharisees clung, there are traditions that openly contradict, or in some way undermine the word of God.

The traditions with which we have grown up can be deeply embedded in our thinking and our actions, especially if, as religious leaders, we have gone on to be trained further in them. In theological colleges we are steeped in traditions of our church and, although we may be encouraged to consider and develop them to appeal to our current social setting, only rarely are we encouraged to check and correct them by comparison with the apostolic teaching. This is, however, exactly what the Reformers were trying to do. Not surprisingly, it proved very difficult and painful and not at all popular with those religious leaders who were determined to hold fast to 'the traditions of the Church'.

The only sure foundation

As Jesus explained to Nicodemus, the leading Pharisee who came to see him after nightfall, it is the Holy Spirit of God who opens eyes to see spiritual things. Without his work in our lives we cannot see the kingdom of God. And so the cure for spiritual blindness, even for the most exalted religious leader, is to humble ourselves before Almighty God and cry to him for mercy, for the opening of our eyes: To ask his forgiveness, and beg for that spiritual enlightening that enables us to see who the Lord Jesus truly is and what he has done. To ask him to open our eyes to the whole vision of the kingdom of God, given to us in his word.

Jesus declared, "I thank you, Father, Lord of heaven and earth, that you have hidden these things from the wise and understanding and revealed them to little children; yes, Father, for such was your gracious will." It is the Lord God alone, who can open eyes and give spiritual insight.

As Master of a slave-trading ship, John Newton cried to God for mercy in a great storm – and his eyes were opened. Aboard ship, isolated from any traditional church teaching, he grew as a disciple simply by a spiritually enlightened reading of the New Testament. Years later, as an ordained minister, his letters of encouragement to his fellow clergy still radiate a simple trust and humble obedience to the Lord Jesus.

John Newton urges us to read the word of God, not only as a religious duty, nor simply for sermon preparation, but, under the leading of the Holy Spirit, to feed and nourish our own hearts and enlighten our own minds in the ways of God. The writings and biographies of God's 'spiritual giants', such as John Bunyan, can greatly help and inspire us in this.

'But,' writes John Newton, 'the chief and grand means of edification, without which all other helps will disappoint us, and prove like clouds without water, are the Bible and prayer, the word of grace and the throne of grace. A frequent perusal of the Bible will give us an enlarged and comprehensive view of the whole . . . and preserve us from an over-attachment to any system of man's compilation . . . I know of no better rule of reading the Scripture, than to read it through from beginning to end; and, when we have finished it once, to begin again.'

A parable for those of us who are led

This is a tiny parable, but an absolutely key one, if we are not to be led to spiritual disaster. We may be blessed with a church leader who walks closely with God in simple trust and humble obedience, and can therefore say, with the apostle Paul, 'Be imitators of me, as I am of Christ'. But such a leader may be succeeded by one 'trained in the ways of ministry' yet without any spiritual insight whatever. If those who lead us are not enlightened, enlivened and thrilled with the kingdom of heaven, and personally hungry to learn more of it, how can they lead others to it, or enable them to fulfil their part in it?

If we are able, and if that is welcome, we can respectfully help and encourage those who lead and guide us. Our Lord certainly helped Nicodemus, and we read in the Acts of the Apostles that Aquila and Priscilla were able to help and enlighten Apollos, as they '. . . explained to him the way of God more accurately.' If that is not possible, we are simply to follow our Lord's instruction and 'leave them alone,' knowing that both they and we are answerable to the Lord God. Jesus plainly taught his disciples concerning the Pharisees, 'Let them alone; they are blind guides.'

It is not for nothing that we find in the second letter of Peter, 'You therefore, beloved, knowing this beforehand, take care that you are not carried away with the error of lawless people and lose your own stability. But grow in the grace and knowledge of our Lord and Saviour Jesus Christ . . .'

Thomas Lye, on being ejected from All Hallows, Lombard Street in 1662 said, 'Where God does not find a mouth to speak, you must not find an ear to hear, nor a heart to believe.'

Just as much as any faithful church leader, to grow in grace and spiritual discernment, and to make sure that our spiritual anchor is secure, those who are led also need to be personally 'steeped in the word of God'. How else will we be warned if we are being misguided? Like the noble Jewish people of Berea, as they listened and weighed the words of the apostle Paul, we do well to be 'examining the Scriptures daily to see if these things are so.'

The teaching of the church, or of a favourite minister or preacher, is offered to help us, but the ultimate responsibility lies with each one of us. We cannot safely entrust the safe keeping of our spiritual life to others. It is our responsibility to keep our own hearts and souls before God. We can only do so by keeping close to the word of God and praying for the Holy Spirit's enlightening. If we fail to do that, we may well find ourselves trusting blind guides, and must not be surprised if we are led astray.

In Summary

This striking saying, brief as it is, has an enduring value as a warning to both those who teach, and to those who are taught. Here is a challenge to those given the responsibility to teach, to keep heart and mind close to the words and ways of God. And to those who hear, to recognise the great responsibility of being discerning. Like the Jewish believers of Berea, it is our constant responsibility to test what we read or hear, and see if it is according to the word of God.

Heavenly Father, we thank you for this short yet significant parable of your Son. By your grace enable us to seek the guiding of your Holy Spirit to enlighten our minds to the truths of your word, and so be able to test all we teach, all we read, and all we hear, by the word of God.

Questions for personal reflection or discussion

1. Why did the Pharisees refuse to acknowledge our Lord or accept his teaching?
2. Have we been led to believe in religious traditions and human opinions that are not in accord with Scripture, and that can restrict our understanding or acceptance of the word of God?
3. Could we come to hold a very unbalanced view of Scripture? For example, delighting in its promises but neglecting its warnings?
4. What dangers are there for our churches if they come to be led by able but spiritually unseeing leaders?
5. What can ordinary believing Christian people do, in order not to be misled? What steps can we take to test the truth?
6. Are there dangers for our country if, in a democracy, we elect spiritually blind or openly ungodly leaders?

Searching questions for those willing to ask them
In the light of this parable, as guides and as those who are guided, would we do well to take time to reflect on the extent to which the following can each contribute to obscuring our spiritual vision, perhaps even rendering us unable to see or to heed the words of our Lord and his chosen apostles?
1) Our position in society and our personal pride.
2) Our established ways of thinking and the traditions of the society in which we live.

3) The traditions of the church whose leaders guide us, and the family loyalties which have shaped us.
4) Our current life-style and way of behaving.
5) The pressures of modern life and the constraints of time.

Perhaps, encouraged to leave the serious reading of the words of our Lord and his chosen apostles to spiritual leaders, we have never made the time to read and ponder the words of Scripture for ourselves. We could be quite unaware of the direction in which we are being led, or of the danger of being misled. Do we really pray for ready eyes to see and unstopped ears to hear the teaching of our Lord and his chosen apostles?

References

The Pharisees offended – Matthew 15:12-14
Making void the word of God – Matthew 15:6-9
Walk humbly with your God – Micah 6:8
Tithe mint and rue – Luke 11:42
Swallowing a camel! – Matthew 23:23-24
Not to abandon the law – Matthew 5:17
The mute, (the dumb), sing for joy – Isaiah 35:4-6
The Spirit of the Lord is upon me – Luke 4:18 and 19-21
John the Baptist – Luke 7:22
You search the Scriptures – John 5:39-40
You shut the kingdom of heaven – Matthew 23:13-14
"Are we blind?" – John 9:32-41
The false prophet Hananiah – Jeremiah 28:15-16
Not planted by God – Matthew 15:13-14
'An appalling and horrible thing,' Jeremiah's warning to Israel in the days before it was swept into captivity under the judgement of God – Jeremiah 5:30-31
My people . . . led astray – Jeremiah 50:6
He alone has seen the Father, and . . . made him known – John 1:18

'This is my beloved Son: listen to him' – Mark 9:7
In these last days he has spoken – Hebrews 1:1-2
The apostles' priority – Acts 6:1-4 and Romans 1:1
Not everyone . . . "Lord, Lord" – Matthew 7:21
Nicodemus – John 3:1-15
Hidden from the wise and revealed to children – Matthew 11:25
Be imitators of me, as I am of Christ – 1Corinthians 11:1
Apollos – Acts 18:26
Let them alone – Matthew 15:13-14
Take care . . . not carried away with error – 2 Peter 3:17-18
Examining the Scriptures daily – Acts 17:11

Footnote

'He also told them a parable: "Can a blind man lead a blind man? Will they not both fall into a pit?"' These words of the Lord Jesus are found towards the conclusion of what has become known as 'The Sermon on the Plain,' so named as Luke records that Jesus gave it standing 'on a level place.' The sermon is in many ways very similar to the account we have in Matthew's gospel of 'The Sermon on the Mount.' However, this little parable, although it is found elsewhere in Matthew's gospel, (Matthew 15:13-14), is not recorded by Matthew as being part of that sermon.

The Wise and the Foolish Builders

This parable is set last because the parable of the Sower, the first of a series of our Lord's major parables, gives us such a clear introduction to all the parables, and this one presents us with a most valuable concluding challenge and note of glory.

"Why do you call me, 'Lord, Lord,' and not do what I tell you? Everyone who comes to me and hears my words and does them, I will show you what he is like: he is like a man building a house, who dug deep and laid the foundation on the rock. And when a flood arose, the stream broke against that house and could not shake it, because it had been well built. But the one who hears and does not do them is like a man who built a house on the ground without a foundation. When the stream broke against it, immediately it fell, and the ruin of that house was great."

Luke 6:46-49 English Standard Version

"Not everyone who says to me, 'Lord, Lord,' will enter the kingdom of heaven, but the one who does the will of my Father who is in heaven. On that day many will say to me, 'Lord, Lord, did we not prophesy in your name, and cast out demons in your name, and do many mighty works in your name?' And then will I declare to them, 'I never knew you; depart from me, you workers of lawlessness.'

"Everyone then who hears these words of mine and does them will be like a wise man who built his house on the rock. And the rain fell, and the floods came, and the winds blew and beat on that house, but it did not fall, because it had been founded on the rock. And everyone who hears these words of mine and does not do them will be like a foolish man who built his house on the sand. And the rain fell, and the floods came, and the winds blew and beat against that house, and it fell, and great was the fall of it."

And when Jesus finished these sayings, the crowds were astonished at his teaching, for he was teaching them as one who had authority, and not as their scribes.

Matthew 7:21-29, English Standard Version

The Wise and the Foolish Builders; the Rock and the Sand

May I invite you to look at the setting, at the detail of the two houses and their builders, and at why Jesus told this arresting parable? We can then look at the challenges it presents, the possible storms and finally at the great significance of the parable.

The setting in which the parable was told
The parable of the wise and foolish men is found in the gospels of both Matthew and Luke. In Matthew it comes as the conclusion and final challenge of what is often called 'The Sermon on the Mount.'

In Luke's gospel, the account of the Lord's teaching is much more brief, however, the thrust is the same and the concluding parable of the two builders is very similar. The teaching seems to have been given on a quite separate occasion and is sometimes known as 'The Sermon on the Plain', as Luke records that it was given in a level place.

An overview of the two sermons
Under the interpretation and traditions of the scribes and Pharisees, God's law had become a narrow, religious, ritual observance. As Jesus interpreted the law of God as it had been given to Moses, he showed that it went much deeper and was a matter of the heart. So, for example, disciples are not only to keep back from actual, physical

murder, but to keep anger in check, and that more subtle tendency to pour scorn on or undermine those who we don't like or don't agree with. Disciples are called, not only to refrain from adultery, but to keep lust in all its subtle forms under control before an all-seeing heavenly Father. True disciples are challenged to respond to those who take advantage or persecute them, not with retaliation but with patience and a willingness to forgive.

In Matthew's account, Jesus draws a sharp distinction between those who want to use a 'veneer of apparent godliness' to further their own social standing, and those who really mean business with the Lord God. And so, very unlike the practice of the scribes and Pharisees in those days, personal praying and fasting are to be in secret before our heavenly Father, rather than opportunities to put on some kind of display to impress those around us. Similarly, giving is to be done discreetly before our Father in heaven. It is not to be used as the Pharisees used it, as a public opportunity to demonstrate their generosity, so that everyone could admire them. Again, Jesus taught a very different view of wealth and possessions; not to view them as 'all mine, for my personal use,' but to see them as a trust from the Lord God to be used in ways that bring honour to his name.

He taught disciples to trust our heavenly Father for all that we need, and to keep back from judging others. He warned that the entrance and the path to life, the Lord God's best for us, is narrow, the way hard and sometimes lonely, and that there are false folk about who would mislead us.

Norval Geldenhuys concludes his comment on the whole sermon by saying, 'Never before or after Jesus did anyone lay down such high standards of how one should live in thought and action toward God and one's fellow-men.' Here is the pattern for God's new creation; everything and everybody living in a right relationship with him and with one another.

The priorities and lifestyle of all true members and citizens of the kingdom of heaven, God's new creation in and through his Son, are spelled out and explained in both the Sermon on the Mount and the Sermon on the Plain – and then the challenge presented, "Why do you call me 'Lord, Lord,' and not do what I tell you? Everyone who comes to me and hears my words and does them, I will show you what he is like . . ." This emphasis on actually putting his teaching into practical everyday living, 'doing what he says', is a constant theme of the Lord and, subsequently, of his apostles throughout the New Testament.

In the light of these solemn words, Jesus told this short parable to stir his hearers to actually live in obedience to the godly way he had set out, rather than just be 'moved by', or 'delighted with', or 'critically interested in' his teaching. Here is a serious call to repentance before God, a change of thinking and living, and to faith in the Son of God. True faith and heeding his words will always lead to holiness of living, such as he had described in the sermon.

In this parable, as Joseph Parker points out, we have our Lord's own view of his teaching. His words are not just elegant sayings for us to admire or assess, but the great foundation stones on which it is essential that each one of us builds.

The detail of the parable itself
May I invite you to look first at the houses and how they were built, then at the builders and their different approaches, and finally at the storms their houses needed to withstand.

The houses We can reasonably assume that the two men each wanted a house as soon as possible, that the houses they intended to live in were similar and that they were built in the same area and so subjected to the same violent storms.

While the sun shone, the houses, when they were completed, were much the same. However, one man had made a fundamental error. He had omitted something on which his house would ultimately depend.

In those days there were no mechanical diggers to prepare the ground, no mobile cement mixers bringing concrete to lay the foundations and no trucks with heavy lifting gear to deliver the material for the walls or to lift the roofing beams into place. It would all be done by hand and so, at every stage, there would be the temptation to make it less laborious to build. The foolish man did make life easier; he did not trouble too much with the great effort of preparing the hidden foundations, he concentrated on the walls and roof. (Only Matthew mentions that he was building directly on sand.)

The foolish man could laugh at the wise man sweating away as he 'dug deep and laid the foundation on the rock,' while his own house was finished and lived in. Not until the storm struck did the wise man have any clear advantage. Until then, the foolish man appeared to be the more efficient and successful builder, and the wise man appeared to be foolish, doing all that extra work as he dug down to the rock.

The builders We are not told why the man who ultimately proved to be foolish, built in the way he did. He may simply have been too lazy to dig deeply! However, he may have had three other very common but characteristic traits that cause us to fail.

Martyn Lloyd Jones suggests that the first of these was haste. Did he want his house now; built as rapidly as possible? Without 'wasting time' researching the area in which he was to build, and without the labour of digging deeply, his house would be built much more quickly and with far less effort.

His second characteristic may well have been that he was 'strong-headed'. Searches, surveys and seeking advice were not for him. He knew what he wanted and clearly had no eyes to see or ears to hear the wisdom of digging deeply and laying the foundation of his house on rock.

His third characteristic, as William Barclay points out, may have been that he was a man for the present moment only. He did not look ahead or see his house building project from a long-term perspective. He saw it only from the perspective of the hot and dry days, without looking ahead to the testing times of the autumn and spring rains.

The man who proved to be wise also had characteristics. He, too, had a clear idea of the kind of house he would like to live in. But he was determined to get it right. Perhaps from his own observation or from advice offered to him, he could see the wisdom of digging deeply enough to lay his foundations on solid rock. In order to achieve this he was willing to spend time and a great deal of effort building his house. He was certainly not lazy, hasty or given to taking disastrous short-cuts.

The storms and floods   Following heavy rain, in a lowland situation, flood waters can rise worryingly steadily, but they often allow time to prepare and escape. In a mountainous or hilly region, as much of Israel is, the scene is very different. When the rain pours down, in a very short time any normally quiet and lovely hollow leading to the valley bottom is filled with a raging torrent as the water runs off the rocky hillsides. This is the kind of flood that would test anyone's house.

The foolish man's house looked at least as good as the wise man's house – when, after all the hard work, that was eventually completed. But, as Matthew records, '. . . the rain fell, and the floods came, and the winds blew and beat against' both houses and a torrent of water 'broke against' them. Only then was each house severely tested.

When the flood waters broke against the wise man's house, it was not shaken, 'because it had been well built.' It didn't fall, 'because it had been founded on the rock.' However, when the flood broke against the foolish man's house, as it was built 'on the ground without a foundation,' it fell immediately, 'and the ruin of that house was great.'

Matthew Henry warns that the foolish man's house '. . . fell in the storm, when the builder had most need of it, and expected it to shelter him,' and it 'fell when it was too late to build another . . .'

Here, right on the surface of the parable is a valuable lesson for the whole of life. It is one, I freely acknowledge, we often learn too late! In any endeavour, from preparing for an examination, to getting married, to taking some great career decision, to building a house or following up some great possibility – stop and reflect. It may be a great idea but beware of haste. Take advice. Look to the times ahead, and spare no appropriate effort or expense. Frustrating as it may seem, take your time so that you can get it right.

If that is the case with every project that we set out to do, how much more is it the case with the whole aim, purpose and direction of our lives? This parable challenges us to seriously heed all that our Lord taught, and to live in God's world, not just for the present, but in the light of eternity.

The Lord Jesus gave no promise that those who are his faithful and obedient disciples will escape the storms of life, but rather that, built on the foundation of himself and his teaching – and on this foundation alone – their 'house' will stand steadfast.

"Everyone who comes to me and hears my words and does them, I will show you what he is like: he is like a man building a house, who dug deep and laid the foundation on the rock. And when a flood arose, the stream broke against that house and could not shake it, because it had been well built. But the one who hears and does not do them is like a man who built a house on the ground without a foundation. When the stream broke against it, immediately it fell, and the ruin of that house was great."

The Wise and the Foolish the Builders; the Rock and the Sand – continued

The parable's application to Jesus' original hearers and to ourselves in our day

It is clear that Jesus told it because he knew that many in the crowd listening to him were heading for disaster. He wanted to warn them with this simple, vivid picture of the two men and their two houses. The people in the crowds were all 'followers of Jesus'. They flocked to him wherever he was. They marvelled to see his miracles and enjoyed hearing his every word. They were amazed by his teaching and by his authority. Just like the houses, at a glance, these people all looked the same, they were all 'his followers', but some were wise and some were foolish.

Like all of our Lord's parables, this parable would discern between the very different groups of people in the crowd listening to him. It would give those holding mistaken views and ways an opportunity to turn from them, recognise who Jesus truly is and heed his words – to believe and obey him.

Peter and John and our Lord's other true disciples would go on to live, demonstrate and teach this godly way of life; the New Testament is full of their writings, and records of their deeds. Yet so many of those listening to Jesus had no ears or heart or willingness to let his teaching touch and change the way in which they thought and lived. Ultimately Jesus' teaching did them no good. They carried on heading towards disaster.

And for ourselves?
We can attend church or chapel; go to Christian conventions, rallies, camps or Bible studies and love to hear God's word explained and expounded by fine preachers and great orators. We feel 'blessed' to

have been present, but are we allowing God, through his holy word to search us and know our hearts? If we come without a willingness for the word of God to 'rebuke, reprove or correct' our thinking or our living, we carry on building our lives according to our own wisdom, or the wisdom of the world around us – but failing to found it on the rock of the word of the Lord.

Beware, then, of listening to the words of the Lord, his apostles or his faithful ministers today as the Lord God described the Old Testament people of God listening to Ezekiel, 'You are to them like one who sings love songs with a beautiful voice and plays well on an instrument, for they hear what you say, but they will not do it.'

There were others in the crowd 'following Jesus' who were also heading for disaster. They had their own reasons to put aside the significance of what Jesus did and to refrain from doing as he taught. These were the privileged religious leaders of the day, in particular the scribes and Pharisees. They had their favoured status and position to consider, and following his teaching would directly challenge the lifestyle they enjoyed. Among their fellow religious leaders, it would also involve terrible loss of face to acknowledge him as the promised, anointed son of David, the Christ of God, let alone be seen as one of his true disciples.

Would being known among our friends and acquaintances as a disciple of the Lord Jesus, be too great a loss of face? Or perhaps we are unwilling to do as he says because it runs against our traditions, the way that we have always done things or thought about things. The words of Jesus might challenge our present life-style. It did for the scribes and Pharisees and, ultimately, they were the foolish ones. They did not do as the Lord Jesus taught; they clung to their established ways – as, but for the grace of God, we will always tend to do.

It was to a large and mixed company of hearers that the Lord Jesus first delivered this gracious but solemn warning. It remains a warning for us, today. Only those who actually do what he taught will be found, in the end, to be the true members of the kingdom of God. Those who, for one reason or another, do not – are courting disaster.

Brief and familiar as it is, for those with ears to hear and eyes to see, here is yet another seriously challenging parable.

All the words of Jesus – or just some of them?
After his resurrection, Jesus gave his disciples an instruction. They were to teach the new disciples they were commissioned to make '. . . to observe all that I have commanded you.' This instruction clearly covers the whole of his teaching. In our own day, it is very easy to be among those who take hold of only some of our Lord's teaching. We love and rejoice in his promises, but pass very lightly over his warnings and his commandments. It is possible to heed the words of Jesus we like to hear, and brush aside the ones we like less. Here we are plainly warned that the greatest error is to hear the words of Jesus, and yet fail to do them.

Each time we encounter Scripture, read, preached, discussed or shared, we are given an opportunity to examine the foundation upon which we are building; to make our repentance deeper and our belief stronger; to more fully trust and more willingly obey him, and so be increasingly ready to face the great storms of life.

Through this brief parable Jesus makes it very plain that the only sure foundation for the true and wise disciple, now as then, is a vital submission to him. He is the one appointed to be the final judge 'on that day'. He is the true disciple's Lord – and so day by day he calls us to be one of those who, in his words, 'Comes to me and hears my words and does them.' Do we have such a humble willingness to walk where he leads and put into practice what he taught, and so shape our whole lives by his teaching?

Quiet and peaceful days
While things were going well, the two houses appeared to be much the same. People in the crowd listening to Jesus seemed outwardly to be

much the same, as do the people in our churches and chapels. But here, for us in our day, is the challenge of the parable. While all is well, we can contentedly find ourselves simply meeting to be uplifted by the singing, hear a 'Bible talk', to meet with friendly folk and to enjoy social activities together. We may also meet to discuss and weigh Jesus' words. But we could be in great danger. Unless we do what the Lord Jesus says, we could be found to have walked the disastrous way of the foolish man when terrible storms break against our lives.

We may enjoy good health and have all we need for a very full and active life. It seems that trial and temptation, difficulties and death come nowhere near us. Indeed, it looks as if they never could come near our door . . . and yet they will. Then, and only then, will the foundation upon which our life has been built be discovered, tested and laid bare.

When the storm breaks

When do you want to get indoors? Not while it is warm and sunny, but when the wind howls and the rain lashes and the pathways become rivers, then you need a shelter from the stormy blast. Then, and not until then, you need to know that the house is well built and a safe place to shelter.

'And the rain fell, and the floods came, and the winds blew and beat against that house . . .' Our Lord does not spell out the nature of the storms. It is sufficient that he has given us warning. However, in this life, like the apostle Peter, we may face dreadful temptation. Like the apostle Paul, we may be badly let down by friends, falsely accused, and mistreated terribly by those who hate us. Like Job, we may suffer the loss of everything that is precious to us.

The Scriptures help us to be prepared, 'I have stored up your word in my heart, that I might not sin against you', 'My flesh and my heart may fail, but God is the strength of my heart and my portion for ever' and the apostle Paul warns disciples that, 'through many tribulations we must enter the kingdom of God.'

'That day' – the final and greatest test of all
Just before he told this parable, Matthew records that Jesus gave a solemn warning: 'On that day many will say to me, "Lord, Lord, did we not prophesy in your name, and cast out demons in your name, and do many mighty works in your name?" And then will I declare to them, "I never knew you; depart from me, you workers of lawlessness."' (Matthew 7:22-23)

'That day' is the day when the foundations – or the lack of them – will be plainly seen. Here is the final and most testing 'storm' of all. The warning was not only for Jesus' hearers, it applies to us today. Matthew Henry notes that it is possible to profess faith and enjoy the many privileges found in the church, to walk with great assurance and even to gain a great reputation in it – and yet at the end to be found to have built on the sand. It may not be recognised by us, or by those around us, until trial and persecution, death and judgement knock at our door. Apparent faith is so hard to distinguish from real and obedient faith until, in this life, the great tests and temptations strike, or until that day when we must all appear before the judgement seat of Christ, when the secrets of all hearts will be known.

When prayed with humble sincerity, how wise and helpful is David's prayer, 'Search me, O God, and know my heart! Try me and know my thoughts! And see if there be any ungodly way in me, and lead me in the way everlasting!'

The great significance of Jesus' words and of this parable
'And when Jesus finished these sayings, the crowds were astonished at his teaching, for he was teaching them as one who had authority, and not as their scribes.' (Matthew 7:28-29)

Who then is it who has such authority? Kenneth Bailey notes, in this parable, a very significant echo of a parable and prophecy of

Isaiah some 700 years earlier. It may seem obscure to us, but its significance would not have been lost on the scribes and Pharisees, experts in the law and the prophets. As they listened to Jesus, they would see, to their discomfort, all too plainly his claim to be the fulfilment of the promise of God uttered by Isaiah.

Isaiah had prophesied that, in the face of a terrifying, all-conquering Assyrian advance, although the people and their leaders had laid their hopes on human treaties with Egypt, these would prove valueless; 'a refuge of lies,' and 'a covenant with death.' Those who had put their trust in them would be – like the foolish man of the Lord's parable – swept away just as storm waters overwhelm a feeble shelter; sweeping away both shelter and those in it.

However, in the same prophetic utterance, Isaiah also foresaw the day when the Lord God would lay in Zion 'a stone, a tested stone, a precious cornerstone, of a sure foundation . . .' Did the Lord's parable of the two builders lay before his hearers the veiled but stupendous claim that he, the Lord Jesus, and his words are the fulfilment of that prophecy? That he is the precious, God-laid cornerstone and the only sure foundation. That building life on the finest of human wisdom or any other scheme must end in disaster. That in the Lord Jesus alone, and in obedience to his words, is found the only safe foundation.

This is no 21st century novel interpretation. The prophecy is quoted by the apostle Peter in his first letter and clearly applied to the Lord Jesus.

Lines from the ancient hymn, translated from the Latin, with its wonderful melody, express it perfectly.

> Christ is made the sure foundation,
> Christ the head and corner-stone,
> Chosen of the Lord and precious . . .

And finally, from the 18th century, John Newton writes, 'Jesus is the only door, the only way of a sinner's access to the knowledge and favour of God. This is the precious and sure foundation which he has laid in Zion: and to presume to build our hope on any other, is to build on quicksand.'

No wonder the people were amazed and astonished by Jesus' words. He 'was teaching them as one who had authority, and not as their scribes.' Here are the commands, rules and warnings of the Son of God before whose throne we must all 'on that day' be judged. To him, our only Saviour and Lord, whether we choose to acknowledge it or not, has been committed all authority, all judgement.

Heavenly Father, thank you for this deeply challenging parable from the lips of your Son, the Lord Jesus. By your Holy Spirit open our eyes to see who he truly is, and then in humility 'come to him, hear his words and do them.'

Questions for personal reflection or discussion

1. 'Why do you call me, 'Lord, Lord,' and not do what I tell you?' These words were spoken to those who gathered to listen to Jesus. Are they equally words to us today?
2. Can we be unwilling to do as the Lord Jesus tells us because this would challenge our thinking, our traditions, or how we are living?
3. Do we fail to do as our Lord tells us because we heed his promises, but do not take his warnings and commands seriously?
4. Perhaps we find ourselves going to church 'to be uplifted by the singing, to meet with friendly folk and to enjoy social activities together' or 'to . . . discuss Jesus' words.' But, without God's word touching the way we live, are we in great danger?

5. '. . . it is possible to profess faith and enjoy the many privileges found in the church, and even to gain a great reputation in it, to walk with great assurance – and yet at the end to be found to have built on the sand.' Can we feel that we are obeying the Lord Jesus, while actually building on some other foundation?

6. Our thoughts, our plans, our decisions, our lifestyle – we are all building. But is it according to Jesus' words? What we can do to make sure that we are building our lives on a solid foundation?

7. Why is it that, ultimately, 'building life on the finest of human wisdom or any other scheme must end in disaster'?

8. Although throughout life we may face personal storms and testing times, what ultimate 'storm' must we face?

9 'Whether we choose to acknowledge it or not,' to the Lord Jesus 'has been committed all authority, all judgement.' Will we do what he tells us?' Before him, will we ultimately prove to have been wise?

References

Prayer to be in secret – Matthew 6:5-6

Giving to be discreet – Matthew 6:2-4

Not to judge others – Luke 6:37 and Matthew 7:1

The path narrow and hard – Matthew 7:13-14

Those who would mislead – Matthew 7:15-20

Rebuke, reprove or correct our thinking or living – 2 Timothy 3:16

Like one who sings love songs with a beautiful voice – Ezekiel 33:32

Teaching them to observe all that I have commanded you – Matthew 28:20

Stored your word in my heart, that I might not sin against you – Psalm 119:11

God is the strength of my heart and my portion forever – Psalm 73:26

Through many tribulations – Acts 14:22

I never knew you – Matthew 7:22-23

Judgement seat of Christ – 2Corinthians 5:9-11

Secrets of all hearts known – Romans 2:16

Search me, O God . . . and lead me in the way everlasting – Psalm 139:23&24

A precious cornerstone, of a sure foundation – Isaiah 28:16 and 1 Peter 2:6

Teaching as one who had authority – Matthew 7:28-29

All authority, all judgement – John 5:22 and 26-27

Postscript

Throughout these parables I freely confess that I have found myself confronted with a far more demanding and robust Jesus than I have ever been accustomed to seeing portrayed in our modern churches. He is so much more than a friend and comforter in troubles, so much more than a teacher of godly ways of living. He is Shepherd, Saviour and the only gateway to heaven. But, as these parables make plain, he is also the absolute Lord and King. As such, he rightly expects our close attention to his warnings, instructions and commands. Like the finest of military leaders, he both inspires and calls for our utter loyalty and total obedience.

The steadfast kindness, love and compassion of the Lord Jesus, and his patient awareness of our frailty are wonderful truths to hold fast. But the Lord Jesus is not only there for our comfort. He is the absolute and sovereign Lord and Master.

Richard Baxter, concluding his sermon on the Wedding Feast, preached in St Laurence-Jury in 1656, simply said,

'I have delivered my message, the Lord open your hearts to receive it. I have persuaded you with the word of truth and soberness; the Lord persuade you more effectually . . .'

Principal Sources

Holy Bible English Standard Version, Containing the Old and New Testaments, Anglicised Edition. Collins, 2002.

Kenneth E. Bailey: *Poet and Peasant* and *Through Peasant Eyes* Combined Edition. Wm. B. Eerdmans 1983; and *Jesus Through Middle Eastern Eyes*. SPCK 2008. – Kenneth Bailey (1930-2016) was a Presbyterian Minister who for forty years worked extensively in the Middle East and served in the Near Eastern School of Theology, Beirut as Professor of New Testament Studies.

William Barclay: *The Daily Study Bible, The Gospel of Luke*. The Saint Andrew Press, Edinburgh, Eleventh Impression 1970. – William Barclay (1907-1978) was Professor of Divinity and Biblical Criticism at the University of Glasgow.

John Bunyan: *The Pilgrim's Progress*. Edited with an Introduction and Notes by Roger Sharrock. Penguin Books 1965. – John Bunyan, (1628-1688) 'The Tinker of Bedford', was a Puritan preacher and writer. For his persistent 'illegal' preaching, he spent some twelve years in prison. It was during this time that he began to write his most well known work *The Pilgrim's Progress*.

John Calvin: *Commentary on a Harmony of the Evangelists, Matthew, Mark, and Luke*. Translated from the original Latin, and collated with the Author's French version by the Rev. William Pringle. Wm. B. Eerdmans. – John Calvin (1509-64) was the great French reformer and theologian. He was forced to flee from France to Geneva where he had a world-influencing ministry.

G. Campbell Morgan: *The Gospel According to Luke.* Marshall, Morgan & Scott 1976 Edition. – G. Campbell Morgan (1863-1945) was a renowned preacher, and the Minister of Westminster Chapel, London. In the early half of the 20th century, he drew great crowds to hear his expositions and interpretations of Scripture, which were thought provoking and not always traditional.

Arthur Carr: *The Cambridge Bible for Schools & Colleges, The Gospel According to St. Matthew.* Cambridge University Press 1882. – Arthur Carr (died 1917) was a fellow of Oriel College, Oxford and Assistant Master at Wellington College.

C. H. Dodd: *The Parables of the Kingdom.* Collins, Fontana Books 1961. – Charles Harold Dodd (1884-1973) was Rylands Professor of Biblical Criticism and Exegesis at Manchester University.

Norval Geldenhuys: *Commentary on the Gospel of Luke.* The English text with Introduction, Exposition and Notes. Marshall, Morgan & Scott 1977 edition. – Norval Geldenhuys was a Dutch Reformed Pastor in South Africa.

A.M. Hunter: *Parables for Today.* SCM Press 1983. – Archibald Hunter is Professor Emeritus of New Testament and former Master of Christ's College Aberdeen.

Martyn Lloyd-Jones: *Studies in the Sermon on the Mount.* Intervarsity Press, Second Edition 1978. – David Martyn Lloyd-Jones (1899-1981) was for thirty years the Minister of Westminster Chapel, London. His expository preaching and writing, undergirded as it was with strong biblical doctrine, has strengthened and encouraged tens of thousands of Christian disciples across the world.

Alexander Maclaren: *Bible Class Expositions, The Gospel of Luke*. Hodder and Stoughton, Fifth Edition 1907. – Alexander Maclaren (1826-1910) was a renowned Baptist preacher, writer and the Pastor of Portland Chapel, Southampton and subsequently of Union Chapel, Manchester.

Leon Morris: *Tyndale New Testament Commentaries, The Gospel According to St. Luke, An Introduction and Commentary*. Inter-Varsity Press 1974. – The Revd Canon Leon Morris (1914-2006) was the Principal of Ridley College, Melbourne and subsequently Visiting Professor of New Testament at Trinity Evangelical Divinity School.

The New Bible Commentary. Edited by Professor F. Davidson, A. M. Stibbs and E.F. Kevan. The Inter-Varsity Fellowship. Second Edition, 1967 reprint.

John Newton: *Jewels from John Newton*, Daily Readings from the Works of John Newton selected by Miller Ferrie. Banner of Truth Trust 2016. – John Newton (1725-1807) was a sea-faring Captain whose heart the Lord totally changed. He became a Church of England Minister at Olney in Buckinghamshire. John Newton was known as 'the letter-writer of the Great Awakening'. He also wrote the hymns *Amazing grace* and *Glorious things of thee are spoken* and a great many others.

Joseph Parker: *The People's Bible, Discourses upon Holy Scripture, Volume 20, Mark and Luke*. Hazell, Watson and Viney 1902. – Joseph Parker (1830-1902) was The Minister of the City Temple, Holborn Viaduct, London. Joseph Parker was a noted 19th century preacher and writer, renowned for his eloquence.

J.C.Ryle: *Expository Thoughts on the Gospel, St Luke, Volumes 1&2.* James Clarke & Co. Ltd. Reprinted 1969. – John Charles Ryle (1816-1900) was for many years Vicar of Stradbroke in Suffolk, where much of his writing took place. He was appointed to be the first Bishop of Liverpool in 1880.

Richard Trench: *Notes on the Parables of Our Lord.* John W. Parker and Son, Eighth Edition, 1860. – Richard Trench (1807-1886) was a biblical scholar whose career included being appointed Dean of Westminster in 1856, and Archbishop of Dublin and all Ireland in 1864.

The Cover Images, the Author, and our other Publications

The Cover

The cover images are from an overland expedition to the Middle East and Jerusalem undertaken by a group of students in 1964. Top row: a country lane near Nazareth; one of us on a borrowed, shepherd's donkey; bottom row: a typical oil lamp; the sea of Galilee – around whose shores and surrounding hills so much of the ministry of Jesus took place.

The Author

Born in Great Malvern, Worcestershire, England, John Belham has a scientific background, but for most of his life has had the privilege of serving with some very wonderful people, first in suburban ministry, then as Rector of a group of country parishes, and more recently assisting with city ministry. Married with four grown-up children, he delights in the Lord God – his word, his people and his creation.

Other Publications

An e-book edition of these explorations of the parables is published with this paperback edition. (ISBN 978-0-9537489-3-8)

At the time of publication several of these parables with accompanying podcasts are available at https://www.parables.org.uk

Exploring and Applying the Lord's Prayer

A book by the same author, highlighting the practical out-working of this greatest of prayers. Chapter by chapter you are invited to explore and apply each phrase, as if you were exploring the rooms of a great mansion. There are questions for personal reflection or discussion.

Lord, teach us to pray . . . the Lord's Prayer explored and applied, published by Parva Press in 2000 (Paperback 125 pages). Available from the publisher. ISBN 0-9537489-0-1

A new edition, published in 2018 by Grace and Truth Publications, under the title, *To Change the World for Good . . . Exploring and Applying the Lord's Prayer* (Paperback 133pages). Available through book stores world-wide. ISBN 987-0-9929465-7-9

The e-book edition, *Exploring and Applying the Lord's Prayer, A Prayer to Change the World*, published by Parva Press in 2021. ISBN 978-0-9537489-1-4

For further details and to hear the accompanying podcasts visit https://www.lords-prayer.co.uk or search online 'exploring and applying the Lord's Prayer'.

Given understanding and a willingness to take it to heart, the Lord's Prayer will not only teach us to pray, it will revolutionise the way we think and the way we live. It is so much more than a gentle murmur. It is a prayer to change the world – beginning with those who pray it.

www.ingramcontent.com/pod-product-compliance
Lightning Source LLC
Chambersburg PA
CBHW062242300426
44110CB00034B/1108